HIRE HONESTY

Then Trust Your Employees

BILL MCCONNELL

ARCHWAY
PUBLISHING

Archway Publishing books may be ordered through booksellers or by contacting:

Archway Publishing
1663 Liberty Drive
Bloomington, IN 47403
www.archwaypublishing.com
1 (888) 242-5904

ISBN: 978-1-4808-3845-1 (sc)
ISBN: 978-1-4808-3846-8 (hc)
ISBN: 978-1-4808-3847-5 (e)

Library of Congress Control Number: 2016917052

Print information available on the last page.

Archway Publishing rev. date: 10/26/2016

Acknowledgements

While developing the ideas for *Hire Honesty* I had plenty of help from co-workers, friends, and family. I would like to give special thanks to a few. Jeff O'toole, Scott Reynolds, Paul Cross, Kent Nelson, and Ray Sleppy slogged through rough drafts of the manuscript and then endured long conversations with the slow-witted author about which passages should be lengthened, shortened, or discarded. Lucas Chakot provided the youthful reflections and insight that bridged the gap between baby-boomer and millennial generations. All their well-intentioned advice and frank comments are reflected in the positive aspects of this book. Any flaws are my doing.

For twenty-eight years the employees of Patusan Trading Company served as guinea pigs in my laboratory of business management. They all deserve my respect and my sincere thanks. I wish the best of luck to Larry Cuong Tran and Randy Jones who continue the Patusan tradition.

Jack Goldschmidt has been a reliable source of information, insight, and guidance at Patusan and at Hire On Corporation. Thanks, Jack, for listening and opining.

At Triple Creek Ranch, Sheri Hurless, Molly Smith, and Kyle Whyard learned the *Hire Honesty* stratagem and then applied it with great success. Without their patience and administrative input the spectacular achievements of that outstanding resort-hotel would not have been realized. Special thanks go to Barbara and Craig Barrett who gave Leslie and me the opportunity to manage Triple Creek Ranch.

While this is a self-published book, I received professional editorial input from two outstanding performers. Elizabeth Evans provided vital opinions and patient advice relating to form and content. Elizabeth took a primordial, amorphous blob of words and squeezed it into the functional format that evolved into a real live—and not too bad—book. Eva Talmadge's fastidious copy-editing was accurate and indispensable. Any persisting typos and grammatical mistakes are the result of my post hoc alterations.

My wife, Leslie, was always there at both Patusan and Triple Creek Ranch to thwart my latent foolishness, for which she deserves the thanks of those thus protected; and then she steered me toward whatever positive outcome eventually ensued, for which she earns my heartfelt gratitude. Thanks too to Rob and Madi for enduring their father's relentless lectures and boorish opinions while I worked out the cognitive kinks in what would eventually become this book about hiring outstanding honest employees like those at Patusan Trading Company and Triple Creek Ranch. Thank you all.

Bill McConnell
Blairsville, Pennsylvania

CONTENTS

INTRODUCTION

I wrote *Hire Honesty* so that employers would have a better way to screen, interview, and hire employees. In turn, you doubtless are reading this because you need a better method of hiring than the one you are using now. Probably you can reflect on one or two ideal employees and you wish you had a whole staff just like them. You think such workers are rare and you would need to be lucky to find more. You might even agree with the old maxim, good help is hard to find, while you struggle with a less than stellar staff.

It's not surprising that you want to improve your employee screening and selection methods since every employer recognizes the value of good employees and struggles with the process of hiring them. My promise to you is this: After you read and apply the lessons of *Hire Honesty*, your business will run smoother, your employees will be happier, and you will be a better manager.

If you want good employees, you need to know which quality makes them good. What is it that makes some workers show up on time, perform admirably, work enthusiastically, get along with coworkers, and make conscientious decisions? That supreme quality, you will soon learn, is honesty. Honesty is the character equivalent of the good-worker gene.

Employee performance and business success depend on honesty from both workers and management, while worker discord and business failure inevitably result from dishonesty. For American businesses, who hire more than one million new employees each week, the need to hire honest workers surpasses in importance virtually every other aspect of business.

Why is honesty important in the workplace? How does an employer recognize honesty? The answers are not simple, which is why so few employers use honesty as their principle criterion in hiring. Instead, they pursue fleeting concepts such as "top prospects," "A-listers," "team players," and "ninety percenters." They parse answers to the "top ten" hiring questions, looking for some mystical revelation that might foretell the future performance of a particular job candidate. Despite those efforts, after they have completed the tedious processes and narrowed their selection to the final candidates, they remain frustrated because their ineffectual methods would not differentiate George Costanza from George Washington, or Tokyo Rose from Rosie the Riveter.

Yet when one experiences an honest workplace, it is apparent that workers and management are infused with good-worker genes. Business ideals such as efficiency, stability, and profitability are evident. Employees are thorough, polite, and conscientious. Management creates plans for the future instead of fretting about labor disputes, absenteeism, and declining productivity.

Workplace honesty is an obvious objective, yet popular hiring methods and management techniques give only lip service to this vital precept, or they ignore it altogether. So, to fix all that, I will introduce the following concepts:

- Honesty as the foundation of exceptional job performance
- The good-worker gene as a metaphor for honesty within the workplace
- The recessive nature of good-worker genes
- The need to separate workers' comfort lives from their sustenance lives

- "Managed conversation" as the instrument for identifying and maintaining workplace honesty
- The "all-about-you interview"
- Trust as the principle motivator for honest workers

I have divided this book into four parts: The Theory, The Tools, The Process, and The Application. The theoretical discussion examines the facts and the rationale behind attaching profound importance to honesty in society, to the individual, and within the workplace. The simplicity of the prescribed tools might surprise you. Like the wheel, "managed conversation" is an obvious device, but it works only when it is used for a targeted purpose. The other tools too are familiar, but we'll learn new ways to wield them.

The search for honest employees involves a specific interview process, the all-about-you interview, which I will explain in detail, using positive and negative examples along with my personal commentary. I invite you, the reader, to join the discussion and use the sample interview dialogues as your inaugural experience with this process.

In application, you'll learn that an honest workplace requires a wholly different management style from the ordinary workplace setting. Honest workers need, above all else, to be trusted.

Hire Honesty is the culmination of forty years of inquiry and thousands of interviews. To develop these hiring techniques, I studied innumerable retailers, manufacturers, international hotels, and small businesses. I conferred with Fortune 500 company CEOs and their employees. I listened to and analyzed the comments of job seekers, actual hires, business associates, and customers.

When I cite my business experience, I do so with humility because my business career, which included twenty-eight years as President and CEO of Patusan Trading Company and five years as

Co-General Manager with my wife, Leslie, at Triple Creek Ranch, is distinctly non-remarkable to anybody except me and maybe those with whom I worked. However, the concepts contained within *Hire Honesty* are truly remarkable. When they were applied at Patusan and at Triple Creek Ranch the effect was immediate and dramatic.

But, it took me a while to figure it all out. When I finally struck upon the notion of using personal honesty as the fundamental tenet in selecting new employees, I applied it at Patusan, an importer and wholesaler of fine oriental rugs. We established production facilities in Nepal, China, India, and Pakistan and then sold our products throughout the United States and Canada. In those international settings the principles of *Hire Honesty* were profoundly successful and roundly applauded.

When the same principles, which by now I had written down and organized into a distinct management system, were applied at Triple Creek Ranch in 2009, that already prestigious resort climbed up the charts until, in 2014, it earned the ranking as the world's best hotel.[1] The same hiring and management methods that proved successful in remote areas of developing Asia were dramatically successful in the sophisticated enclaves of elite vacationers.

The one singular and definitive thing that I contributed to both of these diverse enterprises was my focus on hiring honest workers. I made sure that both companies employed honest people and that made all the difference.

How did I know my honesty techniques were working? Easy. I listened to people, and the one remark that I heard repeatedly from business associates and customers was, "Where do you find these wonderful workers?" From job applicants and employees the remarks were of a similar vein: "This is a great place to work." The "hire honesty" formula was balanced: on one side clients and consumers were happy and on the other side employees and management were prospering. Good-worker genes were being expressed.

By the way, this book is about honesty and anyone who dares expound upon the concept of honesty is open to charges of hypocrisy. I intend everything contained in *Hire Honesty* to be the unmitigated truth. Nonetheless, I am a liar. I have lied. I do lie. I will continue to lie unless I die right away. The same is true of you, dear reader. You have lied. You do lie. You will continue to lie. If you have a problem with those statements, set down this book and simply walk away; then keep on walking until you forget you are human, because only then could you plausibly deny that you lie.

Allow me to balance that dire declaration with this positive one: Doing good work is fun. It is a pleasure to screen, interview, and hire job applicants when that process is done correctly, and when it results in an honest person collecting a well-deserved paycheck. All-about-you job interviews generate instructive and gratifying experiences for both the interviewer and the applicant. Upon implementing *Hire Honesty*'s methods, human resource professionals and small business owners alike will look forward to their next opportunity, and every chance thereafter, to recruit and hire honest workers and then work alongside them as workplace cohesion yields business success.

CHAPTER 1   THE GOOD-WORKER GENE

Have you ever shopped at a furniture store where you were assisted by a conscientious salesperson, settled your bill with a cheerful attendant, then had your furniture delivered by careful furniture movers who offered to help rearrange your furnishings before they neatened the room and departed? It happens, and when it does you ask, "Where did they find such incredible workers?"

As a sales rep, you might have walked into the offices of a corporation where you were greeted by a receptionist who knew you were scheduled to meet with Mrs. Matthews in purchasing, and that Mrs. Matthews was expecting you. The receptionist pointed out the restrooms and the coffeemaker and asked if she could help with preparations for your meeting. When you met Mrs. Matthews, you found she had already researched your company and was familiar with your product line.

Wrapping up, you stood to leave, and Mrs. Matthews said, "Oh, there goes Mr. Hansen, our CEO. Do you have time for an introduction?" You met the company's CEO, who was also polite, enthusiastic, and engaging. In your car, while you were buckling your seat belt and brushing the potato chips from the console, you asked yourself, "How do I get a job with that company?"

This year you took your family to a new resort. At check-in the bellhop said, "I'll place your bags in your room." You thanked him and offered a generous tip, and he said, "Please don't tip during your stay. If you're pleased with the service, simply add a gratuity when you check out."

The receptionist affirmed, "If you decide to leave a tip on your departure, we'll distribute it fairly among the staff." You wondered: Why would the bellhop decline a direct tip now in favor of an uncertain chance of getting one later? Where do you find service workers who decline tips?

Though the venues vary and the circumstances differ, the examples above share a vital characteristic that is easily over-looked. It's almost as if these workers possessed a good-worker gene. In the case of the furniture store, one might conclude the staff just happens to be comprised of naturally cheerful, helpful people. The sales representative might credit an effective train-ing program for the company's friendly efficiency. At the resort, a patron might conclude managers are keeping a close eye on employees, probably through ceiling-mounted cameras, maybe drones. But cheerful people have bad days, training programs work only for people willing to be trained, and security cameras can always be out-witted—yet these workers keep excelling.

Wouldn't it be great if the good-worker gene were real and detectible? This gene would signal that the person would work hard, be productive and reliable, rarely be absent, be cheerful while going about the job, and be friendly and polite to co-workers. Sorry to say, no such gene exists, but a single character trait will do everything one could ask of the fictional gene. That character trait is honesty. Workplace honesty is the key to busi-ness success and worker satisfaction. Honesty serves as a good-worker gene.

From a job seeker's point of view, honesty also serves as a good-employer gene. A job seeker looking for the collective corporate gene that would assure a fair-minded employer and compatible coworkers would find no such DNA. But if that job seeker found an employer who espoused honesty and who hired honest workers, he or she would have found the equivalent of the good-employer gene.

Honesty is not a gene. It is not a trait coded into our DNA. A technician cannot analyze a blood sample and confirm the donor is honest or dishonest, and as we will see, neither can the polygraph operator nor the body language expert. Honesty has nothing to do with our physical being, appearance, heritage, where we were born, or when. Honesty comes about as a conscious decision from within the mind of each individual to behave in a particular way.

So, what is honesty? Defining the word can be tricky. To avoid defining obscenity, United States Supreme Court Justice Potter Stewart is famous for declaring, "I know it when I see it."[2] Following Judge Stewart's example, we could eliminate all philosophical wrangling by simply saying, "I know honesty when I see it." But it is important for us to have a definition that sets a precedent for future decisions and discussions. I offer this practical definition: Honesty is a person's deliberate effort to say, act on, and accept things as they are known or are perceived to be.

> **Honesty is a person's deliberate effort to say, act on, and accept things as they are known or are perceived to be.**

Because honesty is nearly impossible to define, every discussion about honesty is carried out under conditions of uncertainty. From one vantage point, a statement may appear honest, but looking closer, an observer may become less certain. It is similar to measuring the length of a coastline. Looking down from the International Space Station, the coastline appears well defined. From closer, say from an airplane, more of the detail becomes visible and we realize we need to account for the coves and jetties, making our calculation more difficult. Then, as we walk the coastline, we see that the coves and jetties are made up of boulders and cliffs, each with uneven surfaces that must be considered in the overall length. Next, we kneel on the shore and notice that water seeps in around each grain of sand. Then the tide comes in and a wave crashes down, and we start our measurements all over. Like a coastline, honesty is real, but personal judgment is required when measuring it. Thus we grow to appreciate Justice Stewart's dilemma.

The single most important task of any employer is the act of hiring employees. The single most important task of any job seeker is being hired by the right employer. The employer wants to hire the employee who can be trusted to work hard, be safe, get along with coworkers, and look out for the best interests of the company. The employee seeks the employer who will pay well, provide job security, respect personal privacy, and treat all workers fairly. Finding that ideal employer/employee match is vital to the success and happiness of both the employer and the employee.

For an employer, surrounding oneself with honest employees means having the opportunity to do all those things that are fun and exciting about running a business: spending workdays advancing the prospects of the company, managing production, pushing sales growth, seeking new markets, and staying ahead of competition. To the contrary, a dishonest workforce connotes labor disputes, wrangling over wages and salaries, absenteeism, and employee attrition—everything that is miserable about managing. Where dishonesty prevails managers grow weary, their attention span lapses, and they become unproductive. Communication channels become clogged with non-productive considerations, and important messages are thwarted before they reach their targets. But where honesty prevails, workplace satisfaction reigns.

A problem arises when honesty does not overwhelmingly prevail—when it is present but not abundant and not dominant. That is because the good-worker gene is recessive. You might remember from biology class that certain genes are expressed only when they are paired with genes like themselves. That's how good-worker genes are; they function only next to other good-worker genes. In biology some genes are always expressed, even when paired with countermanding genes. Genes whose traits are always expressed are called dominant genes. In the workplace, dishonesty dominates and stifles honesty. Only when paired with other honest workers will employees openly act, speak, and perform honestly, which is why employers must strive to hire only honest employees.

Take the bellhop who declined your proffered tip: What happens if that afternoon you decide to take a dip in the pool and the pool attendant hands you a towel, then sticks out his paw for a tip? You certainly would be disinclined to leave a general tip at check-out. In order for the "tip when you leave" policy to work, everybody at the resort must be honest. Otherwise, the system fails.

After your new furniture has been delivered, you find that the delivery crew has chipped your plaster and stained your carpet. You express your anger in a phone call to the erstwhile cheerful attendant who takes the matter to the storeowner, who offers to repair the damage. But who will perform the repairs? You won't allow that oafish delivery crew back in your home, so you argue with the store owner over which outside contractor will do the work. In the end, both parties have a bad day.

The near-utopian ideal of an honest workplace is achievable because honest people recognize and respect honesty and they reject dishonesty. When an employer establishes honesty as a workplace paradigm, honest workers no longer need to fend off the onslaught of dishonesty. They learn to depend on their coworkers and managers. Once a majority of honest workers and managers has been reached, as a matter of course, dishonest workers are evicted, and dishonest applicants are rejected. From that point forward, good employers team up with good help and the office, shop, factory, mill, or garage start-up can cultivate those matters that lead to real success in business—efficiency, productivity, and profitability.

The skeptic will ask: What about the honest jerk and the honest lazy slob? Alas, an honest jerk is still a jerk and an honest slob is still a slob. I recommend you hire neither. But I'll show that honesty is an antidote to most personal vices, with honest people intrinsically striving to fix their inner defects. If that monkey in your mirror can be regarded with honesty, then your flaws can be repaired and your mistakes atoned.

Summary

What if there were a good-worker gene? How would carriers of that gene perform within the workplace? They would perform honestly. Honesty is a person's deliberate effort to say, act on, and accept things as they are known or are perceived to be. Honesty is the common thread that connects peak workplace performance to workplace satisfaction. Nearly every workplace problem is the result of some level of dishonesty, requiring managers to spend most of their time preventing or correcting damage from dishonest acts. Where honesty prevails, workplaces operate harmoniously as managers and workers concentrate their efforts on improving productivity instead of enforcing workplace rules. An honest jerk is still a jerk, but an honest jerk is rare.

Part I

The Theory

Honesty forms the foundation of virtually all societal institutions and personal interactions, and it functions that way in the workplace too. To understand just how vital honesty is, we need to examine its role within these settings. To use it as a criterion for selecting employees, we will need to recognize it. Since, ironically, honesty is most apparent when it is absent, we will need to understand and recognize lying, the deliberate contamination of truth and honesty. But are all mistruths lies, and are all truths practical and deserving voice? Judgment is required. Part I provides the fundamental understanding of honesty that makes it a practical instrument for building an honest workforce and an honest workplace.

Chapter 2   Honesty and Society

As CEO of Patusan Trading Company, Inc., a small business that imported oriental rugs and sold them wholesale through furniture stores in the United States and Canada, I, an American raised in a traditional small-town, church-going culture, had the opportunity to compare various religions and moral codes first-hand. Frequently I visited Muslim Pakistan, Hindu India, officially atheist China, and the Buddhist Tibetans in Nepal on a single one- or two-month business trip. The cultural comparisons were insightful, and the differences were sometimes stark, but for many years, we carried on extensive business while maintaining loyal professional and personal relationships within those vastly diverse cultures. How could an American farm kid from a Eurocentric, Western culture find common ground among the unfamiliar oriental cultures of Asia? A discussion with Mr. Sufian Ahmed in Ghosia, India, helped me sort it out.

Mr. Sufian, a devout Muslim, was the patriarch of a well-known rug-weaving family whose ancestry traces back to a Persian trader who settled in the Indian village of Ghosia in the sixteenth century. Ghosia lies on the outskirts of Varanasi, an ancient city noted for its contributions to Hinduism, Buddhism, Sikhism, and Jainism. Sometimes called the Jerusalem of the East, archeologists believe Varanasi was established ten thousand years ago. According to Hindu lore, the city was founded by the god Shiva. Around 877 B.C., Jain leader Parshva was born in Varanasi then was raised and educated there. Gautama Buddha preached the Dharma—The Principles—at nearby Sarnath around 500 B.C. On his first Udasi—divine mission of peace—Guru Nanak, founder of the Sikh religion, visited Varanasi to confer with religious leaders of various faiths. As a lifelong resident of Varanasi, Mr. Sufian interacted with the followers of many religions and moral codes in his daily life.

Early in my career as a rug merchant, I sought Mr. Sufian's advice. Over a late-evening vegetarian meal during the holy month of Ramadan, with his laughing grandchildren running here and there, and Mr. Sufian's four obedient sons listening with respectful encouragement, I asked how, in his business dealings, he sorted out the religious customs and social peculiarities of Varanasi. He replied, "It's not difficult. In business and in life, one must look past religion, social status, and appearance to a person's fundamental nature, and ask: Is this person honest?"

His statement stuck with me. From that day forward, in whatever country I happened to be, I made a point of buying products only from honest vendors, dealing with honest shippers, seeking honest bankers, hiring honest salespeople, and selling products through honest outlets. I spent more time talking to my business associates, pondering their words, and watching their actions. I carefully assessed and prioritized honesty, placing it ahead of the mundane considerations of routine business. When deciding upon suppliers, I chose the ones I felt were more honest, sometimes even at a higher cost. When pitching Patusan's services to furniture stores, I chose as clients those stores whose owners were willing to share trust. In my business decisions I weighed honesty on the same scale with profit and I eventually learned that honesty was profitable. The more I put Mr. Sufian's philosophy to the test, the more wise his advice proved to be, and the more my business flourished as my professional associates became trusted friends.

Mr. Sufian's bit of business wisdom was equally applicable to my personal life. As I began viewing daily events through the lens of honesty, my core of family and friends congealed with stronger bonds. I began to recognize honesty in others and I gravitated toward them, while I advised my children to look for the benefits of honesty among their friends and within their personal relationships. In a way, I was transported back to my childhood, when my parents scratched out a living from the family farm with the help of friends and neighbors who looked out for and helped one another. Then and now, the bonds forged of honesty and personal trust are prudent and immutable.

Origin and Evolution of Truth

Let's consider the primal state of truth and watch it evolve from a force of nature into the defining factor of workplace success.

Curiosity, the inherent search for facts, is an essential natural instinct. It drives young animals and infants to play with and taste everything, including things that hurt and taste bad. Even before they are cognitively aware of their surroundings, babies learn that hard, pointy objects cause pain, hot surfaces burn, and loud noises portend bad tidings. Curiosity teaches us that certain elements of our environment can harm us. If we fail to learn, if we fail to connect cause with effect, if we fail to accept the concrete fact that hot means pain, we weaken our chances for survival. Curiosity is life's instinctual quest for honesty.

If nature lied to us, if our brains were not programed to process facts honestly, if hot did not cause pain, but instead delivered physical gratification, our disfigured hands and scarred skin would defend us poorly from the harsh realities of life. Nature is a labyrinth of universal facts that can be survived only through the application of fundamental honesty.

Human beings manipulate their environment for protection, comfort, and power. The same intelligence that allows humanity to make tangible changes to its environment grants it the ability to conceive purely intellectual concepts such as art, philosophy, and mathematics.

Some intellectual creations are positive; others are not. Some novelists and movie producers create fictions that challenge our minds and expand our world. Some manipulators and scammers craft lies and trickery to steal our belongings and destroy our lives. We endeavor to separate those intellectual creations that affect us positively from those that do us harm; for this purpose we employ our wits.

Honesty, with its various incarnations, is the intellectual construct that communicates the natural order of things. The words "truth," "reason," "knowledge," and "science" have been used interchangeably by philosophers. Each word's meaning is nuanced, but all four fall under the intellectual umbrella of honesty. Philosophers struggle to capture the vast complexities of honesty with simple words, words that transform hazy concepts into practical tools. It is worthwhile to consider their musings, because from their efforts we gain useful understanding.

Aristotle said, "Philosophy is the science which considers truth."[3] He thought "the purpose of a theoretical discipline is the pursuit of truth through contemplation."[4] The eighteenth century Scottish philosopher David Hume said, "Reason or science is nothing but the comparing of ideas, and the discovery of their relations."[5] Hume also asserted "a certain curiosity implanted in human nature"[6] was the driving force in humanity's quest for reason. For millennia, humanity's deepest thinkers have been wrestling with the origin and meaning of truth. Though they might argue over the details, they agree on the momentous importance of the fundamentals of honesty.

Honesty has several implicit extensions. Let us consider two: truth and trust. Using old-fashioned similes, truth is to honesty what water is to the ocean—honesty is comprised of truth just as the ocean is comprised of water. There are things in the ocean besides water, but without water there is no ocean, just as without truth there can be no honesty. Some water lies outside the ocean just as some truths are not relevant to every honest statement. Taken to extremes, the simile may break down, but for the most part, it holds water.

Trust is to truth what swimming is to the ocean—trust allows us to navigate within truth. When we learn to swim we have the means of surviving in the ocean, and when we learn to trust we can assimilate truth and honesty.

Social Distrust

Through the ages, philosophers, scientists, and religious leaders had good reason to ponder the importance of honesty and idealize it. Honesty, they inevitably concluded, was essential to a properly functioning society. Without trust, no person could participate in the institutions of family, friendship, faith, commerce, or any of the other interactions necessitated by community living. In a world devoid of trust, each person would remain within his or her cave fearing deceit's shadow might darken the entrance and a fateful life-or-death battle would ensue. So, societies have formed that liberate humanity from the fear inherent to distrust and deceit.

Science historian Steven Shapin puts it, "Society was made through an act of trust; it continued so long as the trust was acquitted; and it was voided when the trust was violated."[7]

Trust is essential to the social order of humanity. In a properly functioning society, we are able to walk outside our homes because we have established a trust within our communities that threats to life and limb have been mitigated by other members of the community, allowing us to focus on the less demanding aspects of living, such as whether to have beef or tofu for dinner.

So we hand the grocer our money in exchange for beef or tofu, which we trust are up to our expectations and are untainted and unspoiled. We purchase gasoline trusting that the pump has been honestly calibrated to dispense gallons or liters in accordance with the posted price on the gauge. We purchase our train or airline ticket based upon our trust that the railroad company or airline will fulfill its promise to honor that ticket and deliver us to our intended destination. The fabric of society is built upon trust, and trust is society's regard for the honesty of others.

It is worth considering just how many tiers of trust constitute even the simplest matters within modern society. Consider that tank of gasoline you purchased. Did you contemplate driving away without paying? Did you consider paying with counterfeit currency or with a stolen credit card? The pump displayed an inspection sticker verifying the accuracy of its gauges, but was the inspector honest, or does he have an agreement with the convenience store to scalp an ounce or two from each gallon, then split the windfall with the store manager? Did the distributor fill the holding tank with contaminated fuel? Did the refinery properly distill the gasoline before selling it to the distributor? Are the safety valves and fire prevention devices functioning properly on the gas pump? Are the welds on the gas tank of your automobile reliable, or did the manufacturer skimp on that detail, increasing the possibility that your tank will explode at the next bump in the road? This list barely scratches the surface of all the potential deceits involved in purchasing a simple staple of our daily lives. Yet we rarely consider them.

French Renaissance philosopher Michel de Montaigne said, "If lies and falsehoods had only one face, we would be better off, for we would recognize the opposite of what the liar said to be the truth. But the reverse of truth has a hundred thousand shapes and a limitless field."[8]

Within society, honesty and trust are expected. Conversely, distrust and skepticism are the hallmarks of disrespect and societal decline. In 1967, Harold Garfinkel published *Studies in Ethnomethodology*,[9] in which he discussed experiments where students pushed the limits of skepticism. They merely pretended to question the credibility of people around them, and the results were not pretty. One can try this in your own life. If you want to ruin your day and that of another, simply question the other's credibility. Your questions can be as innocuous as, "Do you think it will rain today?" Whatever the answer, treat it skeptically. "No? Well, what makes you the authority?" "Yes? How can you be so sure?" The result, if one persists with distrusting rejoinders, will be a confrontation and surely a loss of respect.

One student in Garfinkel's experiment openly expressed skepticism to a bus driver about the route he would take and another distrusted a spouse's reason for returning late from work. Garfinkel reports that both situations quickly erupted into open hostility. Such experiments should come with a don't-try-this-at-home warning, because even moderate expressions of skepticism, such as the raising of a disbelieving eyebrow or the clearing of a questioning throat, can cause resentment.

In September 2004, less than two months before a presidential election, formerly venerated CBS anchorman Dan Rather went public with documents that he said revealed that a candidate had falsified his military records. The news captured national and worldwide headlines. However, a quick glance at purported copies of the original documents, supposedly typewritten in 1973, revealed that the font and character spacing were computer generated in a manner unavailable in 1973. Rather's credibility was destroyed and his career met an inglorious end. The greater loss to the public was that news outlets in general were no longer trusted, and the public was wisely skeptical of the information fed to them by the news media.

Lying by Governments and Armies

Trust is the foundation of any long-term harmonious relationship; distrust, whatever the cause, is the destroyer of harmony. Garfinkel's experiments targeted individual interactions, but distrust wreaks havoc on a large scale too, such as distrust between a government and its citizenry, news services and their consumers, and the educational establishment and its students. Examples of pervasive distrust of government can be witnessed in countries where the currencies are over-valued by the government. In such a country, one US dollar will buy, say, 50 pesos at the official government bank, but 60 pesos from the black marketeer on the street corner. The government insists their peso is worth more than it actually is, while the public is aware that the government is lying.

In 1928, Soviet agronomist Dr. Trofim Lysenko imperiously discarded Mendelian genetics and declared his own dubious theories to be correct. He was roundly applauded within the Soviet politburo, proud to proclaim that communism had moved science forward. But Lysenko had falsified his research, claiming monumental increases in wheat yield, when only slight gains or declines in production were observed. His fraudulent science was taught throughout the Soviet Union, and when wheat yields failed to bear out his claims, he simply inflated the harvest records.[10] The resulting food shortages caused starvation and famine as actual food supplies dwindled in a country of vast food-producing potential. Today, the term "Lysenkoism" is synonymous with consensual, fraudulent science.

When society is infused with skepticism, when erstwhile voters throw up their hands and say, "Ah, what's the use?"—that is when democracy fails and dictatorships fill the void with their secret police, neighbors ratting out neighbors, and domestic spying on private communications. History shows us that dictatorships quickly replace incidental street violence with premeditated police violence, military violence, and debilitating societal angst as the dictator's personal distrust and resulting suspicion infects the total population.

The most convincing example of distrust prefacing the decline of civilization is provided by the events in Germany during the 1930s and '40s, when pathological distrust and paranoia led to one of the world's most cataclysmic eras. The dictatorial ambitions of a few delusional people combined with the calculated false statements of state propagandists working with the tacit approval of a pliant intelligentsia resulted in millions of deaths and worldwide desolation.

Subtle intellectual distinctions were used by Nazi propagandist Joseph Goebbels to rationalize the dishonesty that eventually rained down misery on the mass of humanity. Goebbels liked to distinguish "concrete truth" from "poetic truth."[11] He explained, "Propaganda must not investigate the truth objectively...but must present only the aspect of the truth that is favorable."[12] When the bulk of the populace and the prominent thinkers within society are willing to allow such philosophies as Goebbels's and Hitler's to stand, they stand with the tyrants.

In his *Communist Manifesto*, Karl Marx used wordplay to rationalize his agenda: "Communism abolishes eternal truths... it therefore acts in contradiction to all past historical experience."[13] Saul Alinsky's version of the ideal radical concurs with Goebbels and Marx. In *Rules for Radicals*, Alinsky says, "To begin with, he [the radical] does not have a fixed truth—truth to him is relative and changing; everything to him is relative and changing."[14]

Benito Mussolini's truth was fascism. He said, "Fascism is... an expression of truth in the higher region of the history of thought."[15] In power politics, step one is to manipulate facts; step two is to declare those manipulations to be the "new truth." When society is asked to transform its respect for honesty, and adopt a new, higher, and enlightened edition of truth, those demanding the transformation must be questioned lest all society suffer the consequences.

Civil Ills

Many civil ills exist because society tolerates dishonesty. Prejudice, racism, bigotry, sexism, and the like are, at their core, the result of basic dishonesty. Bigotry, for example, may be the result of one group perpetuating hatred of another group across a period of successive generations. This hatred or distrust may have no existing basis in reality, yet long-standing social conventions impede honest assessment of the root problem.

What is dishonest about bigotry? If we use this commonly accepted definition for bigotry: any intolerance of people, beliefs, or opinions strictly because they differ from oneself or one's own, then the dishonesty lies in one's presumption that the other people, their beliefs, or their opinions are automatically intolerable. The dishonesty, not unlike a willingness to believe a juicy bit of gossip about a bitter rival, lies within the person who would pass judgment without first considering facts. It is personally dishonest to presume to know something that one does not know.

Dishonesty, in the form of baseless presumption without sound knowledge, is at the core of all prejudice.

I suspect this type of dishonesty is what Dr. Martin Luther King sought to rectify when he asked Americans to judge his children by the content of their character and not the color of their skin. Honesty, like justice, is blind, so Dr. King was saying if you have the honesty to strip away baseless bias then you will pursue merit, not color; integrity, not conformity.

The disenfranchisement of women is institutionalized sexism. Presumably, all men have or had mothers, and with few exceptions, those men regarded their mothers as wise, industrious, thoughtful people, who also just happened to have been responsible for providing life and nurture to them. But, from the inception of Greek democracy until recently, women were denied the right to vote by those same men. Was, then, every politically active male throughout history a sexist bigot? I doubt it. Convention often clouds human judgment, but an uncoerced, honest society will correct past mistakes as facts become evident.

The Science Enigma

Let us compare the vital societal roles of scientific honesty to those of honesty in business. As we discussed earlier, in history and philosophy the word science has been substituted for the word truth. I will use this context for science and expand it through philosophical parallels to demonstrate the importance of truth and honesty in business, and to show that social trust is essential to successful business.

It is important for employers to consider the role science plays in the workplace, because not only are the vast majority of all products, jobs, and incomes the direct result of scientific inquiry, but also because the discipline required for scientific thinking resembles the methodical approach employers and entrepreneurs apply in their day to day decision making. After all, a functioning business amounts to a single cell within a micro-economic organism, and economics, as historian Thomas Carlyle told us, is the "dismal science." Dismal, maybe, but nonetheless still science.

The scientific process puts science in an ironic relationship with trust and society. Among scientists, trust comes, paradoxically, not from scientific consensus, but from persistent skepticism.

No scientific theory is beyond questioning. As Nobel physicist Dr. Richard Feynman put it, "Science is a culture of doubt."[16] Because, Feynman says, it's better to "live with the doubt than have answers that might be wrong."

Business too has an ironic relationship with trust and society. While business is self-interested and acquisitive, its selfishness is not sated except by providing goods and services at prices that are acceptable to those who consume those goods and services. Within a free market, competition checks the selfishness of any particular business, because when that particular business violates the trust and becomes too greedy, another business may enter the market with reduced profits and prices and force the greedy establishment to either reduce its prices or cease operations. Thus, emissaries of free markets might reply to Dr. Feynman's statement about doubt and science with a statement of their own about greed and business: Business thrives on a culture of greed, but it is better to live with its greed than to live without its goods and services.

So how does the innate skepticism of science square with society's need for trust, and why doesn't the scientific community explode in a ball of fiery resentment? Steven Shapin, in his *A Social History of Truth*, says, "The very distrust which social theorists have identified as the most potent way of dissolving social order is said to be the most potent means of constructing our knowledge."[17] So scientists learn to be civil even while doubting, challenging, and denigrating each other's theories.

Likewise, with measured civility, society accepts the truth that business is greedy. As scientists must temper their skepticism, businesses and markets must temper their greed. A fundamental trust is necessary for science and business to operate. In business, it is assumed that the goods and services exchanged will meet consumers' expectations for quality and quantity, and it is accepted that the provider of those goods and services will accrue a moderate gain for providing them. It is only when the trust is violated and business's greed surpasses society's reasonable expectations that skepticism grows into a festering distrust of business.

Science requires institutionalized civility, which Shapin calls, "the means to dissent without disaster."[18] The marketplace also requires institutionalized civility with consumers tolerating a limited amount of greed before they go stomping out of the department store.

In a reciprocal to Montaigne's description of a lie as having "a hundred thousand shapes and a limitless field,"[19] when science is corrupted with dishonesty, society's loss is not singular; instead society loses all those immeasurable benefits from what might have been. The suppression or denial of a single scientific fact may prevent the growth of a hundred thousand facts and a limitless field of advances and benefits to society.

When fair and open business is thwarted by doubts arising from unscrupulous players and market manipulators, the loss includes all those goods and services that might have been produced had society's trust in business not been shaken. All those jobs that would have been created by the producers, the peripheral benefits of those jobs, and the subsequent prosperity are all lost. In business, product value must be verified by skeptical consumers who acknowledge and accept the presence of greed but who disapprove of gluttony.

Business, like science, is vulnerable to degradation from those who foul their own domain. Both are assailed by quacks and snake oil peddlers who seek ill-gotten profit with false claims about their discoveries. Generally, such claims are couched in jargon or vague, quasi-scientific terms. In a free market system, caveat emptor—buyer beware—is more often implied than stated, and it is the individual who must exercise the judgment to spurn commercial quackery.

Business people and scientists are attacked from many quarters, and they must repel these attacks by constantly reinforcing the trust of their customers and peers. Society, which is the product of human trust, depends upon business and markets to obtain the goods and services that fulfill its wants and needs. Consequently, employers and business people must strive to thwart unscrupulous shysters who would erode or destroy the public's faith in business.

Summary

Society is built on and sustained by honesty and trust. Starting with our family and friends and radiating out to the community, to the country, and eventually to the world as a whole, trust is essential to productive relationships. Throughout history, the breakdown of trust and the denial of facts have had dire consequences. Those who seek to manipulate society for their selfish goals often start by redefining truth and honesty. Even minor interruptions to a community's trust can cause harm. Science is the systematic search for truth within the natural world. The integrity of science is maintained by a balance of facts and doubt. Business is the systematic search for, and exchange of, the goods and services sought by society. The integrity of business is maintained by a balance of greed and need. Society's trust is essential both for the advancement of science and for the success of business. Without trust, society will turn its back on markets and on science and the consequential loss will be immeasurable.

CHAPTER 3   HONESTY AND THE INDIVIDUAL

The first step to solving a problem is identifying it, which may be the reason Ancient Greeks carved "Know thyself" into the stone on their most holy shrine at Delphi. It is safe to assume that this inscription is not mere graffiti; it implies godly counsel. If the cumulative wisdom of pre-classical Greece can be boiled down to three items[1] and one of those three is "know thyself," then let us consider why, through almost 3,000 years of philosophical soul searching, knowing oneself has been deemed divinely important.

Know thyself, or as Shakespeare would say, "To thine own self be true,"[20] is a command to internalize honesty. The wisdom of the Delphic message lies in its recognition that it is much harder to make honest judgments about ourselves than about others; thus we are commanded to know ourselves instead of "know others." Knowing others requires simple recognition, whereas knowing oneself requires recognition, judgment, and the implicit

---

[1] In addition to "Know thyself," "Nothing in excess" and the Greek letter epsilon (E) also were chosen as advice for the ages. "Nothing in excess" has been passed on as "moderation in all things." But what's up with "E"? Nobody is sure, but some speculate that it is a symbolic representation of the words "Thou art." Together, then, the three maxims could be understood as, "You are," "Know who you are," and "Don't be an idiot." http://vunex.blogspot.com/2007/03/e-at-delphi.html.

assignment of fixing what is wrong. Knowing ourselves is the harder task.

If we are able to be honest with ourselves, we become worthier stewards of the world around us. Since human beings have been assigned or usurped—depending upon your point of view—dominion over so much of nature, our level of honesty has far-reaching consequences. Our responsibility to the world and to ourselves demands honesty, the honesty to manage ourselves properly before we attempt to project our judgment onto nature or other people.

Being honest with ourselves is not easy. Strength is required to adopt the personal checks and balances that constitute personal honesty. These checks and balances go by the names of humility, integrity, and honor.

Humility

We seem to have an instinctual wall of conceit around our psyches, a defensive palisade built to protect whatever lies inside, even if what lies inside is not worth preserving. The psychological wall is constructed of bricks composed of vanity and arrogance. Within our personal fortress, one or two worthy monuments may stand, but when we come to know ourselves, we realize that our wall of self-preservation shelters mostly mirages and straw houses, dilapidated and badly in need of repair or demolition. As an honest person comes to know him or herself, the wall of conceit begins to crumble, revealing the accurate state of reality.

Whether we laugh or cry over our personal realities depends upon our emotional strength at the time of the revelations. During a weakened state, unshrouded truths may be as frightening as any physical threat of nature, and the resultant knowledge may cause us to react fearfully. However, as we become familiar with our failings and develop the strength needed to bear their weight, we check our fear with intellectual and emotional muscle.

As we fortify our wills, we come to know ourselves for the flawed characters we are. Emotional strength allows us to laugh at whom we have come to know. We learn to take ourselves less seriously. Our vanity and arrogance, we realize, are pathetic. Yet, try as we may, even after we fix one layer of problems, more problems appear and they keep appearing, new ones and the same old ones. We continue fixing and still we can't make ourselves right. Eventually, we realize that the burden of knowing ourselves is heavy and never becomes any lighter, but we become stronger. Paradoxically, when we attain humility—when we accept our personal weakness—we acquire personal strength—a goal worthy of Delphi.

Few people exemplify the paradoxical reckoning with humility as well as Benjamin Franklin. In the portion of his autobiography written following a near-death illness when he was fifty-five, he drolly informs his son that of all his conquests over youthful vices, he is most "proud of my humility." While pride and humility are polar opposites to most of us, Franklin's humility, he felt, was a cause for pride. Then, he quips, "I cannot boast of much success in acquiring the reality of this virtue, but I had a good deal with regard to the appearance of it."

Over time, humility's "natural inclination became so easy, and so habitual to me," that Franklin attributed his immense success to this single quality. As to pride, he recommended, "Disguise it, struggle with it, beat it down, stifle it, mortify it…." Triumphing over pride and attaining of humility, Franklin stressed, allows honest people to know who they are, know their faults, and have the strength to shrug off whatever negative thoughts and words others have for them.

The self-confidence borne of humility is attractive to others. Humble self-confidence projects personal strength without the self-important arrogance that abrades the egos of others. Likewise, humility lies at the core of desirable personality traits such dignity, modesty, and reasonableness: attributes rarely evident among attention-seekers, but oh-so welcomed among friends and family. What faults humble people possess, others often find unthreatening, even delightful idiosyncrasies or, at least, endurable peculiarities. Humility humanizes.

Charm is also an outcome of humility. When humility is combined with wit, people are charmed. Without humility, wit is entertaining but not charming. Because their own egos are in check, humble people freely focus their attention on others, putting others at ease, making them feel important, and in the process, charming them. Non-humble people are concerned primarily with appearing important themselves, thereby subordinating the feelings of others—the antithesis of charm.

Humble people tend to understand circumstances and accept the failings of others and are compassionate toward them. The reason many people, like Warren Buffett and Bill Gates, donate to charities while few people, like Mother Teresa, actually perform charitable acts, is that donations require only funding, while compassion requires humility to understand, counsel, and care for those in need. Though charity is vital, without compassion charity is a mere impersonation of caring.

Sincerity is another subset of humility. Why would actor/comedian George Burns say, "Sincerity! If you can fake that, you've got it made"?[21] He was funny, that's why. The quality exhibited by people whom one trusts—their believability—is their sincerity; and, though judgment about another's sincerity is made early in a relationship, time tests the accuracy of that judgment.

Impressions about another person's sincerity are often formed before one has had time to verify the honesty of the other. An intuitive opinion of another's sincerity is formed when, for example, the mechanic says, "Let me see if your car is ready."

The statement may not ring of profundity, yet the mechanic has just acknowledged that he or she lacks the sought-after information and is willing to admit it. The statement also indicates the mechanic is concerned with his or her own veracity. Sincerity, probably the most vital component to the early development of business relationships, is communicated subtly through a combination of outward honesty and internal humility.

Frankness and candidness result from humility. When humility becomes second nature, we don't need to squelch every thought or comment. Being fully aware of their own weaknesses, humble people are free to speak their thoughts about others because humility has stripped insults and thoughtlessness from their thinking. In this way, humility liberates honesty.

In coming to grips with our weaknesses, as humility forces us to do, we also condition ourselves to accept blame for our faults and missteps. A person who recognizes his or her own lack of perfection has had practice accepting responsibility for his or her failings. Humble people possess the strength to accept and carry the burden of failure and guilt. Every employer will recognize the importance of this quality among his or her employees.

Those without humility refuse to shoulder the burden of their failures as they deflect criticism by pointing fingers and placing blame. Ultimately they succumb to defensiveness, judgmentalism, and chronic pessimism.

Because they neither possess humility's strength nor understand its utility the way Ben Franklin did, arrogant, prideful people often mistake humbleness for weakness. These egotists prey on weakness, disadvantage, and vulnerability, and, wrong though they are, they target humble people with their duping schemes. But, as with fictional Atticus Finch in *To Kill a Mockingbird* and real-life Abraham Lincoln in American history, humility often frustrates and prevails over arrogance. While arrogance may achieve a few quick individual gains, within society humility abides.

Humble people recognize humility in others, and seek the company of like-minded people. Over time, the honesty borne of humility instigates those seminal friendships that coalesce into communities and then into societies. In the workplace, humility is a trait expressed by the good worker gene.

Integrity

Integrity is generally regarded as the fullness of a person's internal honesty. Philosopher/writer Spencer Johnson defines it this way: "Honesty is telling truth to others, integrity is telling truth to oneself."[22] As we develop intellectually, either we make a habit of internal honesty or we don't. By habitually telling truth to ourselves, we establish honesty as the default program in our personal conduct.

Take the occasion, for instance, when, at 10:55 p.m., five minutes before official closing time, the pizza shop owner has one shriveled, stale slice left over from the dinner hour rush and a late-arriving customer walks through the door and asks for fresh pizza. Does the shop owner 1) offer the customer the old piece for free, and explain it will take a few minutes until a fresh pie can be baked, 2) reheat the old slice and serve it hoping the customer doesn't notice or complain, or, 3) tell the customer the shop is closed, then, from that day forward, lock the front door at 10:50 p.m.?

A fair-minded pizza shop owner may deliberate the pros and cons of his or her actions, and decide either to serve the stale food and save the cost in time and ingredients, or to honor the sign on the door and its implicit promise that the food will meet expected standards of quality. But the shop owner with integrity will not consider the pros and cons; he or she will not need to. Instead, he or she will automatically bake a new pie or offer the old slice for free.

Integrity allows us reflexively to fulfill the subtle promises of daily life, not only to the satisfaction of others, but also to ourselves. The shop's hours, the name over its door, the price of the product, the acceptance of money in exchange for goods or services—each constitutes a pact with the public. A shop owner with integrity upholds those implied promises. Over a period of maturation, a person practices honesty so that it becomes second nature, and when it does, that is when the person obtains integrity. The person of integrity does not think about right and wrong; integrity guides his or her actions toward honesty as spontaneously as our spoon rises and our mouth opens.

Power of Personal Integrity

A person of integrity holds power over others: not the trifling power of force or control, but the profound power to respect and disrespect, which, coming from a person of integrity, is far more potent than physical power. People crave respect, but being respected by a respectable person is different from being respected by just anybody. The only respect worth having is the respect of people of integrity. Respect from an unknown person, or from someone lacking integrity, is not real respect; it is simply popularity.

If a person of integrity respects another, that is a compliment: if a jerk expresses his or her respect for another, that is not. If you are the person of integrity, the respect you extend to another person is the sincerest praise you can give that person. Withdrawing that respect or denying it altogether is the most damaging reproof a person of integrity can deliver.

Retaliation, revenge, and hostility are devices used by those who lack integrity. When a person of integrity withholds respect, the injury of that consideration alone exceeds any other forms of reckoning. Thereby, integrity renders vindictive action unnecessary.

Everybody makes mistakes, including people who possess integrity. When judging the honesty of another the adjudicator assumes a momentous responsibility. So the judging of others should be a careful, thoughtful process. However, mistakenly withholding respect is far more easily corrected than is an act of overt retribution.

Honor

Honor is often regarded as an old-fashioned word, but it shouldn't be. Honor represents a commitment to personal integrity and a willingness to share an alliance of trust. Whereas integrity is internal, honor is shared.

The notion of honor is sometimes stereotyped as a sort of blind fanaticism associated with archaic military code. However, honor is neither fanatical nor archaic when it represents a community's willingness to adhere to a code of shared honesty. Honor is the trust between people who recognize one another's integrity, and as such, it constitutes a fundamental dynamic within any group with a common purpose.

In the military, where people often put their lives into the hands of others, honor is vital to the trust and morale of the group. In a situation where split-second decisions are made that may result in peril and loss of life, it is vital that the corps has the utmost trust in the men and women making those decisions. When being ordered into battle, one needs to know that a person of honor has made the fateful decision to go forward. Officers must make honest evaluations of crucial situations and act in the best interest of the corps, and not for personal reasons.

Military honor is more than the hackneyed bravado portrayed by movie producers. As the integrity shared by a select group of men and women who risk their lives for our protection, it is essential to all free people that men and women of honor lead our military.

Stepping back from the ledge, honor in business has vital but less fateful consequences than military honor. A decision to seek personal gain at the expense of the company, such as that of a salesperson who trolls for a bribe or a spiff, will ultimately hurt others. It is a violation of honor when a person considers accepting a personal windfall to the exclusion of coworkers or when a company preys on an unwitting public. Honest people will represent their products, services, and prices with honesty and accuracy. Honorable businesses will spurn any suggestion of dishonest activity, and dishonorable companies are, thankfully, generally short-lived.

Likewise, honor between companies is fundamental to long-term business relationships. When employees from one company trust a supplier or vendor from another company, both companies can advance their businesses. When an interruption to the routine order of business occurs, both companies work to resolve the issue rather than spar over who is responsible or who will pay, because shared trust resolves issues as a matter of course. Since companies and corporations are made up of people, the honor of the individuals comprising those companies extends to the companies themselves.

Relative Truth

We have all heard that "truth is relative." In discussions about honesty and truth, "relative truth" is nearly always mentioned then followed by quotes from Greek philosopher Protagoras: "Man is the measure of all things,"[23] or Nietzsche: "Truths are illusions."[24] The argument proceeds that one person measures truth one way, and another measures it another way, just as a note posted on an office door reading "I'll be back in a minute" does not necessarily mean the person will return in sixty seconds. Such discussions qualify as trivial or merely academic until we reexamine the words of Marx and Goebbels, whose trivializing of truth and honesty produced horrendous results.

Philosopher/economist Dr. Thomas Sowell addresses relative truth this way: "Truth is valued precisely for its value in interpersonal communication. If we each have our own private truths, then we would be better off (as well as more honest) to stop using the word or the concept and recognize that nobody's words could be relied upon anymore."[25] Dr. Sowell wants us to say what we mean and mean what we say in our everyday lives. Quibbling over relative truths on vital issues, while relative truth is merely a semantic matter, compromises integrity. Within society, truth and honesty serve practical roles that lie beyond the obscure debates of philosophers.

Plato and Aristotle found fault[26] with Protagoras's relative truths, pointing out that his theories exempt him from honoring his own statements, and furthermore, they are semantically self-confirming and rationally non-falsifiable. If man is the measure of all things, and Protagoras is that man, then everything he claims is true must be true, even when he is lying.

If the definition of truth is elusive, speaking of relative truth as if it were a certainty sets a snare of contradictions that will entangle all but the most obtuse, who simply refuse to admit they are entwined in their own device.

Some who speak of relative truth are splitting hairs over diction, while others are conflicted by the concept of honesty. These fear the uncertainty of honesty's metaphorical coastline so they never bring their ship to shore. The waves and the shifting sand confuse them, and their view of the harbor is blocked by an intellectual fog. Because they refuse to acknowledge the existence of a definable shore, they bob indecisively at the mercy of the wind and tide, which finally cast them upon life's rocks. Honesty's castaways perform poorly in the workplace.

Other Benefits of Truth. Who Knew?

The benefits of honesty can be physical as well as psychological, thereby improving job performance while reducing absenteeism. In 2014, a study conducted by Dr. Anita Kelly and Dr. Lijuan Wang at the University of Notre Dame in South Bend, Indiana,[27] found that honesty carries more dividends than just improving one's popularity and dependability. It also improves one's health. The study monitored 110 adults through a period in which most were mandated to "speak honestly, truthfully, and sincerely—not only about the big things, but also about the small things."

Periodically, all participants were given polygraph tests to monitor their compliance with their instructions. They were also given regular, thorough physical exams during the course of the study. The control group was given the same examinations, but was not advised to maintain a code of honesty. The findings showed that the group adopting honesty and sincerity suffered significantly fewer health problems than the control group. Among the no-lie group, both mental health and physical health improved, with substantial reductions in stress as well as reductions in colds, sore throats, and headaches.

Dr. Kelly speculates that lying causes emotional stress that develops into physical maladies. Truthfulness relieved stress and improved the health of those who adopted a more honest life style. An honest workplace is a healthier workplace, and a healthier workplace is surely a more productive workplace.

Summary

Individual honesty starts with knowing oneself, and from that beginning arise humility, integrity, and honor. Humility is the personal strength that acknowledges and manages one's weaknesses. Integrity is internal honesty. Honor is sharing honesty with others.

One might think that recognizing one's own weaknesses would cause a vortex of pessimism, but the opposite is true. Honesty and humility are developed and strengthened over time. Like any regimen of exercise, with practice, it becomes easier for each individual to act with integrity and thereby reap the benefits of personal honesty, such as confidence, charm, and popularity. These positive developments are reason for optimism. Humble people tend to attract others of similar mindset, and the individuals within the resulting community reinforce one another's honesty. Personal honesty is easier to maintain as societal honesty becomes entrenched.

Protagoras and Nietzsche put forth theories that challenge the importance of individual honesty by hypothesizing that facts are often uncertain; thus, they conclude, honesty is relative. Yet the practical aspects of honesty remain the foundation of any individual's self-worth, as well as that individual's worth to the community.

Chapter 4   Honesty in the Workplace

We've looked at honesty and society and at honesty and the individual, now let's focus on the workplace where misunderstandings often arise from the divergent points of view of the employer and the employee. We'll examine those opposing perspectives then strip away the surface difficulties to get to the underlying problems, which typically are the result of dishonesty.

The social forces within the workplace are distinct from those associated with family, friends, and personal lives. The interpersonal protocols, dignities, and mores of the workplace, while complementary to our private lives, are assessed according to different criteria. After a few days absence from work, for instance, one would not greet a coworker with a hearty handshake and a hug, as one would a close friend or relative, regardless of how interdependent your workaday lives had become. The workplace induces productivity instead of attachment, sustenance ahead of sensitivity. We separate work lives from personal lives so that a worker's family and friends can enjoy benefits of the workplace without bearing its burdens.

Though many of us form tight friendships with our coworkers, workplace bonds are more akin to team participation than to family bonding. Workplace relationships provide sustenance, while personal friendships and family bonds provide comfort. As we'll discuss in a later chapter, these considerations become vital when managing an honest workforce. When hiring the honest workers who will eventually populate that workforce, it is important to recognize the priorities of those workers.

Workplace Provides Sustenance, Not Love

The sustenance/comfort dichotomy was demonstrated in the laboratory by Dr. Harry Harlow in the 1950s at the University of Wisconsin. In a study entitled "The Nature of Love,"[28] Dr. Harlow used orphaned baby rhesus monkeys, highly intelligent animals, to demonstrate that the need for creature comfort was distinct and separate from the need for sustenance.

Harlow's baby monkeys were fed from bottles attached to rough wire mock mothers, but they had the choice of cuddling with softly padded mock mothers. The baby monkeys nearly always bonded to the comfort mother and only visited the sustaining mother for feeding. When stress in the form of loud noises and flashing lights scared the babies, overwhelmingly they ran to their comfort mothers and abandoned their food source. In addition, in the presence of their comfort mothers the young monkeys reacted more calmly to the scare tactics. Harlow's classic research has been interpreted to mean that we are biologically wired to prioritize comfort and support ahead of sustenance.

While Harlow's baby monkeys demonstrate the actions of mere laboratory animals, one need not look far to find correlating examples in human society. Our friends and family are dear to us for different reasons than our coworkers are valued. We cherish friends and family because they fulfill our longing for companionship, support, and love. We choose to excuse and compensate for our friends' faults, we enjoy their impulsiveness and idiosyncrasies, and we happily provide for their needs, or they provide for ours. Family relationships entail obligations as well as choices.

In the workplace we do not want to deal with peculiarities, faults, and weaknesses, and our coworkers do not want to compensate for ours. Instead, we want to complete our work with the highest rate of return and professional satisfaction so we can leave work and spend time within our comfort environment, with our friends and families.

In the workplace, we offer and receive support and personal assistance, but these merely fulfill our need for sustenance. The factors that often bolster workplace productivity—things like the routine of regular production and the fatigue of working long hours to fill unexpected purchase orders, as examples—would strain most non-workplace relationships.

Spontaneity and quirky humor are the hallmarks of friendship and the stimulus for family ties, but within the workplace they may become counterproductive. This is important to remember, particularly for small business owners who are tempted sometimes to hire friends, and within larger companies where a person might try to do a friend a favor and recommend him or her for a job or a promotion within the company. The workplace provides sustenance while friends and family provide comfort; it's best not to confuse the two.

However, honesty is one common quality that bolsters solidarity both at home and at work. In our comfort setting, honesty allows us to relax in a non-stressful, unchallenged atmosphere. At work, honesty combines with commitment, ability, and humility to produce a highly productive atmosphere. To describe the human qualities that efficiently deliver sustenance we will use the words "dependability," "competence," and "leadership."

Dependability

Dependability is the combination of honesty and commitment. When a worker accepts an assigned task and then performs that task in the agreed-upon manner and timeframe, that worker is dependable. When an employer makes a commitment or promise to his or her workers and then fulfills that commitment in the agreed upon manner and timeframe, that employer is dependable. Dependability in the workplace is simply a matter of doing what one says, and, as such, dependability is fundamentally dependent upon personal honesty.

Competence

Competence is the combination of dependability and ability that elevates job performance to a laudable level. Ability may come in the form of knowledge, learned skills, creative talent, or any other faculty needed to perform a designated task well. The competent worker or employer is the one who is dependable and determined to establish a high level of achievement. Thus, the competent operating room nurse performs his or her job by arriving on time, being properly prepared, and by deftly executing his or her duties. Competence requires both ability and dependability, and dependability, we recall, requires honesty.

Sometimes incompetence is harder to explain than competence, because the reasons for incompetence may be obscure. For instance, incompetence can result either from a lack of ability or from a lack of dependability. Not every person with ability is dependable, and not every dependable person has ability. The incompetent nurse might possess the necessary skills but be unprepared, or lack the necessary skills but be prepared. If you are the patient, regrettably the result may be the same for you.

The person who has ability but who lacks the honesty necessary to be dependable presents a dilemma for management, especially when his or her ability to perform a certain duty creates the misperception that he or she is also capable of performing supervisory duties. As we will discuss in Chapter 15, Supervising an Honest Workplace, when employers overlook honesty and choose managers based solely upon their ability to perform a specific function, the results can be devastating to morale and to business.

The opposite of the worker with ability, but who lacks dependability, is one who is dependable but lacks ability. Sometimes this problem is associated with "the Peter Principle."[29] First described by Laurence J. Peter in 1969, the Peter Principle refers to a person who has reached the limits of his or her ability and who lacks the aptitude to advance professionally. When a deficiency in ability becomes evident, an honest but incapable person will admit the problem and seek its remedy. It is the responsibility of higher management to provide the necessary coaching to overcome the deficiency or to assign duties that the honest person is capable of performing. As a last resort, the honest but incapable person should be dismissed, but an honest worker is a terrible thing to waste.

Honest but incompetent managers sometimes arise when parents hand the reins of management to offspring, as in many small businesses and, for example, at Ford Motor Corporation where Henry Ford's son, Edsel Ford made several notorious management decisions. If the incapable manager possesses integrity and humility, he or she will admit to the professional inadequacies and seek remedies. This constitutes an opportunity for advancement for other honest people within the business who choose to assist the manager in overcoming his or her deficiencies. An honest manager is also a terrible thing to waste.

Sometimes managers lack both ability and dependability yet they end up in positions of authority, possibly through deceit. This situation is especially damaging because managers wield power and if they are deceitful, they can harm co-workers and the business as a whole.

Unless removed immediately, a manager who is both deceitful and incapable, but has somehow played the system and landed in a position of authority, constitutes a death sentence for business. Such a person will scheme to conceal both his or her dishonesty and his or her inability. The result is invariably a workplace nightmare of failed production, suspicion, allegations, and blame. As the noose of deceit and failure tightens, such a manager inevitably becomes more dictatorial and distrustful of coworkers. The whole company or industry may become a festering culture of dishonesty and ineptitude. The legacy of such institutionalized animus includes the subprime banking crisis of 2008, Enron Corporation, and Solyndra. In each case deceitful incompetence destroyed the livelihoods of vast numbers of innocent people, including management, staff, stockholders, customers, peripheral businesses, and, most damaging of all, the faith of the public.

Leadership

More books, essays, and lectures have addressed the issue of leadership than just about any other characteristic of human endeavor, but defining leadership is not complicated. In the workplace, leadership is comprised of competence and humility.

I want to point out that in this discussion, leadership is not synonymous with power. By some definitions, the toughest dude in a band of thugs is a leader. Sometimes circumstances align so that a particular person holds sway over events and personnel, and hence that person has power. These circumstances may be the result of belligerence, misappropriation, happenchance, or privileged birth, which is different than the power of leadership, which is derived from merit and earned respect.

In my definition, leadership is magnanimous; it is the principled leadership derived from internal honesty, ability, and shared ideals: the type of leadership that people follow as an act of conscious will, rather than for fear of reprisal or imminent physical threat.

Some leaders are virtually powerless, and many, many powerful people are distinctly devoid of leadership. Distinguished leadership may manifest itself in the form of a person who quietly stifles malicious gossip, who encourages a young person to strive and pursue dreams, or in one who offers a suggestion to improve corporate productivity—all without seeking advantage or power. In this way, leadership permeates society through small and persistent steps. When such leadership is recognized by others and imbued with well-deserved power, society moves forward.

In 1759, Scottish philosopher/economist Adam Smith stated his opinion of leadership in the workplace this way: "The man whom we believe is necessarily, in the things concerning which we believe him, our leader and director, and we look up to him with a certain degree of esteem and respect."[30] Smith focuses on believability, or trustworthiness, as the foundation of leadership, but, to maintain the respect of their coworkers, true leaders are more than trustworthy: they are humble. Without humility, competence fails to provide leadership.

Leadership happens when the leader concentrates his or her attention on another person or other people, which is impossible when one is thinking primarily of oneself. An ironic situation occurs when a person declares that he or she wants to become a leader; in other words, that person wants to concentrate his or her thoughts upon him or herself, thereby thwarting the ability to lead. Becoming a leader requires a person to quell the internal urge to greatness and encourage others to accomplish their goals and develop their abilities. Until one's ego is under control, leadership is impossible. Prospective leaders must first accomplish humility, then, if they possess the requisite competence, they are fit to lead.

For some people, leadership is difficult to realize because their high level of competence creates a feeling of superiority, which extinguishes humility. In fact, ability and humility tend to act in opposition. As outstanding ability draws the lauds of coworkers, a worker's or manager's ego can quickly run out of control. As the praise reaches higher levels, the strain on humility is intensified to the point that only truly strong individuals are capable of constraining an insistent ego, which is why there are so few leaders in the world.

We all want to feel important, and there is one sure way of achieving that goal: make other people important. Short of sacrificial acts of bravery, the best way to make other people important is by being attentive to them. The person who satisfies others' egos will quickly become the most important person in the room. That person will be sought out for advice, as a sounding board, and for emotional support, and be regarded as a friend and confidante by nearly everybody who knows him or her. There is no quicker or easier path to leadership than to bolster the importance of others.

What about the intangible trappings of leadership such as charisma, determination, and assertiveness? Again, each one is a subset of honesty. Charisma, the innate human quality that attracts the respect of others, comes in many incarnations, but without honesty, the respect is fleeting. Determination and assertiveness are factors within competence, but they do not enhance leadership unless they come from a trustworthy and humble individual; otherwise, they are merely veiled aggression.

Honesty and Workplace Cohesion

As discussed earlier, honesty and trust are essential to the cohesion of society and social order. They are also vital to workplace productivity. An atmosphere of trust allows information and productivity to flow unimpeded, while distrust places barriers and interrupts business operations. In 2014, a study concluded at Aalto University School of Science in Finland[31] effectively demonstrated the importance of honesty and trust within the workplace.

By measuring various levels of honesty in the exchange of information and resources between individuals and subgroups, the Aalto researchers were able to determine the cohesiveness of the overall group. It was not surprising that they found that a high level of honesty within the channels of communication increased cohesion within the larger group.

The study determined that not only did total group cohesiveness increase directly with the level of honesty, but that dishonesty fragmented the larger group into tightly knit cliques of honest and dishonest persons. Dishonesty essentially balkanized the larger community. The study further concluded that after fragmentation had occurred, most communication between cliques was carried on by "moderately deceptive agents" whose presence was marginally tolerated by interacting parties.

The researchers found that as honesty within the community decreases, "Moderately deceptive agents maximize their betweenness and become very central in the network, acting as bridges between groups."[32] These deceptive agents become more interactive with the various groups, while the honest workers form "small tight communities with truthful interactions." Thus the dishonest members of the study became more influential, while the honest members huddled together in an effort to fend off the plague of dishonesty.

Introducing dishonesty into the workplace not only sunders the community, but it perversely empowers the dishonest elements, elevating them to the status of communication conduits and arbitrators. In their capacity as workplace communicators, dishonest agents are able to stifle productivity and shift power to themselves. The dishonest groups were factionalized further as various levels and modes of dishonesty were accepted or rejected by the deceivers. The study also found that exclusively dishonest people were excluded from all groups but served as communication links between the most deceptive cliques.

The Aalto study effectively depicts the dysfunctional social hierarchy of many factories, offices, and corporations. Within those companies where honesty is compromised, cliques form and operations become factionalized. Management invariably finds itself embroiled with problems arising from failures of personal integrity while the day-to-day challenges of business go untended.

However, where honesty is the dominant culture, where workers can trust the information and resources supplied to them by their coworkers, workplaces operate smoothly as inclusive, intra-dependent businesses.

Summary

Workplaces provide sustenance, which is distinct and separate from the environment of friends and family, which provide comfort and love. As important as honesty is to the structure of society, it is more singularly important in the workplace, where it provides the foundation of productivity and efficiency, and, ultimately, personal sustenance. Those human qualities that are integral to business success, such as dependability, competence, and leadership, are built upon a foundation of honesty and humility.

Without humility, a leadership vacuum will prevail and productivity will plummet.

A fundamentally honest worker functions best within an environment that respects honesty. Consequently, those workplaces that attract dishonest or marginally honest coworkers, either through poor hiring choices or because of the one time, short-term nature of a particular business, will prevent honest workers from having rewarding careers. It is important for honest workers to seek like-minded coworkers and employers.

A study conducted at Finland's Aalto University showed that workplaces where honest communications prevail tend to maintain a high level of harmonious productivity, while where dishonesty prevails, harmony dissolves into isolated cliques and factions and the power of dishonest agents increases as they become the conduits of communication.

CHAPTER 5   JUDGING HONESTY

Now things get personal. Judging anything is personal. But, when we are judging the honesty of another person, first we must judge our own honesty, and that can present unwelcomed personal challenges. In business, unexpected circumstances and complicated situations tax our judgment, as mine was tested on one occasion at Patusan.

An interior designer from a furniture store phoned Patusan Trading Company and requested that a particular rug be sent to her store. Her client had seen the rug during one of our exhibits, but had waited until now to buy it. Real hand-knotted oriental rugs are individually produced in a time-consuming and precise process and are, in that way, unique pieces of art. The designer had written down the rug's identification number and indicated that her client was particularly interested in owning a rug that was constructed of a combination of wool and silk. We tracked down that particular rug and there was a problem: it was not made of wool and silk, but of wool and rayon. "But your salesman said it was silk," the designer told me.

At Patusan, we set ourselves apart from the shadier elements of the oriental rug industry by meticulously adhering to a policy of complete honesty. It was clear to all our salespeople that no product misrepresentation would be tolerated. Our prices were firm, we were always respectful of our customers, and we did not lie about our product. I needed to talk to the salesman.

Though this particular young salesman was hardworking, enthusiastic, and highly productive, and though he had never given me reason to doubt his honesty during his five years of Patusan employment, I had decided before the meeting started that he would be fired unless he had a completely cogent reason for his mistake.

It turns out, he didn't. He said he had been showing silk rugs and failed to explain that this one rug out of all of them contained rayon and not silk, a lie by omission. He did not think the customer would pick that particular rug, but she did. After years of trusting the man, of growing to genuinely like the guy, of counting on him to overcome the rigorous challenges of our distinct style of business that required unmitigated honesty, I felt I owed him more than a summary dismissal. But I felt I must dismiss him or employees and customers would think I had abandoned our stated principles.

I laid the groundwork for his discharge by detailing the merits of honesty in business and reminding him of Patusan's commitment to personal integrity and the tenets adopted from Mr. Sufian Ahmed early in Patusan's history. I reminded him, too, of the many times when we could have taken advantage of customers, but hadn't, and of the times when our squeaky-clean image had earned lauds and additional business. I commented on the simplicity of our honest business model. I explained that those commitments and those principles are so important that I could not trade them for either his ability as a worker or for our personal friendship.

I asked pointedly, "Did you intentionally mislead the customer?" His answer was evasive. He could have said no and asserted his innocence, but he didn't. He could have said yes and our conversation would have been essentially over, and I could have proclaimed my decision to dismiss him. Instead he stalled and began discussing the philosophical aspects of honesty, its cultural ramifications, and how his commitment to honesty was tantamount to adopting a religious creed.

Again, I asked, "Did you intentionally mislead the customer?" He would not deny it.

After nearly an hour of this emotionally draining parting of ways, I sat back in my chair and prepared to make my predetermined pronouncement. But he spoke first.

"I'm not saying this to preserve my job," he said. "I am saying it because of the respect that I have for this company, my coworkers, and all that we stand for. I will never again lie in a business transaction regardless of whether I am working here or elsewhere."

This frank statement told me two things: That he had indeed lied to the customer, and that he was absolutely committed to not lying again, otherwise he would have simply denied his first lie, which he had just spent a painstaking hour deftly not doing. He had lied once, but his conscience had kicked in and he was not willing to lie again even to save his job.

I changed my mind, and I'm glad I did. He called the designer and her client, explaining and apologizing for his breach of trust. Several years later, this worker left our company and started his own highly successful business while establishing himself as a pillar in the community and while upholding his pledge to honesty. He remains a close friend. We both had learned valuable lessons from our weaknesses. He had recommitted to personal integrity, and I had learned that some people deserve the chance to hit the reset button.

Ironic, isn't it, that the author of a book on workplace honesty would highlight a case where dishonesty was excused? The uncertain nature of truth and honesty requires tolerance and reasoning to judge just where that fuzzy gray line lies and whether to condemn those who violate it. Good people do step across it then jump back. We exercise personal judgment to determine if they penetrated too far, stayed there too long, or crossed the line too often. In business and in life, before we are worthy to judge others we must first candidly judge ourselves.

Not every untruth constitutes a lie or a violation of social trust. To judge lies we must recognize them. As you might expect, some very intelligent thinkers have paved the way. Their musings help us identify those employees who possess the good-worker gene.

Recall that, philosophically, science is truth. In *The Logic of Scientific Discovery*,[33] philosopher and scientist Dr. Karl Popper points out that scientific theories cannot be validated except by establishing criteria that prove them false. Popper explains, for example, that as scientists we may see a white swan and conclude swans are white. We may see a second white swan and feel confident in our conclusion. We may count a thousand swans, all of which are white, and feel certain that all swans are white. But our theory on the plumage of swans would be wrong if a single black swan exists.

By Dr. Popper's definition, a non-falsifiable, and therefore non-scientific, statement would be to say, as they paddle amidst lily pads on a quiet pond, "The swans are happy." They may look happy and they may even be happy, but we have no way of knowing for sure if they are happy. Unless a valid method for psychoanalyzing the mental state of swans is devised, the statement "The swans are happy" lies beyond the realm of science.

Probably Dr. Popper would object to this over simplification of his theory of falsification, and he might have rejected its usage as a tool in the pedestrian purpose of hiring employees. But his theory is tailor made for estimating a person's honesty by discovering how often and to what end he or she acts dishonestly.

We defined honesty as a person's deliberate effort to say, act on, and accept things as they are known or are perceived to be. We define lying as a deliberate effort to say, act on, and accept things as they are known or perceived **not** to be. We all act dishonestly to varying degrees, but, within the context of the workplace, moderating the degree to which we lie is crucial to maintaining workplace honesty.

No matter how we define lying, thoughtful, unbiased judgment is required to ascertain fact from falsehood, jest from injury, and innocence from malevolence. For that reason, our practical definition of lying will include a contingency that the liar deliberately attempt to damage another person, encourage erroneous decisions, or seek unmerited personal advantage. The addition of these conditions helps us to separate conversational lies from damaging lies.

Dr. Robert Feldman, a psychologist from the University of Massachusetts, wrote in his book *Liar in Your Life* that the average person engaged in a "getting to know you" conversation typically tells three lies within the first ten minutes.[34] This, if true, would probably disqualify every job applicant ever to apply for a job, and render unworkable the pretext of seeking honest job applicants. But do all Dr. Feldman's lies qualify as destructive, false information that damage other people or deliver unmerited personal advantage? Are those three lies told in the first ten minutes of a "getting to know you" conversation intentionally destructive? Well, that depends.

White Lies and Prosocial Lying

Every practical definition of lying entails some degree of moral evaluation. Not all deliberate lies are intentionally destructive; some are intentionally constructive, such as "Thank you for the delicious apple pie," which implies the apple pie tasted good, when, perhaps, it didn't. The statement, which contained a deliberately false impression, expressed gratitude for good intentions, which in this context trumped the need for honesty. Generally, such falsehoods are called white lies. Sociologists and psychologists refer to white lies as prosocial lying. It might be said that prosocial lying is merely another form of politeness.

One of the conclusions from the earlier mentioned Aalto University study was that prosocial lying "may even enhance the cohesion of the society as a whole and help to create links with other people."[35] Such prosocial mistruths are stated with the intention to encourage, gratify, or convey politeness but with no intention of deceiving. The receiver accepts them as gestures of civility and not as profound statements of fact. Though they are false statements, they are understood by both parties to be rhetorical ploys.

Dr. Feldman disagrees. He argues that all lies "involve some degree of victimization."[36] He feels that even the lies of everyday conversation beget more lies, and though these lies may produce short-term benefits, in the long term they are damaging. One might wonder how Dr. Feldman answers the question, "How are you?"

Some lies are destructive others are not. They are mistruths stated for reasons other than deceiving or manipulating, and they are welcomed by their receivers with, as poet Samuel Taylor Coleridge put it, "a willing suspension of disbelief."[37] These untruths are nothing more than polite social intercourse, more intent on encouraging the happiness of the participants than on propagating falsehoods.

What about "brutal honesty"? After making a deliberately hurtful comment, we sometimes hear a person say, "Well, I was just being honest." This could be called "anti-social honesty." Every second of every day, we are surrounded by lamentable truths, and if we verbalized our thoughts on each one, we would do little more than insult and complain. Brutally honest observations may be factual, but in a personal sense, they are not honest. Deliberately hurting another person with brutal honesty is a shameful violation of humility, the foundation of personal honesty.

British poet William Blake spoke of brutal honesty this way:

> A truth that's told with bad intent
> Beats all the lies you can invent.[38]

Marginal Lies

Though lying cannot be quantified in a practical way with high scores given for real doozies and lower scores given for minor truth-stretching infractions, lies must be judged. In this section on marginal lying or potentially destructive lies, those lies which are on the edge of propriety will be examined. Sometimes an untruth does not constitute a lie, but where does one draw the line? Each untruth must be judged within its particular circumstances. Within our comfort environment, marginal lies may be less consequential that within the workplace. Let's consider the types of untruths regularly encountered that, on one hand, may be prosocial and, on the other, destructive lying.

Exaggeration can involve relatively innocuous puffery or it can entail deliberate manipulation for gain. Puffery is simple embellishment for dramatic effect and often for humor. Simple idiocies like "So I told the boss to go jump off a bridge" constitute puffery. Puffery escalates to deceit when the message is intended to convey an untruth about actual events, as when the puffer follows with, "I really did." When a tendency to exaggerate becomes chronic, distrust becomes a problem.

Bragging lies on the borderline between exaggeration and fact. Bragging violates most social codes not because it is dishonest, but because it shows a disregard for basic humility, an essential component of personal honesty. Dizzy Dean may have been one hell of a baseball player, but he was no genius, which was probably the reason why, in 1937, he said, "It ain't bragging if you can do it."[39] Bragging is bragging precisely if you can do it; if you can't do it, you're lying. Bragging is nothing more than self-praise, a way for non-humble people to quench their thirst for the approval of others. Most bragging entails exaggeration. While maybe The Dizz wasn't exaggerating, he was bragging.

Because bragging usually relates only to the bragger and does not interfere with the sustenance of others, it may amount to nothing more than an annoying personality flaw, albeit one that transmits a notion of personal insecurity and arrogance. A bragger on your team will not help you win either the ball game or the contract. For that reason, the tendency to brag is lumped in with exaggeration as a form of dishonesty that is unwelcomed in the workplace.

Humility Trumps Boasting

Here's something braggers might want to consider: The belief that self-promotion makes favorable impressions is wrong. In job interviews, we're told to toot our own horns so we look confident and accomplished. While tooting might be the conventional wisdom, an orchestrated demonstration of humility is better than tooting. Studies have shown that self-promoters are viewed as incompetent and unlikeable by their conversation partners.

In 2014, Irene Scopelliti of the City College of London and her colleagues at Carnegie Mellon and Tilburg Universities reported finding not only that self-promotion creates ennui and scorn among listeners, but also that when self-promoters ramp up their bragging, they tend to misread reactions and think listeners are interested when they are decidedly not.[40] Scopelliti concluded that egocentrism leads "to the opposite consequences than the ones the self-promoter strategically intended." Direct and unabashed self-promotion damages an applicant's chances of landing a job.

Instead, a job candidate should strive to create a favorable impression while maintaining an air of humility. This is achieved by humbly demonstrating the manner in which the applicant's personal accomplishments match the needs of the prospective employer. In the process, the applicant wholly presents his or her accomplishments and qualifications, but with a focus on benefiting the prospective employer instead of hyping personal achievements.

For example, instead of boasting, "I doubled birdseed sales at Sally's Backyard Bird Emporium," the interviewee should present his or her accomplishments with more humility. "Though the products are quite different, selling is a skill whether selling bowling balls or birdseed. With the help of your accomplished staff, I hope to double bowling ball sales the way I doubled birdseed sales for my former employer."

Exaggeration and puffery are standard practice in advertising and sales. In the domain of marketing, products are described with attention-grabbing superlatives, which are then qualified with fine print or whispered disclaimers. On the grand scale, such exaggeration amounts to nothing more than grabbing attention among a crowd of competitors, but on an individual level a boundary line must be clear. An advertising agent or a salesperson who employs puffery in the promotion of products needs to recognize the need to scale back to frank honesty in closing a deal. The most effective advertising and the most effective salespeople are those who can emphasize a product's value without exaggerating it. Without respect for honesty, salespeople cannot detect where the line is or when they have crossed it. Among those hired to promote and sell products, personal honesty is a vital attribute.

Name-calling is often overlooked as a form of exaggeration. Name-calling allows the name-caller to defame a person allegorically without expressly stating the other's faults. Thus a person who is boorish, rude, and condescending is called a pig, and a person who is shy, thoughtful, and reserved is called a wimp. Often these impressions reflect the temperament of a name-caller, who, when calling another a wimp, might him or herself be a boorish, rude, condescending person. Some people resort to name-calling when they lack specific information or have reached their intellectual limits.

French philosopher Roland Barthes is credited with first calling **gossip** "murder by language."[41] Not everybody sees it that way, however. Dr. David Livingstone Smith, psychologist at the University of New England in Portland, Maine, contends that gossip helped bind human beings into social groups, thereby providing the evolutionary advantage that raised humanity from lowly cave dwellers to participants in a complex society.[42] Eons ago, gossip may have coaxed some prehistoric busybodies from their caves, but within a civilized society, gossip serves more the role noted by Barthes: social destruction. Gossip is the act of conveying imprecise information about another person to damage the other's reputation or for the entertainment of the conveyor, and, as such, it is a pervasive form of dishonesty.

The problem with gossip is that it is rarely victimless. Even bland gossip tends to target somebody. "Susie loves Johnny" is rarely intended to compliment Susie or Johnny and usually it is uncollaborated by either, and thereby constitutes information designed more to manipulate than to inform. Such gossip is nearly always used as a weapon by the weak and insecure to dominate another person or persons.

So why are human beings so addicted to gossip? Three major reasons come to mind. First, for the listener, the thirst for information spawned by natural, evolutionary curiosity is satisfied.

Second, for the purveyor, gossip creates a sense of power over the subject of the gossip. Third, the entertainment value of gossip provides the gossiper with a feeling of authority and control over the audience.

Entertainers enjoy controlling the emotions of their audiences, but liars manipulate that control to destroy the lives and reputations of others. Gossip is an insidious form of dishonesty that damages people and the workplace.

Bart Simpson has particularly strong preservation instincts. To protect himself from the wrath of his teacher, Mrs. Krabappel, and Principal Skinner, he adopted the self-defense tactics of "I didn't do it; nobody saw me do it; you can't prove anything."[43] Never mind that Bart's first statement is mitigated by his second statement and his third statement offers his defense for having lied in his first statement. He's living a good life as a clever ten-year-old cartoon kid, and he provides an excellent example of **lying for self-preservation**.

We learn to lie for self-preservation at a very young age, usually about the second time we stick our fingers into the icing on a cake or break a valuable dish. It is nearly instinctual to invent some excuse for our inexcusable actions. If we get away with it while we're young, it may become ingrained into our psyche as a successful verbal defense mechanism. Most post-adolescents recognize that self-preserving lies, such as, "I wasn't speeding, Officer," are futile. Adults accept responsibility for their actions. Since mature human beings make the best coworkers, the hiring of Bart Simpson acolytes is ill-advised.

A disingenuous person, as the name indicates, is one who is not genuine. We all deal with **disingenuousness** and people who present false personal images. In the olden days of the television show *Leave it to Beaver*, Eddie Haskell was the quintessential fake. In one scene Eddie is interrupted by Beaver's (Theodore's) mom: "Wally, if your dumb brother tags along, I'm gonna—Oh, good afternoon, Mrs. Cleaver. I was just telling Wallace how pleasant it would be for Theodore to accompany us to the movies."[44]

Humorist author Dave Barry also takes a well-aimed jab at artificial people when he says, "A person who is nice to you but rude to the waiter is not a nice person."[45] Many disingenuous people have difficulty maintaining their false image for an extended period. They may fawn over the interviewer while seeking a job, but they will invariably reveal their true nature to the receptionist or during a second interview. Disingenuousness is not a nice character trait. It is a type of lying and betrayal.

A **poseur** is someone who poses or pretends to be someone he or she is not, or have something he or she does not have, or know something he or she does not know, and it is a blatant form of disingenuousness. In the context of employment, most poseurs will fall into a category of posing as experts in a field when in fact their knowledge is lacking.

The degrees of posing can run the gamut from someone pretending to know where he or she is when lost in traffic to a people like Doctors Fleischmann and Pons, who in 1989 claimed to have discovered cold fusion when they had not. In the case of the disoriented driver, the issue may be nothing more than wounded pride, barely worthy of the label of fib. In the case of the misguided electrochemists, their fifteen minutes of fame dramatically ended along with their professional reputations. In the workplace a poseur is likely to be exposed when real world challenges result in failures of planning, performance, and production, costing coworkers and management untold losses.

From a job seeker's point of view, the honest candidate wants to demonstrate the necessary aptitudes without fabricating or exaggerating his or her actual knowledge. So, an interview creates a dilemma for any person concerned with maintaining his or her integrity: whether to stick strictly to the facts and expose oneself as marginally qualified, or to exaggerate and lay claim to the experience necessary for the job and risk exposure as a fraud. From an employer's point of view, the former scenario is immensely preferable, as gaps in knowledge and experience can be filled; gaps in integrity cannot.

Poseurs are particularly damaging within the sales arena. Conventional wisdom deems that disingenuous, smooth-talking, silver-tongued, yammering, BSing, glib, slick liars make the best salespeople. Nothing could be further from the truth. No doubt this perception evolved from the need to put poseurs to work somewhere, and rather than endure their ineptitude in-house, they were foolishly shunted outside to deal with the public where they invariably do far more harm than good. Besides being the revenue generators, often salespeople are the public persona of a company. A poseur acting as a salesperson damages not only the sales volume, but also the business's image.

Poseurs often cluster around businesses where sales transactions are quick and one-time, such as used cars, telemarketing, and flea market booths. Any prolonged association would expose the poseur and deter sales. Where long-term relationships with clients are vital, such as with professional account managers, poseurs make ineffectual salespeople. When hiring salespeople, an employer must weed out the poseurs or expect contentious relationships with clients.

Narcissistic lying falls on the borderline between strong personality and personality disorder. When tolerable, the flamboyant or extroverted narcissist demonstrates a strong personality; when aggressive or self-deceiving, the narcissist crosses the line into personality disorder, possibly requiring psychiatric attention.[46] This discussion focuses on the socially tolerable, mostly-just-annoying narcissist.

Psychologists tell us that narcissistic personalities are motivated by a craving for public praise; they will try to convince themselves and others that they are something that they are not. Narcissists possess a sense of personal greatness that is constantly in need of reinforcement whether or not it is deserved. Even high praise often fails to satisfy the lust for glorification. For many narcissists the need for praise is limitless and unquenchable. If praise from others is not forthcoming, then the narcissist will provide the service him or herself with boasting about actual or invented accomplishments.

Sometimes very accomplished society types and professionals are tolerably narcissistic. Psychiatrist Charles Ford, MD, points to entrepreneurs[47] as particularly likely to possess narcissistic personality traits. Entrepreneurs might point to the medical profession as a hotbed of narcissism. Many successful people exhibit a functional narcissism by which they operate professionally as ambitious, adaptable workers because their narcissism is tempered with an understanding of the importance of humility. These tempered narcissists recognize their personal flaw, but they may be unwilling or unable to contain it completely. Generally, such people can be regarded as possessing a quirky personality instead of a flawed character. In small doses, narcissism may be forgiven.

Tolerable narcissists tend to be glib, casual, and convincing in their conversations. Sometimes, to appear magnanimous, they will heap praise on others, but typically a narcissist's praise is carefully tailored to reflect positively on the narcissist. They will say something like, "Professor Jones is the leading authority in his field, unequalled in his accomplishments, and in command of the most productive laboratory in the country, which, by the way, he begged me to manage for him." Often such reflective praise is quickly followed with statements of self-aggrandizement along the lines of, "And he would never have discovered the cure for cancer without my help."

Narcissism in the workplace is likely to become a problem when a situation requires cooperation and teamwork. On such occasions the narcissist will feel his or her contributions are greater and worthy of higher praise than others. The narcissist may feel unwarranted resentment against fellow workers and, conversely, coworkers may resent the narcissist. Because a narcissist's longing for glorification can rarely be sated, a narcissist can sour workplace atmosphere as resultant bickering and tension mount and cohesion declines.

When the narcissist is the boss, he or she will view him or herself as entitled, special, and dominant. Subordinates will work thanklessly as they try to perform at levels that satisfy the insatiable ego of their boss. A narcissistic employer constitutes an obstruction to a competent worker's career path, and is a valid reason for seeking employment elsewhere.

Because they often regard job interviews as an excellent opportunity to present their superiority to someone who will appreciate it, narcissists are easily recognized during the interview process as they drone on and on about themselves.

Breaches of Logic

One subtle but vital way that honesty shapes our lives and our workplaces is through logic. Logic is a system of reasoning that reveals and preserves truth.

A hiring manager needs to recognize and exercise logic. When evaluating candidates' respect for honesty, he or she will need to recognize then judge the logic or reasoning ability of the candidate. When deciding which candidate to hire, he or she will exercise logic in making that decision.

A person who respects and practices logic is likely to recognize and value truth and honesty, while a person who ignores or thwarts logic may be purposefully deceptive. Logic can be complicated, and its misuse may reflect unintentional misunderstanding instead of deliberate dishonesty. Let's look at logic, so that when it is either used or flouted we can recognize and judge the circumstances.

Logical argumentation is an analytical process by which participants present premises to infer or deduce accurate conclusions. Used here in the classical sense, argumentation does not refer to those angry arguments, or quarrels whose misplaced purpose is to vent pent-up emotions, or the tedious, mildly amusing disagreements over such topics as whether Tom Brady or Peyton Manning was the better quarterback. Logical argumentation is the constructive process that sometimes is listed under the headings of rhetoric, logic, and reason as well as argumentation.

Arguments are generally divided into two types: deductive and inductive. Deductive arguments are less practical and therefore less common. They allow only a single conclusion to be drawn from the information, or premises, provided. Premises are the foundational facts that point the way to a higher truth, or conclusion. The example of deductive reasoning that has been passed down for 2,500 years follows: All men are mortal. Socrates is a man. Therefore, Socrates is mortal. The beauty of deductive arguments is the certainty of their conclusions, which is the reason they are useful in precise sciences like mathematics.

Most conversations, on the other hand, take the form of inductive argumentation, where conditions of uncertainty and differences of opinion are resolved by establishing shared premises, then attempting to draw a common conclusion from those premises.

From this premise: The sun has risen in the east every morning throughout history; we draw this conclusion: The sun will rise in the east tomorrow. There are other possible conclusions. One could argue that tomorrow's sun will rise in the north, but that argument would be weak, because no evidence exists to validate it. Still, the argument requires that the participants exercise a degree of judgment and share some worldly knowledge to agree upon the conclusion.

When the premises of an argument do not agree with the conclusion, the argument is said to be fallacious. Such lapses are called fallacies of logic. Sometimes a simple lapse in judgment or a misunderstanding of facts accounts for mistakes and false statements. When this happens, the errors can be recognized and rebutted, and they do not cross the threshold of deceit. Other times, fallacies of logic are employed expressly to deceive.

Fallacies of logic breach reason, and "Reason," David Hume tells us, "is the discovery of truth or falsehood." Hume continues, "Truth or falsehood consists in an agreement or disagreement either to the real relations of ideas, or to real existence and matter of fact."[48] Our ability to reason is a measure of our skill at understanding and furthering truth. While preserving truth denotes integrity, skillful reasoning signifies intelligence. When intelligence conspires to thwart reason, that act constitutes deliberate dishonesty.

An example of a logical fallacy follows. Human beings are smart because they have large brains. Elephants have larger brains than human beings; therefore, elephants are smarter than human beings. The argument fails on several levels. Brain function and physiology are complex scientific topics, and brain size may not exactly correlate to smartness. Without a shared definition of "smart," our conclusion is baseless. If smart means reading the newspaper, completing the Sudoku, and pondering the latest findings in the realm of astrophysics, then elephants aren't smart. If it means fitting into the complex social hierarchy of an elephant herd and warding off attacks from prowling African lions, then elephants are smarter than human beings.

It is not always easy to recognize when logical fallacies are being abused, which is why it is important to understand their subtleties. Skillful liars will take advantage of these subtleties to influence the opinions and actions of others, so a working knowledge of logic and the fallacies of logic help us understand the liars' techniques.

Sometimes, scheming liars apply logical fallacies this way: "I worked as Senator Smithers's campaign manager. Senator Smithers is a powerful and influential politician who can pull strings to get things done. Therefore, you should hire me as your new marketing director."

What was wrong with that logic? The blatant name-dropping is annoying, but also the conclusion is illogical because it fails to connect working for Senator Smithers with the qualifications essential to manage a marketing department. The lapse in logic could indicate poor reasoning skills, or it could be a calculated attempt to influence the interviewer's judgment by wielding the authority attached to Senator Smithers's name as a veiled threat of political retribution if the job is not proffered. The applicant appears willing to forego logic and advocate an unreasonable conclusion.

Another job applicant might say this: "I worked as Senator Smithers's campaign manager. Managing a successful political campaign is similar to managing a marketing department. Therefore, you should hire me as your new marketing director." This job applicant is conscious of connecting the premises with a conductive inference to reach a relevant conclusion, indicating not only respect for reason, but also an ability to communicate in an orderly, constructive manner. This applicant appears more reasonable, and probably is more honest than the first.

People who are careful to build their arguments with sound reasoning are likely to have a conscious and profound respect for truth, and recognize the value of reason in their daily lives. Hence, they are likely to be committed to honesty and accuracy. Those who flout the rules of reason and logic are generally less committed to truth.

Fallacies of Logic

Let's consider some of the more common fallacies of logic so that we can better recognize when logic is being flouted. Fallacies can be grouped into three loose classifications: fallacies of irrelevance, ambiguity, and redundancy.

Fallacies of **irrelevance** make inferences that do not affect the premise nor effect the conclusion, such as this ad hominem fallacy: "Tom says increased market demand moved fuel prices higher, but he owns stock in an oil company, so his opinion can't be trusted." Tom may or may not be trustworthy; however, his statement about fuel prices may be valid regardless of his investments. The speaker infers that Tom's judgment is impaired by a conflict of interest, but the substance of Tom's argument is about the cause of higher fuel prices. Apparently, the speaker disagrees with Tom's conclusion, but rather than refuting the substance of his argument, the speaker attempts to thwart honest debate with useless digressions.

The fallacy of the ascribed motive is one of the more provocative examples of irrelevance. The ascribed motive allows one person to impugn another by speciously attaching a vulgar motive to the other's actions or words. As is the case when Tom says, "Sally chooses plastic bags at the grocery store; she doesn't care about the environment." Or this one: "The company's health insurance plan has raised its deductible; this company doesn't care if we live or die." By ascribing a false motive, the accuser falsely claims the moral high ground and vilifies the target.

As we demonstrated in our discussion on the smartness of elephants, **ambiguity** can arise from false premises and result in false conclusions. What does smart mean, anyway? Sally earned class honors in calculus: she's smart. Sally walks to the parking lot and locks her keys in the trunk of her car: draw your own conclusion. Sometimes fallacies of ambiguity use the multiple meaning of words to make inaccurate conclusions.

The straw man fallacy is a classic example of implicit ambiguity. An example of deliberately undermining a premise with a flimsy inference, then obtaining a fallacious conclusion, follows. "The last time we handed out bonuses, Tom bought a bass boat. Tom doesn't need another bass boat, so no bonus for him." Using the bass boat as an allegory for waste, the obvious inference is that Tom is wasteful with his money. To the speaker, the bass boat implies Tom is wasteful, whereas to Tom it may mean the hard-earned reward for lifelong thrift.

Restating the premise as a conclusion is a form of logical **redundancy**. Such arguments often start with a false premise, then, using different words, restate the false premise as the argument's conclusion. These arguments are often circular, following a format of "I say it's right. I'm your boss; that makes me right."

Redundant fallacies can run in reverse. "You never praise me for my work" implies both a lack of gratitude from the boss and a praiseworthy job performance from the worker. The boss may feel the recent pay raise, promotion, and additional time off is praise enough, while the worker is looking for a gregarious slap on the back and public commendation. On the other hand, since the promotion, the worker may have performed poorly and failed to fill the promise of effective leadership. In essence the worker is saying, "I deserve praise, and you are unappreciative."

Fallacies of logic are not often served up on silver platters. Usually they appear out of the fog of a confusing conversation, in retrospect, after the pace of the discussion has proceeded a few steps farther down the road. In the quest to determine truthfulness, familiarity with fallacies of logic allows for quicker recognition of honesty and provides more time for thorough follow-up questions.

Summary

Not all mistruths are lies, and personal judgment is required to differentiate damaging lies from non-damaging lies. Many elements of daily conversation entail statements and rhetoric that could be interpreted differently depending upon the context and environment in which they are spoken. Many mistruths are socially acceptable and others are forgivable. However, deliberate lying that harms another person, encourages erroneous decisions, or seeks unmerited personal advantage is damaging and damnable. Some personality traits teeter between harmless idiosyncrasies and deliberate deceptions. When present in the workplace, these traits, bragging being one, can damage harmony and productivity. In certain circumstances, breaches of logic may indicate a misinterpretation of logical premises, while in other cases they may indicate deception. Those who follow the principles of logic in their daily lives are generally well versed in truth recognition and more practiced in its use. The onus of judging the honesty and dishonesty of others is a heavy burden to be borne by responsible people.

Chapter 6   Deliberate Lying

The business arena provides liars with the ideal forum to show-case their talents, which is why so many liars yearn to be in business. They enter business for the same reason Willie Sutton robbed banks: "That's where the money is." One way for liars to enter their chosen arena is through the open doors of employers offering jobs. When a deliberate liar applies for a job, interviewers and hiring managers are the business world's first line of defense. To deny liars entry we must recognize their methods.

Deliberate deception differs from the marginal lying dis-cussed in the previous chapter in that deliberate deception ful-fills the definition and our contingencies for lying and is, thereby, categorically damnable. Oddly, this simplifies the problem of managing deliberate deception, as no judgment is required: one merely needs to detect the lie. However, when the deception is deliberate, one is often dealing with an accomplished liar. Here we enter the realm of liars who are practiced, efficient, and con-vincing. Deliberate deception is a skill honed with experience. These liars have invested heavily in their lies and they are com-mitted to making their targets believe them.

A deliberate liar is someone who uses dishonesty to damage another person, encourage erroneous decisions, or seek unmer-ited personal advantage.

Liars have learned that lying empowers, and often they get the guy or the girl, the promotion, the contract, or the triumph in a personal argument. Few things in life exemplify personal power better than a successful career, and if a liar can use his or her skills as a liar to enhance a career, concerted effort will be made to achieve that end. Now we'll study deliberate lying so we can recognize and thwart those would-be deceivers.

Part of the rationalization for lying for career enhancement is the notion that it is acceptable to dupe an employer. The "us against them" mentality that permeates many workplaces provides a pass for those who are willing to lie. In interviews, it is important to look for the workplace divider, the person who maintains an attitude that employees are working inherently against the employer. Such employees are often willing to use that division as a justification for their lying. Employers sometimes use the same tactic, while rationalizing that their lies are essential for the future of the business.

Plausibility is the underlying foundation of all lies. Liars hope to pass off their lies as valid, so they must make them believable. Good liars are hard to detect because they know when to back off. A liar in control of his or her impulses will stop before crossing the line into implausibility. After all, a liar who doesn't control his lying gets caught. There the advantage ends. Good liars don't get caught.

Take, for example, a person who faces stiff competition for a high-paying job as a hospital administrator and who enhances his or her resume with a fictitious public service award from a small town in a distant state. If that particular false resume entry is uncovered by the interviewer or interview committee, the liar will need to have an explanation ready. It is likely that from the moment the deceit enters the liar's mind the wheels are in motion to compound the fabrication with a plausible, though false, explanation. The liar will scheme to cover himself or herself with possible corroborators, false documentation, or a shrugged dismissal: "Since you asked, I have to admit it happened so long ago that it was hardly worth mentioning."

To make a lie plausible, the liar must comport him or herself as though he or she believed it. In *Why We Lie*, Dr. David Livingstone Smith stresses the importance of self-deception to successful lying, explaining, "In hiding truth from ourselves we are able to hide it more fully from others."[49] The liar's meter becomes whether he or she would believe the lie if he or she were on the receiving end. The further liars stretch credulity the more they invest in believing their own lie and the more staunchly they must cling to it. It is not so much that they actually believe the lie as it is that they make the victim believe they do. This helps explain the hysteria in which some liars cloak their lies.

As Montaigne pointed out, "the reverse of truth has a hundred thousand shapes,"[50] and each shape carries its own template for lying. The task of recognizing lies and their vectors may appear daunting, but it becomes less so as we hone our recognition skills. Therefore, employers and hiring managers need to engage in the conversations and communications that flush liars from the weeds and into plain view. We will examine this process more fully in Chapter 8, Managed Conversations.

The Liar's Game

What about the scheming liar who lies for no better reason than because he or she can? Psychologist Paul Ekman is credited with coining the phrase "duping delight"[51] to describe the thrill scheming liars derive from lying. Most of us know such a person, someone who compulsively invents and spreads falsities without pangs of guilt or qualms of immorality. Recklessly, these bald-faced liars dare their listeners to challenge their inventions. In *Lies! Lies! Lies!*, Ford points out that as the feeling of power derived from successfully lying for advantage is reinforced, it can approach the level of addiction, even to the point where the lie serves no purpose beyond sensational gratification.[52]

Duping delight can be intensified if shared with an audience, if the trophy is impressive, or if the dupe is a particularly appealing target, like a company with a generous pension plan.

Like all lies, a degree of moral judgment must be exercised to quantify duping delight. Light teasing, practical joking, and bluffing in sports and games are deceptive schemes that result in duping delight, but in a manner that is generally not damnable. On occasion, the workplace is the setting for such informalities, but the line is clearly crossed when duping delight diminishes job performance.

For the sheer sport of testing how far credulity can be stretched before the lie is discovered, the liar plies unsuspecting victims with manufactured stories and accusations. If possessed of integrity, talent, and discipline, this person might have been a novelist, movie director, or productive in another creative vocation, but without honesty, all the liar can show for his or her creative mind is a legacy of lies. Such a person may relish a job interview to showcase his or her talent for lying.

Let's look at a few specific lying techniques that employers and interviewers might encounter. After all, when we are familiar with the methods, we can recognize their users.

Lying by Omission

Paul Ekman, author of *Telling Lies*, points out that liars prefer passive lying to active lying; they prefer to conceal the truth rather than make up a lie.[53] Concealed truths, also called lies of omission, are lies told not by verbalizing, but by deliberately failing to verbalize. Ironically, it seems even committed liars are burdened with some degree of innate morality, which causes them to avoid overt lying when a passive lie will do. Lies of omission also have practical utility: they allow the liar to avoid many of the mental pitfalls of active lying. Active lying requires keeping track of the myriad ramifications, while lies of omission, when exposed, merely require an admission of ignorance or oversight.

The father demands, "Why didn't you tell me you wrecked the car?"

The son replies, "You didn't ask." In the resulting quandary of parental vexation, the father may forget to ask too about personal injuries, damage to other cars, or about the speed, alcohol, and drugs involved. The son has decided the best lie is to not-mention the accident.

In job interviews, lies of omission commonly occur when the interviewee omits negative employment experience from the resume. When, through involuntary information leakage,[54] the interviewer discovers important facts are omitted, the liar can always claim, "I didn't think it was important," or "I must have forgotten to mention that particular job."

False memory lapse is another form of the lie of omission. Many liars prefer to claim falsely, "I'm sorry, I don't remember." As implausible as the claim may be, we all think separately and we're not privy to other people's memories, so we have no way of verifying the lack of memory.

Diversionary Lying

In place of a faulty memory, a person might choose to lie with the artful dodge, a diversionary tactic intended to lead the questioner away from the substance of a question. As in, "Did you obtain your degree?" Diversion: "During my senior year I was elected captain of the volleyball team and that took up much of my time, but we did win the conference championship. You might remember reading about it in the newspaper." An astute interviewer will recognize the tactic and lead the interviewee back to the original topic.

Lying through exaggerated truth is another technique of diversionary lying. Since this is a handy vehicle by which to add a humorous twist, it is often overlooked or excused. When, for example, a potential employer is asked, "Why did the person who previously held this job leave it?" and the HR professional responds, "Because we stopped paying him," the answer, while accurate, erects a padded obstruction to that line of questioning.

Jargon

For shyster mechanics determined to dupe unwitting motorists and for pseudo-scientists scheming for grant money, a favorite method of lying is to cloak lies in abstruse jargon. When, out of desperation, an out-of-town driver takes his or her malfunctioning automobile to the nearest repair shop, the mechanic might insist that the vehicle needs a new (but made-up) mitogulation regulator, which, lucky for the wayward traveler, the mechanic has in stock in the back of the shop. Since the driver isn't familiar with the device or the cause of the car's problem, he or she pays the $1,795, and leaves town unaware that a broken twenty-dollar fan belt was the cause of the problem.

The interviewee may answer a simple question with a string of obscure technical terms for the sole purpose of frustrating the questioner. When asked, a sincere person will generally reword the answer in a comprehensible manner. A less than sincere person will often continue with the jargon. If a second interview is granted to an interviewee whom the interviewer suspects of using jargon to mask ignorance, the technical experts attending the second interview should be alerted to the candidate's tendencies.

Gaslighting

Gaslighting is a malevolent form of lying where one person retroactively tries to manipulate facts to cause another person to have self-doubts. An example of gaslighting is a boss who claims to have given an important document to an employee even though he is aware that he failed to do so. Yet the boss pretends to re-create the presentation of the document, perhaps saying, "Don't you remember? We were on the elevator at the time," in an effort to convince the employee that he or she has a flawed memory.

Gaslighting compounds the liar's intentional lie with an effort to convince the victim that he or she is emotionally or functionally unstable. This becomes a particular possibility when the gaslighter is in a position of power and authority and the victim is young, impressionable, or vulnerable.

Though this type of lying fits easily into situations of power disparity, coworking peers can experience gaslighting too. Gaslighting is a particularly heinous form of intellectual bullying. When a coworker is guilty of this type of lying, supervisors or managers should be made aware of the problem.

It is not the intention of this discussion to define or diagnose **pathological lying** or provide psychological insight into the mental states of individuals. When a liar starts to believe his or her own lies, the condition is known as pathological lying. When lying gets to this level, psychiatric consultation is needed.

Legal Issues Related to Lying

Fraud, defamation, libel, and slander are legal terms that refer to lying. When lying results in direct, measureable damage to others, the offenses may be actionable in court, either as civil or criminal offenses. What, exactly, the damage happens to be is usually sorted out by the court system. But if a deception or falsity deliberately injures the reputation, property, or business of another, that lie may constitute an illegal act.

Fraud is a deliberately false statement that causes harm to another person, either by allegation ("Your car's transmission needs to be replaced," when the mechanic knows it doesn't) or concealment ("This car is in perfect running condition," when the salesperson knows the transmission needs to be replaced). For fraud to be proven in court the statement must be demonstrably false, known by the originator to be false, intended to deceive the victim, believable by the victim, and it must have caused damage or injury to the victim. Each of these five elements of fraud is conditional and may be difficult to prove.

A person defending against charges of fraud could claim the statement was not intentionally false and only a misunderstanding, or the other person is too gullible and should have known better, or the other person was not really harmed by the statement.

Sales puffery and statements of opinion and belief are not statements of fact and, therefore, are not fraudulent. When the salesperson says, "This car runs like a top," the statement is an allegorical opinion and not a fact. Likewise, when a job applicant says, "I'm the best person for this job," that is a statement of belief and not a fact.

Telling lies about another person is called **defamation**. When those lies are spread through writing or electronic media such as via television, radio, or the Internet, they are called **libel**. When they are spread via spoken words, they are called **slander**. Like fraud, defamation may be the basis for legal action if the lie contains elements of falsity, malicious intent, and measurable injury to the maligned party.

The act of making dishonest statements on a resume or job application is sometimes called resume fraud. Conversely, employers who entice employees with false promises are guilty of employment fraud. The aim of the interview process is to un-cover resume fraud and root out dishonest job applicants, so that their dishonesty never becomes a problem within the workplace. The due diligence of the future employer is generally expected to expose resume fraud and eliminate the applicant from the hiring pool, so resume fraud rarely is subject to legal action.

With employment fraud, unless the job applicant diligently vets his or her future employer before being hired, the employee is likely to be on the payroll before the dishonesty is discovered, as when an employer promises a commission on sales, then refuses to pay it. Employment fraud, when it meets the criteria for legal action, is more likely to end up in court, since the em-ployee has more to gain and the fraudulent employer more to lose, making it all the more foolish for an employer to attempt it.

Fortunately, most lying does not reach the level of fraud or defamation, and the petty lies that are told in our daily lives are more puffery and innuendo than actionable maliciousness. Also, most workers and employers lack the time and resources to legally battle the injustices suffered in day-to-day living. Consequently many deliberate lies go unpunished, but their damage is still felt.

Employers cannot make effective business decisions based upon the faulty information provided by liars, and through lost productivity and worker discontent, liars at work inevitably cause anxiety at home. Employers want to keep deliberate liars off the payroll, and potential employees want to avoid the miserable feeling of helplessness and entrapment that comes from working for a known liar. Within a workplace where honesty is the norm, anxieties over fraud and defamation are obviated.

Summary

Falsehoods that damage another person, encourage erroneous decisions, or result in unmerited personal advantage are called deliberate lies. The workplace provides a venue that can empower and enrich an accomplished liar, and so, within the workplace, liars are driven to greater levels of deceit. Hiring managers and employers, as well as potential employees, need to be aware of liars' methods. Some liars rationalize their lies with an "us against them" agenda, where the employer or employees are regarded as the enemy against whom any method of vengeance is acceptable. To some liars, the delight gained from duping a coworker is reward enough. Where deliberate liars prevail, workplace harmony is destroyed and the effects are felt beyond the workplace, within the comfort zones of family and friends. Some lies, such as fraud and defamation, cause direct, measurable damage to others and are actionable in court.

Chapter 7   How to Spot a Liar and What to Do About It

We have talked about social lies, marginal lies, and deliberate lies; now let us look specifically at the ways of detecting those lies. For employers and employees alike, the real irony is that many of the conventional, popularly recognized, and even legally mandated methods do not work. Success in lie detection, like success in so many other things, entails patience and subtlety.

Since the dawn of civilization, a reliable way to detect lies and liars has been sought, but never found. Many people have claimed the ability to detect lies and liars, but for the most part, they too are liars. But, despite the obstacles to lie detection, we can identify liars and minimize the damage that they do.

Polygraph Testing

Let us talk briefly about polygraphs because they are still being used and because they illustrate some popular misconceptions about lie detection. Polygraph or lie detector tests, which are required by some companies and governmental agencies, measure physiological indicators such as pulse, blood pressure, respiration, and perspiration to gauge the level of stress a person feels when asked or when answering various questions. A polygraph does not measure truth, mental concepts, or brain activity. A person may hear a question about his or her ex-spouse and the mention of the name alone could cause blood pressure to rise and palms to sweat. Likewise, an effective liar can calmly speak falsehoods all day long and not raise the armature of the polygraph, as was the case with notorious spy Aldrich Ames, who was polygraphed numerous times without being caught in his lies.

Prior to his CIA-administered polygraph test, CIA double agent Aldrich Ames, who exposed numerous American spies in the Soviet Union resulting in dozens of arrests and executions, was advised by his Soviet spy master, "Get a good night's sleep, and rest, and go into the test rested and relaxed. Be nice to the polygraph examiner, develop a rapport, and be cooperative and try to maintain your calm."[55] Ames heeded the KGB's advice and the CIA failed to detect his lies. Ultimately it was the extravagant, million-dollar lifestyle on a lowly grunt's CIA salary that exposed Ames.

In the case of polygraphs and truth sera, it is the threat of participating that snares most unwitting criminals and liars. Today's spies are aware of the failings of these techniques, but the ignorant crook, not so much, which is why polygraphs are still used among some law enforcement agencies.

A polygraph is most effectively used as a way to create angst for the person being tested. The machine's reading of physiological responses might show an increase in stress. When that occurs, the examiner doesn't know that a lie has been told, he or she knows only that the person's stress indicators rose. They may have gone up for any number of reasons. Take for instance the question, "Where were you on the Friday night that the First National Bank of Peoria was robbed?" Well, that might have been the day your long-lived family dog finally succumbed, which could cause stress-related readings on the polygraph. The examiner will not know why your stress level went up. When you answer, "I was burying my dog," the examiner may suspect you are lying.

The reverse might also be true. If you were the dastardly villain who really did rob the First National Bank of Peoria and the examiner asks where you were that Friday night, you might answer, "My dog, Ol' Mangy, died that day, so I stayed home and buried him under the apple tree in the backyard." The examiner might sympathize with you, excuse your elevated stress levels, and set you free.

But the more likely scenario would be that the examiner asks the suspect where he or she was on Friday night. Regardless of the answer, the examiner claims his machine detected a lie. The line of questioning would then follow a course of assumed guilt with the hope that the mounting angst would cause the suspect to confess.

In fact, on occasion criminals are advised by certain unscrupulous advisers to curl their toes and bite the insides of their cheeks to create artificial stress readings, thereby throwing the examiner off track. Convicted spy Aldrich Ames offers this advice to his fellow liars: "There's no special magic. . . . Confidence is what does it. Confidence and a friendly relationship with the examiner . . . rapport, where you smile and you make him think that you like him."[56] In brief: polygraphs are not lie detectors; they are simply tools of interrogation that detect lying only when the test-taker succumbs to the examiner's emotional trickery.

Truth Serum

Truth serum, or sodium thiopental, trade named Sodium Pentothal, is a barbiturate once used by psychiatrists and interrogators—and still used by movie producers—to get unwilling participants to tell the truth. In reality, the narcotic effect loosened recipient's tongues but it did not make them tell the truth. They blabbed all right, but not necessarily about anything pertinent to the questions asked. The theory was that if you could get a person to drop his or her guard, like a glib drunkard, they might let vital information slip out; but, like the drunkard, they were just as likely to let slip falsehoods as facts. So, after a short time, the ineffectual[57] "truth serum" fell into disuse by psychiatrists and interrogators, but not by Hollywood.

Tells and Body Language

One often reads of a politician, sports figure, or celebrity who performs a "tell," or makes a suspicious sign, when lying. They wrinkle their brow, look at the floor, inhale deeply, wring their hands, scratch their nose, or make some other subconscious movement or sound that unintentionally coincides with their lying. Many of these tells are codified into conventional wisdom to the point that some of us make conscious efforts to avoid making similar movements so as not to appear to be lying. By avoiding speech hesitations and by keeping hands out of sight, one may sound and appear more honest, or at least more confident.

Do tells actually indicate the presence of a lie? The answer is a clear cut maybe. Many so called tells are simply coincidental tics, speech anomalies, or the effects of nervousness. Occasionally a person who is not prepared to lie, or who is unpracticed at lying, will give a nonverbal indicator. Just as often a person will recognize the suspicious sign before making it and intentionally halt the involuntary action. Generally, observers recognize most nonverbal indicators of lying after the fact, after the lie is revealed through an explicit event, like the surfacing of a stained dress.

If body language is a language, then it is possible to tell a lie with it. Consciously or subconsciously, people alter their body positioning in ways that reflect their thoughts, attitudes, and emotions. So-called experts at reading body language claim the ability to reveal the contradictions between the lies made in oral statements and the facts expressed in body language, but successful liars can hide their body language tells as convincingly as they hide their oral tells. One would expect that a president, say, standing before the people and falsely denying perjury-related charges would equivocate and reveal the truth with subconscious contradicting body language. Instead, a strident liar can assertively wag his finger in the face of the nation in a manner that is completely in keeping with his oral lies. Successful liars lie as well with their body language as they do with their oral language. Body language is not the great code cracker that many wish it were.

Thwarting Bias

In determining the truth or falsity of a statement, two mistakes can be made: one can accept a falsehood as truth, or one can reject truth, thinking it false.[58] One mistake is as wrong as the other. Accepting a falsehood as truth is an obvious concern. Rejecting a true statement as false, possibly due to a latent bias, is potentially more damaging. The consequence could be that an honest person suffers unnecessarily. Silhouetted against a setting sun, even white swans may appear black to Dr. Popper. As lie detectors, we must be patient and avoid the costly mistake of hearing a truth and declaring it false.

Social bias, bigotry and paranoia are maladies that can cause a person to disbelieve truth. It is bad enough that irrational biases degrade worthy social institutions, but in the workplace bias and bigotry damage honest individuals and thereby limit the field of honest associates. Bias and bigotry that result in unwarranted distrust erode the foundations of business.

However, many people are hardwired to believe what they are told. Psychologist Robert Feldman uses the term *truth bias*[59] to define a person's natural inclination to trust and believe those around him or her. Research shows that most people trust what others tell them, even if the others are unknown, and even if the person is aware that the others might have reasons to work counter to them.

Confirmation bias is a willingness to fall for the lies one wants to believe. For example, a person might see a cute, fuzzy, white polar bear and think something that gentle-looking must be friendly. When the polar bear comes slowly closer and crouches down, the person mistakenly concludes, "Ah, look, he likes me." A well-groomed, business-suited man carrying a briefcase portrays an image of professionalism, and when the interview begins, the interviewer may willingly believe false information that reinforces his or her preconceptions.

Face-to-face interviews can be biased if the interviewer forms a professional opinion, positive or negative, based upon the appearance of the interviewee. We are all familiar with the stereotypic scene of a male office manager hiring a female personal assistant based upon the woman's attractive appearance. The man asks, "How fast can you type?" The woman answers, "I can't." He responds, "That's great. Can you start tomorrow?"

To guard against confirmation bias, it is essential for the interviewer to remind himself or herself to set aside prejudices and gauge the interviewee's job worthiness based solely upon the content of the interview, resume, and work references.

Telephone interviews can be biased if the interviewer likes the tone and timbre or the interviewee's voice, or, conversely, if the interviewer doesn't. Accents too elicit biases; and in a phone conversation the effect of an accent or colloquialism is often exaggerated. An annoying feature of phone interviews, aside from potential bias, is that bad reception often leads to poor communication and that failure is often blamed on the interviewee.

Liars versus Dupes

Throughout human evolution, an ongoing tug of war has raged between liars and their potential dupes.[60] Since the first time a liar—call him Sleazeball—succeeded in trading a sick goat for a healthy lamb, liars have been scheming for advantage over possible suckers. From that morning when the first dupe—call him Gulliball—awoke to find his recently acquired goat lying dead outside his cave, dupes have been swearing they will never again be cheated by a liar.

As lie detection procedures improve, liars improve their methods of avoiding detection. After his unpleasant experience, Gulliball will be less trusting. On the other hand, because he benefited from duping Gulliball, Sleazeball will be more willing to lie in the future. Gulliball becomes more wary and Sleazeball becomes more determined. Society's future looks bleak and riven by distrust.

Gulliball is not alone. Research shows human beings are not good at detecting lies. In research published in 2008, using meta-analysis from over 200 relevant studies, psychologists Charles Bond and Bella DePaulo confirmed that human beings are rarely able to recognize veracity.[61] Their study showed that people were able to distinguish truth from lying about 54 percent of the time, when a rate of 50 percent is expected by chance.

In another study in 2009, Christian Hart, D. G. Fillmore, and J. D. Griffith showed that when participants were asked to determine liars from non-liars by watching videos in which some actors were lying and others weren't, the participants guessed correctly slightly *less* than half the time.[62] They could have done better by tossing dice. When the participants searched specifically for telltale behavioral changes and suspicious signs among the actors, they were able to improve their performance slightly, correctly identifying liars only 55 percent of the time. We are not naturally equipped with an effective way to catch liars.

The balancing act goes on, but of this we can be sure: If Gulliball was watching the video and Sleazeball was one of the actors, Gulliball would not believe Sleazeball. Sleazeball lied to Gulliball once, and Gulliball would be a damn fool if he allowed it to happen again. Even if Sleazeball were telling the truth in the video, Gulliball would declare him a liar. Our memories help prevent our repeating past mistakes.

Protection from Liars

Human beings may not be good at distinguishing truth from lying, but by remembering who has lied to us in the past, we are granted a statistical advantage going forward. The best way to protect ourselves from liars is to unveil the liar, then dismiss whatever he or she says from that moment on.

Many of the above-mentioned studies focus on detecting lies within a relatively short time or through indirect interaction with their test subjects, and that is why they fail to detect dishonesty. It takes time to unveil dishonesty. Over time, in social settings, we can engage in prolonged casual conversations and personal interactions that eventually reveal the honesty of others. In a workplace, scheduled interviews take the place of casual conversations, professional evaluations replace personal contact, and time is limited. So a system of interviewing is needed that will accomplish within the meted time that which would likely have taken longer in a social setting.

The amount of time needed to determine a person's veracity depends upon the person and the circumstances, but, according to Paul Ekman, the more time one person spends communicating with another, the more likely lies will be revealed. "Good interviewers know their main task is to enable the interviewee to talk,"[63] Ekman reports. In social settings conversations can range over any topic the participants choose. In the workplace the topics must relate to work and sustenance. This allows both parties to focus their attention within a narrower range and to concentrate their time on delving deeper into specific topics.

Lying requires considerable effort: effort to create the lie, effort to tell the lie convincingly, effort to remember the lie, and even more effort to manipulate future statements to conform to the lie. All that effort is tiring, and therein rests the answer to uncovering lies. Within the constraints of time, the most reliable way to determine if a person is lying is to fatigue the liar into exposing the deception.[64]

While a job interview is of limited time, the nature of the event allows participants to delve deeply into specific work-related topics while dispensing with many time-consuming social niceties. We protect our workplaces from the ravages of dishonesty by exposing the liars, then disassociating from them.

Summary

Though many have been tried, no surefire lie detection method exists. Alas, human beings fare poorly in their efforts to detect lying. Liars are always altering and improving their techniques as their dupes devise new defenses against the next onslaught from the liars. However, we are equipped with memories that help us to remember those who have lied to us in the past, and so through experience we reduce the chances being duped again. After the liar has been exposed, the dupe must make the decision whether to disassociate from that liar. Conversation is a passive way to assess another person's credibility.

PART II

THE TOOLS

To find and hire honest workers we need certain tools. Fortunately, these tools are cheap, readily available, and simple to use. Managed conversation is an interviewing technique that requires only minor modifications to the casual conversation of our daily lives. We're already familiar with resumes and job descriptions, now we just need to know how to use them. Then we will combine rapport building, open questioning and veracity testing with information drawn from a wide range of resources to measure the honesty of job candidates during interviews. It's all quite simple, if it is done properly.

The tools:

- Managed conversation
- Resume
- Job description
- Interviews

Chapter 8   Managed Conversation

Employers and hiring managers have a new tool at their disposal: managed conversation. In the workplace, as in society, honesty and dishonesty wage an ongoing battle. In that battle, honesty's first line of defense is conversation, because conversation extends the history and depth of our relationships and provides time for sorting out who can be trusted and who can't. In essence, conversation protects the fortress until those clamoring at the gates can be judged friend or foe. Managed conversation provides employers with both the means of selecting honest employees and with the means for managing them.

It may be hard to imagine in this era of social media and texting that, as a means of discerning honesty, face-to-face conversation exceeds other forms of communication because, unlike the aforementioned methods, conversation communicates much more than sounds and images. Conversation is efficient in both accuracy and timeliness.

Omitted from written exchanges, for instance, are the pauses of uncertainty and the fluency of confidence: clues that allow listeners to gauge the speaker's veracity. Public addresses deny listeners spontaneous follow-up questions. Likewise, the clues provided by body language and the inconsistencies resulting from cognitive load are not apparent in other forms of communication. The back-and-forth exchange of words combined with behavioral clues and speech anomalies that are detectable only when in another's company make conversation a superior means of assessing veracity.

Even with conversation as a tool, we must guard against being duped. To prevent duping and to encourage the open exchange of ideas within the workplace, we engage in managed conversations. Managed conversations differ only slightly from casual conversations. While casual conversations range freely over any topic of interest, managed conversations, whether scheduled or spontaneous, target a specific topic or purpose and are constrained by time. Casual conversations are suited to our comfort environment, and managed conversations are characteristic of the workplace. To be proficient in managed conversations, interviewers and employers should first understand the fundamentals of casual conversation.

Casual Conversation

In his timeless classic, *How to Win Friends and Influence People*, author Dale Carnegie made the observation that to be a good conversationalist one must be a good listener.[65] A good listener hears, pays close attention, inquires deeper, and encourages continued commentary from the speaker. A good listener encourages the talker to expound upon his or her experiences, thoughts, and feelings.

To become a good listener, simply remember this: It's not about you! It's not about your job, your bad day, your vacation, your homerun, your pet, your divorce, your ailments, your IQ, or anything else relating to or involving you. It's all about the other person.

When the talker mentions a silly thing his or her dog does, it is not a signal for you to mention the silly thing your dog does. Instead, a good conversationalist will ask, "What other silly tricks does your dog do?" The conversation is about his or her dog, not yours. If the talker wants to continue chattering about the mutt for the rest of the evening, and the listener wants to make a favorable impression or has nothing better to do, he or she will ask more questions and listen intently to their answers. The ensuing discussion will delight the talker simply because the topic is his or her choice.

If the talker feels the listener's interest is sincere, the flow of the conversation and the exchange of information and ideas will continue. If the talker feels the listener's interest is insincere or that personal trust might be violated, the conversation will stall. Therefore, the listener must show deference to the talker's privacy, respect for his or her knowledge, and concern for his or her dilemmas. Good conversationalists secure the talker's trust and preserve it.

Effective conversation resembles a verbal dance more than a verbal wrestling match. When the other party mentions that his or her dog sits on command, sometimes we feel compelled to one-up with, "Oh yeah, well, my dog sings opera with René Fleming." A good conversationalist does not try to dominate or counter the other person's verbal moves—that would be wrestling. Instead, a good conversationalist tries to enhance, elevate, and strengthen his or her partner's conversation, the way a dancer assists his or her partner's grace and elegance to the benefit of their mutual performance.

As in dancing, when our partners misstep, we aid their recovery by finding the beat, setting the pace, or adding a flourish that boosts the combined performance. Our conversational partners may be awkward and unfamiliar with the verbal dance steps, and it is our task to help overcome those obstacles and continue dancing. In dancing, when the team is in step, the reward is an elegant performance. In our personal comfort zone, the reward for well-performed conversation is enjoyment, comradery, and bonding. In the workplace, the reward for well-performed conversation is the accurate and efficient exchange of information and ideas that generate more overall sustenance.

Ultimately, though, a well-performed conversation is a rewarding, enjoyable experience. The listener listens because he or she is engaged and entertained. Primordial curiosity is satisfied with the exchange of information, and, if that exchange pleases the listener as well as the speaker, it doesn't matter whose dog does what. It is the personal interaction that we enjoy and that binds us together. Frequent and enduring conversations allow us to better understand and trust others. The better we are at conversing, the more accurately our thoughts and ideas are woven into society's fabric. Conversation provides the fiber from which honest society is woven.

Casual conversations flow smoothly when greased with who, what, when, where, why, and how questions and they are impeded by is, are, did, and do you questions. The former—active questions—require thoughtful and explanatory responses, while the latter—passive questions—generally call for yes or no answers. In workplace discussions and job interviews, questions that start with, "Please tell me about. ..." keep conversations moving while allowing the manager or interviewer to guide the conversation in a specific direction.

Attentive conversationalists will pick out specific words used by the talker and occasionally repeat them back when asking follow-up questions. When the talker says that Mondays were hectic at his old job, the listener might ask, "Why were Mondays more hectic than the other days of the week?" Then follow-up: "Did you agree with management's handling of hectic Mondays?" By using the candidate's own words, the conversation remains focused on him or her, and it signals that he or she is being listened to closely.

Managed Conversation

Managed conversation is casual conversation with a specific purpose and a limited timeframe, making it essential in workplace communications and job interviews. In a managed conversation, the conversation manager controls the topic, duration, and tone of the conversation while the other party provides information, answers, and feedback. The conversation manager is usually the boss, supervisor, or interviewer.

Unlike casual conversations, managed conversations are about sustenance, with the accurate exchange of facts and ideas as the primary goal. With the manager specifying the topic and length of time spent conversing on that topic, such exchanges entail honesty and brevity: honesty because facts are required when making workplace decisions and brevity because in the workplace time is money.

As we mentioned in our discussion about the science enigma, open questioning and veracity testing need not be contentious. When honesty and truth-seeking are the underlying purposes for a conversation, as they should be in every managed conversation in the workplace, then personal temperament and emotional sensibilities are, theoretically, laid aside. Still, people being emotional animals, the conversational manager should recognize the slights that might stir personal sentiments and steer the conversation accordingly, or privately counsel the offended party. But in an atmosphere of honesty and trust, inquiries that challenge statements and beliefs will be accepted as routine and welcomed as positive efforts to advance the common good of the business.

While topic and duration deliver the essence of these conversations, tone enables productivity. A supportive, temperate tone encourages open communication and downplays the conversational manager's authority. It should be similar to the tone of a casual conversation: that is, the conversational manager should listen carefully, ask follow-up questions, encourage the speaker to greater depth, all while showing deference and respect.

As an example, a manager might approach the problem of a malfunctioning machine with, "Sally, how's the widget machine running this morning?" instead of, "Sally, did you fix the widget machine like I told you?" While the first example encourages Sally to provide her explanation of the machine's performance, the second demands a yes or no answer and delivers the implication that Sally doesn't do her job unless told. The first example asks for an opinion and invites commentary; the later conveys contempt and slams shut the gateway to insight.

Listen to the workplace conversations around you and you'll agree that the preceding raw example, which appears singularly aggressive as you read it, falls within the norms of many work venues.

Likewise, starting an interview with "Tell me about yourself" (as surveys show, many interviewers do) smacks of condescension, of an officious bureaucrat tapping an impatient foot while a vending machine spatters bad coffee into a flimsy cup.

In interviews and in managed conversations, it's all about the other person. The information that the manager seeks comes from that person; that person's honesty and workplace compatibility become evident through the conversational process; the decision to hire or not comes from what that person says and the ability and understanding that he or she conveys. Therefore, it is vital that the method for obtaining and adjudicating information, ability, understanding, compatibility, and honesty is optimally effective. Managed conversation opens the gateway into a coworker's or a job candidate's mind and allows thoughts and ideas to flow.

Rapport, Open Questioning and Veracity Testing

Let's break down managed conversation into its components, then consider how those components disclose the conversational clues to honesty.

The three facets of managed conversation are rapport building, open questioning, and veracity testing. The amount of time
spent on each facet depends upon the goal of the particular
conversation. In a job interview, for example, it is essential to
establish rapport before moving on to open questioning and
veracity testing. In conversations between longtime employees,
rapport and veracity are already established, so open questioning makes up the core of communication.

Rapport building establishes a baseline of acquaintance[66]
and helps sort out the conversational inferences. (We'll talk later
about conversational inferences.) It allows the conversing parties
to find the common ground and a comfort zone from which
they can begin exchanging ideas and information. The time
spent building rapport depends upon the circumstances and
the level of familiarity of the participants.

In the day to day affairs within an honest workplace, rapport
will have already been established, and, like riding a bicycle on
the boardwalk, only occasional peddling is needed to maintain
momentum. During job interviews, rapport building is essential
to establishing effective communications. Consequently, rapport-building questions will be more numerous early in an interview than later on. As the interview proceeds through the
cycle of questions and answers, and as tension ebbs and flows,
the interviewer may return to rapport building statements and
questions as needed.

After rapport has been established, **open questions** provide the actionable information and ideas of daily business.
Managed conversations in the workplace consist mostly of open

questions where the manager asks the questions that supply the information used to make managerial decisions. The reliability of the information gleaned from open questioning depends upon the veracity of the people involved in the exchange. When the conversation manager has confidence in the answers, business moves forward. When the validity of the information is suspect, then the manager must proceed to the veracity-testing phase.

In job interviews, because the interviewee's level of veracity has not yet been established, open questions cover a wide range of topics until the interviewer chooses to focus on particular issues or events. The ensuing questions narrow the scope and delve deeper, following up with more questions until enough facts and information are collected to allow the interviewer to proceed to the final, veracity-testing phase.

In a managed conversation, open questioning is followed by the **veracity-testing phase**. In a workplace where honesty prevails managers rarely need to spend time asking questions that reinforce the purported facts exchanged in the conversation. But when the validity of the person answering is unverified or suspect then veracity testing is necessary.

In the workplace, managed conversation takes the form appropriate to the circumstances. When a manager speaks to an informed, familiar employee, open-questioning may dominate while rapport building and veracity testing are disregarded simply because the employee is a trusted confidante. At times, the open-questioning phase of a conversation may encompass an entire day's agenda while conversation managers, peers, and subordinates discuss at length topics of business. When the conversation manager is speaking to an unfamiliar employee, maybe one who has been recently hired, rapport building will necessarily be an important part of that conversation. If the conversation is with a person whose bona fides are not yet established or who has provided questionable information in the past, then the veracity-testing phase will dominate. Every effective managed conversation conforms to the particular situation.

The Sussex Study

In a study performed on behalf of the government of the United Kingdom by researchers at the University of Sussex and the University of Wolverhampton, and published in the *Journal of Experimental Psychology* in 2014, managed conversation was demonstrated to be twenty times more effective in veracity-testing situations than commonly used "suspicious signs" methods.[67] As discussed in Chapter 7, How to Spot a Liar and What to Do About It, suspicious signs such as nervousness, body language, and speech hesitations have been shown to have minimal correlation to veracity. University of Sussex researchers Thomas C. Ormerod and Coral J. Dando showed that security screeners at airports were able to identify deceptive passengers with remarkable success by engaging those passengers in informal but managed conversations.

More effective than scripted questions, documentation checks, and monitoring for suspicious signs, managed conversations in which parties were casually asked open questions such as "Tell me about where you work?" followed by focused questions such as, "What do you do at Widget Manufacturing Inc.?" were effective in determining veracity. The questions were individualized to each person and follow-up questions were spawned by the responses to earlier open questions. Thus each person's questions were novel, unscripted, and unpredictable, much like casual conversations in our personal lives. In essence, the Sussex study confirmed that managed conversation holds the key to determining honesty.

In a curious sidebar, researchers at University of Sussex found that education level among interviewers had no bearing on their ability to determine veracity.[68] An educated person is as likely to be duped as an uneducated person, which may explain why the college professor is so often conned by the grifter.

Conversation Managers' Advantages

In a managed conversation, the conversation manager has these advantages that aid him or her in measuring the veracity of the other participant:

1. Pre-knowledge
2. Interviewee uncertainty
3. Conversational steering
4. Cognitive load
5. Post conversation fact-checking
6. Memory

Before beginning a managed conversation or interview, the manager can collect information about the topic to be discussed. This **pre-knowledge** allows the interviewer to compare candidate-supplied information with known facts.

The subordinate or job candidate is not necessarily aware of the depth or breadth of knowledge possessed by the interviewer. This creates **interviewee uncertainty,** which makes it difficult for the interviewee to know what information is new and what is already known by the manager. The uncertainty complicates attempts to dupe the manager, because all misinformation provided by the subordinate must be mentally logged, as he or she will not know which is likely to be challenged later in the conversation.

The manager **steers the conversation** in a direction of his or her choosing. In the veracity-testing phase, this direction may fall in an area where the manager's pre-knowledge is extensive so the interviewee's statements can be affirmed or challenged, or it may return to an area where the interviewee has made prior statements that can be reexamined for contradictions. The interviewee does not know what direction the conversation is going and consequently is unable to rehearse lies and recite prepared answers.

By effectively steering the conversation, the conversational manager restricts the verbal maneuvering of the subordinate. Some deceivers try to direct the conversation away from topics that might reveal their deceit. The manager will steer the conversation back toward pertinent topics. Deceivers sometimes recognize such redirection as an indication that their deceit is evident. When that happens, deceivers often clam up, while honest people tend to continue delivering requested information.

Well into the managed conversation, after numerous issues and opinions have been discussed, a deceptive interviewee's **cognitive load** will be substantial, and his or her memory taxed. If dishonest statements have been made, chances are the deceitful person will confuse or forget what had been stated earlier, and contradictions will become apparent. At the same time, honest answerers will likely enjoy rehashing and reinforcing their valid statements. Where confusion arises, truth speakers will willingly clarify the issue. Throughout a lengthy managed conversation, honest interviewees tend to become more comfortable, dishonest ones less.

After the managed conversation or interview, the conversation manager has the option of **retroactively checking facts** with experts and, in the case of a job interview, former employers and coworkers through contact with work references. As a managed conversation progresses and the subordinate becomes aware that statements will be cross-checked post-interview, questions are likely to be more carefully answered and earlier false statements revised.

The conversational manager can use **memory and nota-tion** to confirm that false statements have been made. A clear memory and accurate notes are essential to the conversation manager, because the burden of judgment weighs heavily on those who must take decisive action. Once falsehoods have been exposed, it is up to the manager to make the appropriate deci-sion that will prevent future mistakes and problems.

Conversational Clues

As with casual conversation, when a managed conversation bogs down it is time to search for the impediment. In a managed conversation a faltering performance may indicate a reluctance to provide solid facts and well-reasoned opinions because those facts and opinions run counter to the selfish interests of the speaker.

The idea that honesty enhances the conversational dance was given further credibility in 2008 when Frank Horvath and colleagues at Michigan State University published their find-ings concerning the "behavioral analysis interview." They cited a characteristic which they called the Sherlock Holmes Effect,[69] whereby honest interviewees fully cooperated, readily supplied requested information, and willingly provided insight and facts that aided the interviewers, and in so doing they advanced the effort to solve crimes. Guilty persons, they explain, "cannot share as much relevant information because that would ultimately lead to their detection, something they want to complicate, not simplify." An honest person will participate enthusiastically in a managed conversation while a dishonest person holds back when he or she views the conversation as a potential threat.

During a well-conducted managed conversation, as clues appear that can be pursued with open questioning and ve-racity testing, impressions are formed that eventually gel into well-founded opinions of the other person's honesty. Indications of intentional lying eventually emerge in the marginal forms that we discussed earlier: exaggeration, omission of fact, and so on. Rarely will dishonesty reveal itself in an "aha, gotcha!" moment.

As the managed conversation continues, the clues that at first became detectable will develop into trends and then grow apparent. They might start as a tendency toward using superlatives, such as "I always do this" or "I never do that," which may simply be throwaway figures of speech. But later in the interview you might learn about an incident that contradicted the initial statement. Further questioning may reveal that the contradiction was an explainable exception, or, sadly, that it was deliberate distortion. By perceiving these subtleties, conversation managers eventually accumulate information to form the larger impressions from which reliable judgments are made.

Likewise, by its nature, honesty does not reveal itself in a "eureka" moment, because one can always lapse into dishonesty. Honesty reveals itself through an enduring consistency. It has its own distinctive signs such as magnanimity, humility, and cooperativeness. During a managed conversation, honesty will become evident through the absence of the clues of dishonesty.

Honest and dishonest people act differently. Over the course of society's history and prehistory, the characteristics of dishonest people have been deemed disagreeable and the characteristics of honest people agreeable. Because these characteristics are so predictable in their implications, when listed side-by-side, they may appear naïve or idealistic to certain skeptics. Such skeptics may call such a list "a groundless concoction of moralism." To those skeptics, I suggest going back and starting this book over at chapter 2.

Again, I caution that these clues are not definitive of either honesty or dishonesty; they are steering devices, mere indicators. However, taken together, like viewing the coastline from a distance, we perceive a reliable outline from which we can make accurate management and hiring decisions.

These are some conversational clues of honesty and dishonesty:

Honesty	Dishonesty
Accuracy	Affectation
Compassion	Ambiguity
Cheerfulness	Bigotry
Civility	Boredom
Conciseness	Breach of logic
Contrition	Concealed names
Cooperative purpose	Defamation
Curiosity	Defensiveness
Earnestness	Disingenuousness
Empathy	Duping delight
Enthusiasm	Exaggeration
Expertise evident	Gaslighting
Fidelity	Gossip
Frugality	Impatience
Generosity	Incongruity
Genuineness	Insensitivity
Giving credit	Jargon
Humility	Lassitude
Industry	Maligning others
Justice	Name-calling
Logic	Narcissism
Magnanimity	Non-specificity
Moderation	Omission of facts
Optimism	Omission of failure
Orderliness	Persecution complex

Honesty	Dishonesty
Patience	Pessimism — *no solety*
Politeness	Pettiness
Resolution — *look at Facts*	Posing
Respectfulness	Presumption
Sincerity	Rudeness
Specificity	Scapegoating
Sympathy	Sour grapes
Temperance	Unnecessary wordiness
Thoroughness	Using superlatives
Understanding	Vagueness

Conversational Inferences

The suspicion of dishonesty—even a whiff of dishonesty often will cause a conversation to falter, but sometimes other factors besides dishonesty cause conversational glitches. We regularly abbreviate the conversational process with inferences, mental shortcuts that require certain assumptions on the part of the conversation's participants. Conversational inferences are the unspoken assumptions that supply those premises that are excluded from the conversation.

For example, John might make the argument "Tom is a nice guy," which contains unspoken inferences. John infers, "I know Tom well enough to judge his character," and "I'm a good judge of character, so you should agree with me." John assumes his listener will share his inferences and, therefore, his conclusion.

While they serve to condense conversations and arguments, inferences cause confusion when participants in the discussion infer differing premises leading to contradicting conclusions. From his argument "Tom is a nice guy," John assumes his listener shares his inferences, but another listener, let's say, Sally, may infer differently. Maybe Sally doesn't think highly of John, and that fact shapes her conclusions about Tom. To Sally, John's endorsement casts Tom in a bad light.

Upon commencing a conversation, participants intuitively take stock of their shared conversational inferences. People who trust and understand one another generally draw similar inferences and their conversations tend to run smoothly. When inferences are not shared, conversations bog down as the participants recalibrate their words and assumptions. Inferential discord may be caused by differences in age, gender or socio-economic status as well as from bias and prejudice. Conversely, when old friends reunite after a long separation, within a few minutes they may resort to that familiar pattern of inferences that cast their friendship in the first place.

Introductory conversations and job interviews require patience while rapport is established and conversational inferences are sorted. Care must be taken to avoid mistaking nonconcurrent inferences for illogical thought or for dishonesty.

Summary

In our comfort environment, casual conversations roam freely over any topic; in the workplace, managed conversations focus on particular topics and serve specific purposes, and they are constrained by time, because in the workplace time is money. Listening attentively, focusing on the talker, and asking follow-up questions are fundamental to both casual and managed conversations. Conversation establishes trust between participants, but in the workplace an authority figure generally manages the conversation. Managed conversation employs a pattern of rapport building, open questioning, and veracity testing, with the amount of emphasis on each phase varying depending upon circumstances. In an honest workplace, open questioning dominates managed conversations. During job interviews, early focus is placed on rapport building and later on veracity testing. Conversation managers should be aware of the subtle indicators of deceit. Shared conversational inferences allow conversations to proceed smoothly. When social factors reduce the number of inferences, conversations are impeded. .

Chapter 9   Writing Job Descriptions

The job description is a powerful tool in a job interview. It serves two ways: first, to inform the candidate of the job's requirements and duties; and second, to aid the interviewer in evaluating the candidate's ability to perform those duties. Many employers fail to recognize the importance of job descriptions and the vital role they play in hiring honest workers.

In particular, smaller companies often fail to write appropriate job descriptions. This oversight might result from uncertainty about a new position's requirements and responsibilities, or it might happen because the employer has been too busy to write one. These excuses do not remove the need. Without a job description, the employer could face frustrated employees who are rightfully confused about their responsibilities, and these can escalate into legal battles. Even a vague job description that says little more than "this person will perform various duties involved in the production and sale of widgets" is better than nothing.

The job description provides a guideline for the interviewer to follow, enabling him or her to touch on every major aspect of the job and to interact with the job candidate regarding those aspects. With both parties participating in a line-by-line review of the job description, the interviewer can measure the candidate's reaction to each aspect of the job, and the candidate is apprised of the relative importance placed on the specific requirements and duties. Such a reading informs the job candidate while it allows the interviewer to assess the candidate's qualifications and honesty.

If, for example, a job requirement is the ability to work harmoniously with others, the ensuing conversation may provide an opportunity for the interviewer to engage in a managed conversation where, perhaps, a candidate's particular experience is communicated, a former employer's practices are introduced and discussed, or a candidate expresses a revealing fact or opinion that is relevant to the hiring decision. The job description is a tool that enables managed conversation to focus entirely on workplace applications.

Let us consider how to write a job description so that it describes the job and provides an excellent interview platform.

A job description should consist of these essential parts:

- Job title and objective
- Essential qualifications and requirements
- Other qualifications and preferences
- Job duties and responsibilities

The job title and objective are considered together because they are often redundant: the objective essentially providing a detailed explanation of the job title. The objective should summarize the idealized big-picture goals of the position. Though job objectives are presented in vague terms, they serve as thresholds to the in-depth discussions that follow. In essence, the job description's objective serves as an interview icebreaker that gives the interviewer an opportunity to reestablish rapport and open questioning.

In certain cases only a few words separate the stated objective of a corporate CEO from that of an assembly-line worker at the same company. Both objectives would likely include words that stress the importance of a smooth-running operation.

Successful candidates either for the CEO position or for a position on the assembly line will answer the question, "Will you perform the duties of this job diligently and thoroughly?" with the same eager affirmative.

Essential qualifications and requirements should contain a concisely worded list of the education, experience, and skills needed for the job. This list should include only absolute requirements, and not generalities. The interviewer should use this list to pointedly ask the job candidate if he or she fulfills each requirement, and then to ask the candidate for supporting statements or documentation. The ensuing conversation often provides insight into the candidate's particular work history, which can be referenced later, during the veracity-testing portion of the interview.

Other qualifications and preferences on a job description should include the general needs, such as "ability to work cooperatively within a team" and the like. Also, if no experience is required, but three years is preferred, that point should be listed here. While not as specific as essential qualifications and requirements, this section is as important. If a candidate is hired and later discharged for failure to work cooperatively, for example, the employer is able to cite the job description as evidence that working cooperatively was an acknowledged facet of proper job performance.

The list of duties and responsibilities should be as inclusive as possible while not restricting business flexibility and growth. For example, if a dentist's office is equipped with a Cavitron Touch, Steri-Mate 360 scaler, it would be more appropriate to state, "Proficiently operate scaling equipment," than to require proficiency on the specific machine, lest the machine be replaced and a hostile employee, facing retraining, cry foul. A broad and inclusive list accommodates business growth and flexibility.

Also, a list of job requirements that is unnecessarily specific may chase off desirable applicants. Sometimes employers waste time looking for a fully trained employee when training one would have been less costly in money and time.

Summary

The job description serves two important functions: it informs the candidate about the job and it serves as a tool for the interviewer to evaluate the candidate. A job description should include four parts: the job title and objective, essential qualifications and requirements, other qualifications and requirements, and job duties and responsibilities. The candidate and the interviewer should engage in a detailed discussion of its contents in a managed conversation.

Job Description Examples

Now we'll look at job descriptions from two fictitious companies, Brownwell Corporation and Chestnut Ridge Dentistry. These very different companies represent the broadly different ways that jobs are posted and presented. Later, in "Chapter 10, Reading Resumes," we will meet two job seekers who are applying for these jobs. Then, in "Chapter 12, The All About You Interview" we will meet the interviewers and see how they go about interviewing these candidates.

Brownwell Corporation is a multinational (fictional) engineering firm that has been involved in some of the world's most monumental construction projects. They have a rigorous hiring process that begins with a job posting followed by multiple interviews and background checks. Job openings are usually posted on the company's website and on industry job boards intended for viewing by industry insiders, thus the wording is somewhat arcane.

Chestnut Ridge Dentistry (also fictional) is a typical small business with five employees and very little turnover. Consequently, this company has less experience interviewing and hiring than Brownwell. However, because the owner of this small business is intricately familiar with the job duties of his staff, the job description is more comprehensive.

Of the two job description examples that follow, the civil engineer job posting represents the typical variety that a job seeker might encounter at a large company. The structure and industry-insider wording, such as "work schedule C," give this one the appearance of an in-house posting. In Brownwell's case, as it is with many companies, a few changes to the job posting will allow it to serve as the job description.

Often, the hiring process in large companies entails several interviews with various people from multiple departments. Routinely applicants are required to complete and sign numerous forms, disclaimers, and agreements that cover liability issues related to drug use and criminal history. Sometimes job-seeker assent to these agreements is relegated to routine procedure akin to "sign this form then go stand in that line" for fingerprinting and urine samples, and the requirement to do so might not appear on the job description.

Smaller companies, like Chestnut Ridge Dentistry, also need protection from drug-related and criminal history liabilities, but they may lack the facilities or wherewithal to run tests and background investigations. By stating on the job description that drug tests and background checks will be required, small companies may deflect applicants who would have problems complying with those requirements.

The dental assistant/hygienist job description shows a thorough and appropriate job description format for a small company. It supplies substantial information about the position for the job seeker, it covers employer liability by requiring employee disclaimers, and it provides a platform from which to conduct the job interview.

Sample job description, Brownwell Corporation

The wording of Brownwell Corporation's job posting is essentially the same as their job description. We'll see it again when applicant Carter Johnfeld is interviewed.

Job Posting
Brownwell Corporation
Civil Engineer, (EIT, PE), #140041
Location: Pittsburgh, PA
Position Title: Civil Engineer
Relocation Authorized: Family
Citizenship Requirements: USA or Canada
Other Requirements: BS or equivalent in Engineering or
Structural Analytics

Three years engineering experience

EIT or PE certification or equivalent
license

Pre-employment drug screening,
background check

This position will be located in Pittsburgh, Pennsylvania,
and the project is planned for southern Lake Huron,
with site offices in Sarnia, Ontario, Canada. The project
operates on work schedule C, Monday to Friday, 8 hours
daily.

More requirements listed below under "Requirements."

Most job descriptions would not include work schedules, but it is included on this job posting.

Role Overview:

- Evaluate, select and apply standard engineering methods, procedures, and criteria using independent judgment, adapting and modifying when necessary.
- Perform evaluations and technical consultations and guidance on the analysis and design of bridges and their structural components with clear and specific objectives within the variables of the Civil/Structural Engineering discipline.
- Perform and evaluate structural analysis, design, engineering mechanics, thermal analysis, fracture mechanics, shock analysis, vibration analysis, material dynamics, and related tests and technologies while following international codes and standards.
- Review and evaluate material specifications and vendor proposals for compatibility with overall structural requirements.
- Assess adequacy and independently verify suppliers' structural evaluations and technical reviews.
- Assist Project Engineer and Lead Engineer with earthwork/site design as needed.
- Provide technical direction to designers and less experienced engineers.
- Represent the company at technical and design meetings with suppliers and other prime contractors.

This list provides a good outline for discussing the candidate's education, abilities, and experience. With some experience in the field of engineering, a competent HR professional can pass judgment on these matters, but technical expertise will need to be confirmed by an expert.

General Requirements:

- Experience with bridge planning, design, and construction, including the principles of stress, fracturing, material compression, thermal expansion, shock, vibration, geo-structure, and fluid dynamics.
- Experience in computer-aided design and engineering techniques.
- Proficiency in ANSYS or GT STRUDL software.
- Excellent written and oral communications skills.
- Excellent analytical and problem-solving skills.

The requirements listed above are specific while these are more general. It will take an engineer to judge a candidate's proficiency in these.

An HR professional can judge these skills.

Sample Job Description, Chestnut Ridge Dentistry, LLC

Job Description

Chestnut Ridge Dentistry, LLC   Effective Date:
789 Ridge Road   1 November 2016
Vintongrift, PA 15888
Phone: (724) 555-8667

Dental Assistant/Hygienist

Position Objective:
To diligently and thoroughly perform the duties
of Dental Assistant/Hygienist in an efficient,
friendly, and professional manner while working
cooperatively with patients, management, and
coworkers.

This statement of objective
provides a starting point for
discussion.

Essential Job Qualifications and Requirements:
- Current Pennsylvania Dental Assistant/Hygienist
  License.
- Knowledge and information about medicine and
  dentistry needed to diagnose and treat dental
  conditions, maladies, injuries, and diseases.
- The ability to make precise and coordinated finger
  and hand movements, such as those required to
  proficiently clasp, assemble, and manipulate small
  and delicate instruments.
- The visual acuity to accurately and effectively
  examine and ascertain patients' dental health and
  condition.
- Personal sensitivity and empathy to understand
  patients' anxiety, fear, and discomfort; and the
  willingness and ability to assuage the patients'
  concerns.
- The willingness and ability to communicate
  clearly and succinctly in writing and orally, and to
  maintain accurate records and organized files.
- The knowledge and understanding to operate the
  tools, instruments, and machinery associated with
  dental assisting and dental hygienists including
  magnetostrictive ultrasonic scalers and full-mouth
  ultrasonic debridement.
- Current CPR and AED certification.
- This position requires passing the SAMHSA-10
  drug test.

A point-by-point discussion
of this list will allow the
interviewer to compare the
candidate's experience to
the requirements.

Introduces drug-free policy.

Other Qualifications and Preferences

- Compatibility and empathy to work harmoniously with patients and coworkers.
- Communication skills to explain such things as proper dental care and hygiene and use of the implements associated with maintaining and promoting dental health.
- Ability to work cooperatively within a team.
- Ability and willingness to stay focused and anticipate patients' and the dentist's needs.
- The ability to work with, calculate, and accurately convey mathematic information.
- Familiarity with Dentafix software.
- Willingness and ability to communicate effectively by telephone and computer, to make accurate notes, and to perform office and clerical duties.

When discussing these broad statements, the interviewer can refer to the candidate's resume and to statements made earlier in the interview when discussing that resume.

Duties and Responsibilities of the Dental Assistant/Hygienist:

The Dental Assistant/Hygienist is expected to follow the instructions of the dentist and office manager with consistency and dependability while working harmoniously with patients and coworkers.

Establishes chain of authority.
Important to mention that flexibility is a necessity.

The general responsibilities of the Dental Assistant/Hygienist at Chestnut Ridge Dentistry, LLC, are shown below, but, in consultation with management, these duties and responsibilities may change from time to time.

Various duties incumbent to the position of Dental Assistant/Hygienist include, but are not limited to:

- Greet and manage patients
- Prepare patients for dental procedures
- Clean patients' teeth
- Apply local anesthetics
- Apply fluoride treatments
- Take, develop, and mount radiological images
- Prepare dental examination rooms, dental instruments, and trays for use by dentist
- Advise dentists of patient preferences, needs, and state of dental health
- Monitor and maintain inventory and stocks of essential supplies and instruments needed for day to day job performance
- Perform and assist dental lab work
- Update and maintain properly filed patient records
- Assist in scheduling, rescheduling, and billing for services

This list provides an opportunity to review the applicant's experience and proficiency in performing each duty. If weaknesses were detected in the resume review, this may be the time to revisit them and engage in a deeper discussion.

- Build and promote strong, long-lasting patient relationships
- Perform other functions as management deems necessary to the professional performance of the job of Dental Assistant/Hygienist
- Assist management in achieving the aims and goals set forth for by the company

Chestnut Ridge Dentistry, LLC, is a drug free workplace. Illicit or illegal use or abuse of prohibited drugs, alcohol, or substances, the presence of such substances, or performing compensated labor while under the influence of such substances or while having detectable levels as outlined by SAMHSA is strictly prohibited. Violation and the suspicion of violation of this rule may result in summary dismissal.

Reinforces determination to enforce of drug free policy.

(Applicant's signature)   (Full name printed)   (Date)

The signer has read and understands the contents of this Job Description for the Dental Assistant/Hygienist position and agrees that he/she is willing and able to perform these duties.

Signatures confirm mutual understanding and acknowledge that job requirements, duties, and drug testing have been discussed and accepted.

(For Chestnut Ridge Dentistry, LLC)   (Date)

The above signed, representing Chestnut Ridge Dentistry, LLC, has discussed the job requirements of Dental Assistant/Hygienist with the Applicant.

The Chestnut Ridge Dentistry job description provides the better platform for interviewing a job candidate because its list of requirements and job duties is more inclusive. A candidate for Brownwell's position will be interviewed first by a human resources professional then by peers who are familiar with the specific engineering skills required, consequently the job description is less detailed. However, Brownwell would be better off if their job description were more thorough, because then it would serve better as a guide for the interviewer's managed conversation.

Chapter 10 Reading Resumes

We now know that managed conversation provides the information from which we will make our hiring decisions. The next tool in our chest is the applicant's resume, which will be our guide through a central portion of the interview. To use it effectively in the hiring process, we'll need to look closely at the resume and see what it tells us about the author.

As interview tools, resumes are preferable to job applications. Resumes are wholly the creation of the applicants, whereas job applications require applicants to provide information in a format dictated by employers. While a job application provides file-folder documentation, the resume constitutes an opportunity for the interviewer to walk on the applicant's turf; it provides insight into the applicant's character and supplies an essential tool for gauging the applicant's honesty.

Interviewers should view a resume from the applicant's standpoint. When moved to sit down and prepare a resume, most resume writers soberly reflect on their professional accomplishments; they look back on their working lives and take stock. Their resumes encapsulate years of studying, long hours of labor, gratification for jobs well done, disappointment at opportunities missed, and hope for the future. As such, to a potential employer the resume may be a beacon shedding light on professional talent or merely a few blots of ink on a single sheet of Canadian pulp. It is up to the writer to direct the light where it will create the best impression, and up to the reader to maneuver that beam for an accurate view into the working life of the applicant. That is why an applicant's resume is such a valuable interview tool.

A well-written resume is, in a sense, an advertisement, which, if effective, will make a future employer want to sample the product. Like a good advertisement, a resume needs to strike a balance between fact and potential, creating excitement without over promising. If the product is oversold, if its claims are too extravagant, if it looks frivolous, or if it is the wrong product, the author never gets the chance to demonstrate its worth. The advertisement must be enticing yet accurate.

When a resume first lands on the desk or computer of an employer it probably represents that employer's initial contact with the job applicant, and that is where the evaluation begins. The vital decision whether to interview that applicant is made based upon that piece of paper, so it is important that the resume has a sober, professional appearance and contains the right information.

A resume should look like a resume and not like an autobiography or a poster. It should contain information relevant to employment, and be formatted for readability, using concise wording, bullet points, and convenient spacing. It should not be cluttered with unnecessary information or clip art doodads.

The interviewer should assume that every word on the resume has been given careful consideration; if it's on the resume, it must be there for a reason. A lean, stripped-down resume that provides just the facts, ma'am, is more likely to be noticed and read than a cluttered, wordy one. The interviewer will ask the questions that provide pertinent work-history details.

Interviewers should understand that resume structure will vary with the age, work history, and experience of the applicant. Fresh out of high school or college, a job applicant should provide a detailed list of work-related experiences, including all positive information about summer jobs, education, sports, clubs, and personal interests that fits on a page of reasonably sized font. When work experience is lacking, the interviewer must consider other activities that indicate an applicant's level of responsibility and honesty. The company hiring a young or inexperienced worker is taking a risk on an unproven human commodity, and so the interviewer needs to look for indicators that show such an applicant is worth that risk.

An older, accomplished applicant often demonstrates his or her confidence with a shorter resume. After all, a resume summarizes, not lists, accomplishments. A professional life should come to an apex, or maybe two, with the achievements making the telltale statement. For example, a self-assured applicant might simply put, "Purchasing Director, Modesto Branch, Joe's Appliances," without describing every rung of the corporate ladder at Joe's Appliances. If you, the interviewer, are interested in the details, ask about them.

Some occupational fields, such as art, academia, and journalism, require portfolios and lists of publications. These should be attached as dossiers to the resume.

Previewing Resumes

Keep in mind that we are looking for honest candidates and we learned earlier that judging honesty is a complicated process that requires compiling information then regarding that information from various perspectives, and those differing perspectives may confuse us or cause us to draw divergent conclusions. For that reason, an employer who is analyzing resumes must take the time and exercise the understanding that accommodates many contingencies. But sometimes dishonesty is obvious on a resume, such as when the resume states that the candidate earned a college degree, but research proves otherwise. When such is the case, it is usually wise to discard that resume and move on.

Knowing that a job candidate likely has put great effort into producing a resume that condenses his or her professional life, an interviewer has an opportunity to learn much from it. A resume should be read closely, checking content, names, places, timelines, and stated facts. What were the writer's intentions with each statement? Why is it included? What questions does it raise? What conclusions can be drawn? Spending a few minutes scrutinizing a resume can save an interviewer hours that would otherwise be wasted interviewing unworthy candidates.

Resumes are generally broken down into four sections:

1. Contact information and objective
2. Work history
3. Education
4. Personal interests and community involvement

Each section should be read carefully and examined for clues to work performance and professionalism.

Contact Information and Objective

Within personal identification, look for the applicant's full legal name, contact information including telephone number and email address, and possibly a street address. Legal names may change and sometimes a person strongly prefers to be called by a name other than his or her legal name. If a nickname is given, it is advisable to note it and use it during the interview to establish rapport.

A thoughtful candidate will provide a phone number that is answered during business hours, or note otherwise. They may also note if they prefer texting and the regularity with which they check their email. Attention to these considerations on the part of the candidate may indicate competency.

It is important to consider that an applicant may avoid giving a physical street address, especially if that address could raise eyebrows, such as a location in a seedy part of town or temporary housing such as a college dormitory. But sometimes employers require preemployment motor vehicle records, criminal background checks, and drug testing, which require street addresses. These requirements should be discussed with the applicant during the initial interview.

Sometimes resume writers are advised to begin their resumes with a statement of objective in the vein of, "I seek fulfilling employment in the field of geology," which is generally obvious, as the applicant is probably applying for a job as a geologist. Some recommend a resume title such as, "Ditch Digger, 10 Years' Experience." Some information may be gleaned from these statements. My experience is that most job seekers do not put much thought into their stated objectives, but instead add them to their resumes as matters of form.

Work History

Except for those applicants who have little or no work experience, work history will account for the bulk of the resume. The content, organization, and consistency of this section should be examined closely. The usual format lists most recent jobs first then works backward. For each job, look for employer's name, candidate's job title, dates of employment, and, usually, supervisors' names. Below this, usually job duties and accomplishments are listed.

If the interviewer is unfamiliar with the candidate's previous employer, he or she should look it up, study the company, learn what it produces, its number of employees, locations of offices and branches, everything that can be learned about the company. This information will be essential to a thorough interview.

Note the job title. What does it mean? Some companies are very structured and title-conscious while others are not. How are titles obtained at this employer? Is the job title consistent with job duties described?

The employment timeline is one of the most indicative sources of information available on every resume, and it should be the first thing that an employer examines. Either the timeline runs contiguously or it doesn't.

Is the employment timeline complete and consistent from one job to another? Does the completion of the applicant's education coincide with his or her succeeding employment? Are all the dates presented in the same format or do some show the exact day while others show only the year? Do gaps or overlaps appear in the timeline? If so, it may indicate an explainable break from the workforce, such as military service, a sabbatical, or an illness; it might be an unintentional error; or it may indicate the deliberate omission of an unsatisfactory work experience. Employment timelines provide useful information and they are great topics for interview questioning.

Are supervisors' names listed? If so, it amounts to a tacit invitation to contact them. This may be viewed as an expression of confidence on the part of the job applicant. Are some supervisors listed and others not? It can be expected that supervisors from the distant past would not be listed. If the candidate has worked at more than one place in the recent past, and if supervisors are listed at one place but not another, it could be worth asking why that is so.

While the section for listing job duties, accomplishments, and commendations should contain a few brief bullet-pointed statements, resume writers often fill this space with lots of unnecessary but nonetheless useful information. A production supervisor at Widgets Inc. should point out the fact that he or she managed the day shift of thirty workers operating ten widget machines. It is unnecessary to provide remarks such as "maintained regular operations" or "met schedules," which are often thrown in here. The interviewer would expect that a production supervisor would maintain operations and meet schedules.

But, by pointing out these job functions, the applicant might be indicating that operations were not always maintained and schedules were not always met. This gives an astute interviewer some insight into where to take his or her interview questions. Not unlike nervous glances during a casual conversation, excessive wording on a resume may indicate topics that warrant further discussion. When evaluating work history, the list of job duties, accomplishments, and commendations should be read closely.

Education

Educational accomplishments are more relevant for recent graduates. Look for dates of attendance, degrees and certificates earned, along with relevant courses. For recent graduates, employers should look for indications that applicants have the energy and range of interests to keep them engaged in the workplace, such as being employed while attending school, involvement in extracurricular activities, and sports.

Educational claims should be confirmed. For recent graduates, this may be as simple as checking lists of graduates published by the institution. If a candidate claims to have participated in a club's activities or on a sports team, often those rosters are available on-line. It may be more difficult to confirm educational accomplishments from nonaccredited or nontraditional institutions. It is advisable to request that the candidate provide official confirmation of degrees such as diplomas and certificates earned when it is not possible to check through other means.

Often applicants who have not completed their degrees will omit the dates of attendance or provide some other clue to their non-completion. Not infrequently, job candidates falsify their academic credentials. Usually it is not difficult to discern this fraud, so in a sense such dishonest characters are performing a service for their prospective employers by exposing their dishonesty.

Personal Interests and Community Involvement

Personal interests and community involvement are often mentioned on resumes. If they are, the applicant is essentially inviting the interviewer to ask about them. These topics can be useful in rapport-building discussions, and they can provide valuable insight into the interests and professional commitment of the candidate.

For instance, a water-quality specialist reinforces his or her attachment to the cause if he or she is also a fly-fishing enthusiast. A prospective banking executive who belongs to the local country club rubs elbows with potential clients. When the list is exceedingly long or if personal interests potentially tilt the scales away from workplace performance, that too is noteworthy.

References

Candidate-supplied references provide insight into the candidate's priorities. As we'll learn in Chapter 13, Contacting References, during the interview process the interviewer will select references from among the candidate's former supervisors or coworkers. The candidate's list is useful only if it coincides with that requested by the interviewer. If it does, that could be an indication that the candidate is confident that his or her former supervisors and coworkers think highly of his or her job performance.

Often college professors and advisers gauge their own success by how many students find jobs after graduation, and therefore they are likely to be biased. Likewise, recommendations from family and friends are often unreliable. The interviewer should contact only references who can impartially attest to the candidate's honesty, promptness, reliability, and productivity within the workplace.

There is a lot of talk about character references—people who have not shared workplace experience with the applicant, but who are willing to vouch for the applicant's strength of character. Unless the interviewer and the reference share definitions of "character," little can be gained from a character reference. Usually character references are wealthy or influential acquaintances who are unfamiliar with the candidate's work performance. If an applicant has no prior work experience, such as a high school student looking for his or her first summer job, a character reference may have some value; but if the applicant fails to perform, few employers blame the reference, so the reference has little at stake.

Candidates who hope to capitalize on their social connections to gain employment may also think such connections should influence their rate of promotion and pay scale. When a candidate supplies a list of character references, the interviewer may gain valuable insight by discussing the people on that list with the candidate, but will likely learn little about the candidate's workplace performance from them. Most honest job seekers would not want to work for an employer who makes hiring decisions based upon a candidate's social or political connections, as these employers would also be more likely to grant meritless promotions and unearned pay raises to unworthy workers. Work references should come from the workplace and nowhere else.

Cover Letters

Many resumes come with attached cover letters. Some cover letters provide only a prosaic version of the resume, but sometimes they explain an issue relevant to the hiring decision, such as the candidate's reason for leaving their most recent job, or an explanation pertinent to fulfilling a particular job requirement. Either way, a cover letter lets an interviewer know something about the candidate, even if it is only that he or she wastes time writing wordy cover letters.

Resume Sorting Software

Some software providers market resume-sorting products. Search-engine-optimized sorters supposedly sift through stacks of resumes to find the most qualified job candidates so that employers need not do it. These computer programs search the contents of resumes looking for words that match the words found on the associated job descriptions. The merits of these programs are questionable, since it is possible to game the system by seeding resumes with words known to be sought by the computers.

Most resume sorting software perform quantitative tasks, while the momentous decisions associated with hiring honest reliable workers is inherently nuanced, judgmental, and qualitative.

Summary

A resume is an excellent tool for interviewers because it provides valuable insight into the honesty of a prospective employee. Prior to the interview, the interviewer should carefully study the resume paying close attention to the accuracy, consistency, and thoroughness of its author. Timelines should be examined for continuity and lapses. The interviewer should research the information and claims about employers, education, and personal interests, including awards, achievements, and the community activities that appear on the resume to determine validity of each. Resumes that contain contradictions, lapses, and unsubstantiated claims should be regarded skeptically or disregarded altogether. If the decision is made to interview the resume's writer, the interviewer should prepare for that interview by reviewing all pertinent information and research findings. Software and search engines that sort and qualify applicant's resumes are easily fooled and they are not satisfactory substitutes for human judgement.

Resumes Samples

Now we will meet Carter Johnfeld and Jackie Kondin, two ordinary (wholly fictitious) job seekers whose achievements and mistakes we will examine closely. Our job seekers will be applying for the hypothetical jobs described in Chapter 9, Writing Job Descriptions. In Chapter 12, The All About You Interview, we will analyze Carter's and Jackie's performance as they go through the various steps in the interview process. Carter will be interviewed by experienced human resources professional Pauline White, and we'll evaluate her performance too. Jackie will be interviewed by Dr. Mauch, dentist, who wants to fill a vacancy in his office and doesn't have a lot of time to spend on job interviews. After the interviews, we'll contact the candidates' workplace references and hear what they have to say about Carter's and Jackie's job performance.

In a column on the right, I will make comments throughout the interviews. See if you agree with my observations. Think about how you would have handled each circumstance, and what statements you would have made or what questions you would have asked. In the end, see if you agree with my decision to hire, or not, the job seekers.

CARTER JOHNFELD, EIT
234 Coal Run Road | Vintongrift, PA 15888 | (724) 555-4234
| CJJ17@lehigh.edu

OBJECTIVE
Find a fulfilling career as a civil engineer with a creative, dynamic company that challenges my abilities and my mind.

Well stated but purposeless.

SKILLS PROFILE
Conscientious worker
Exemplary analytical, statistical and mathematic skills
Creative problem solver
Team player and compatible coworker
Big picture prospective

How does this list differ from any other person's? No need to spend interview time here.

EMPLOYMENT HISTORY
Tomlin Engineering May 2014 — Present
Pittsburgh, PA
Tampa Bay Bridge Project team member
Materials stress and expansion analyzer
Computed material strength and stress capacity then compared to project requirements. Applied findings to project plans. Coordinated with architects, geologists, environmental consultants and contractors to find most feasible bridge designs.

Working here more than two years. Started at graduation (see education below). Why looking for work now? Focus interview questions here.

Jacobs Engineering May 2013 — Aug 2013
King of Prussia, PA
College Internship (6 credits + pay)
Structural integrity evaluation, repair and replacement on Walt Whitman Bridge, Philadelphia, PA
Served on team that evaluated structural weakness due to weathering and usage, then proposed necessary repairs or replacement of structure and surfaces.
Worked under the supervision of senior engineers and demonstrated CAD and GIS proficiency.

Summer job while in college (see below). Was this internship real work experience or make work? Find out in interview. GIS certified?

Summer Jobs Summers 2008, '09, '10, '11, '12
Carl's Lawn Care, Vintongrift, PA Mowed and tended lawns May to August 2011 & '12
McDonalds, Vintongrift, PA Order taker, grill person, shift mgr. May to August 2009 & '10
Sam's Sno-Kone, Vintongrift, PA Server, attendant June to August 2008

Worked every summer through college. Was invited back at Carl's and McDonald's.

EDUCATION
Carnegie Mellon University Aug 2014 — Present
Pittsburgh, PA
Enrolled in classes
Currently taking a 4-credit course, CE464, Advanced Infrastructural Systems
Accumulated 16 credits toward master's degree. Thirty credits are needed.

Accepted into CMU master's program. Not for dummies. Grad school while working full time—no slouch.

Lehigh University Aug 2010 — May 2014 *Allentown, PA* BS, Civil Engineering GPA 3.14 Fundamentals of Engineering Certification **ACTIVITIES** Varsity Baseball, Lehigh University, freshman and sophomore years. Varsity letter recipient Assistant coach, Little League, Coraopolis, PA	Went straight through. GPA good, not great; bad if Lehigh is a grade inflator. Teamwork. Why not play jr. and sr. yrs? How did he manage summer jobs and baseball together? Check rosters.

Let's unpack Carter's resume. Except for the ineffectual list of skills, Carter's resume is clean and concise. The space wasted on skills could have been better used listing specific aspects of engineering honed in his current job, or he could have reduced the number of words and increased the amount of white space, resulting in a more readable document.

Apparently he completed his undergraduate degree in four years while working every summer, then he was hired by Tomlin Engineering immediately after graduation. After that, he seems to have jumped right into his graduate studies. There are no gaps in the timeline. Many commendable traits are indicated. He worked consecutive summers for the same companies, so his employers must have liked him. Apparently he was successful in baseball, which requires teamwork, discipline, and a good dose of humility (In sports there's always somebody better than you).

What about the 3.14 GPA? Since the mid-1990s, I have seen very few GPAs below 3.00 and, improbably, most seem to be 3.25 and higher. It would be worth asking around to find out if Lehigh University's engineering program sticks to an old-school grading system, harkening back to the days when a B was a hard-earned, good grade. Though Carter's grades put him safely above 3.00, I wonder if he struggled academically. Maybe so-so grades in college are translating into poor job performance at Tomlin Engineering. Could that be the reason he's looking for work now? But he is enrolled in Carnegie Mellon's highly competitive Engineering Master's program, so- . . .

EIT means engineer in training, the designation given to engineers who graduate from an accredited program and pass the EIT exam, which is required in most states before working as an engineer. He must have taken and passed his EIT exam upon graduation from Lehigh. We'll have lots to talk about with Carter. Overall, this is a great resume for a young person. I would definitely want to interview Carter Johnfeld.

Jackie Kondin   Dental Hygienist
123 Coal Run Road
Vintongrift, PA 15888
Email: jkondin@yawho.com
Cell phone: (724) 555-4123

Employment History

Dental Hygienist/Assistant, Loyalhanna Dental
Associates   July 2015 to Present
Ligonier, PA

| Four-month lapse since last job. Working here now? |

Job Duties:

Treat patients   Assist doctors
Perform oral impressions   Restore composites
Perform dental radiography   Maintain records

Compare to job description.

Dental Hygienist/Assistant, Conemaugh Family
Dentistry   Dec. 2013 to Feb. 2015

Johnstown, PA

Clerk, Kiski Farm Supply   Summers 2008, '09
Vintongrift, PA   May 2010 to Jan. 2011

Received degree in May, started work in Dec. 2013. Worked here until started Bradford, including while at WCCC

Education

<u>Bradford School</u>,   Jan. 2011 to May 2013
Pittsburgh, PA

Major: Dental Assisting Associate's Degree

Relevant Courses:

Dental Hygienics I, II & III Dental Radiology I and II

Four-handed dentistry   Pediatric dentistry
Patient psychology   Chairside Assisting I, II,
                        III & IV
Externship   Dental office
                        management
Dental insurance coding   Dental anesthesia and
                        analgesics

After 3 years working in the field, a list of courses is not needed. Dedicate more space to work experience.

Westmoreland County Community College
Aug. 2010 to Dec. 2010

Youngwood, PA
One semester   Dean's List
English, College Algebra, Psychology
Kiski Valley High School Diploma, May 2010

Interesting—one semester, then leave. Might be worth asking about.

Community Activities

Relay for Life   Event organizer (volunteer) 2009, 2010

Habitat for Humanity Volunteer 2010

Community connection—good sign. Confirmation?

References

Dr. Melanie Johntson, DDS   email: mjddm@
yawho.com   cell: (724) 555-9876
Hon. Don Whire, PA Senate   email: sen.
donwhire@pa.us.gov office: (717) 555-8765
Cynthia Holt
email: cholt23@yawho.com
cell: (724) 888-7654

Did Jackie have workplace experience with all 3 people? Find out. Name dropper?

My first impression is that this resume is cluttered with too much information and it is weighted too heavily toward education when it should show more work experience. After three years in the workforce, a list of "relevant courses" is irrelevant. Probably Jackie has casually updated an earlier version of her resume without removing obsolete information.

She has provided plenty of timeline information, but that information may be damaging since it shows several gaps. It looks like Jackie worked while in high school and during her one semester in college. Then she spent one and a half years at Bradford School studying and training to be a dental hygienist/assistant. The timeline shows a lapse of seven months after graduation, when either she did not work, or she had a job and omitted it from this resume. She left Conemaugh Family Dentistry in February and started at Loyalhanna Dental Associates in July. Does that four-month lapse indicate that her departure from Conemaugh was unplanned? The resume shows Jackie is still working for Loyalhanna, so why is she looking for work now?

Having worked for two different employers and looking for a third in three years is not necessarily a bad thing, but it requires an explanation. If her reasons for switching employers are credible, she probably should have noted them on the resume. Those gaps could be a reason for an employer not to interview her.

It will be interesting to ask about the references Jackie chose: Who are they, has she worked with them, and why did she include them?

Jackie might be an excellent dental assistant/hygienist, but her resume does not show it. Let's see how she does in the interview.

CHAPTER 11 ON INTERVIEWING

[handwritten notes in margin: "• yes — google them, Linkes' in on Facebook, Twitter • Make it enjoyable, all about your interview!"]

When done properly, interviewing job candidates is fun. Human resource professionals have the enviable task of engaging in managed conversations with personnel vying for entry into their club—er, workplace, if you insist. For the interviewers these job interviews can and should be informative, entertaining, and fortifying. If interviewers are not having fun, probably they're not doing it right. Maybe they're not focusing on the candidate, who, despite the fun the interviewer is having, is probably feeling quite a lot of stress. Let us look at the proper way to conduct an interview, so these occasions can be productive and gratifying for both the interviewee and the interviewer.

The purpose of job interviews is to assess which applicant will become the best employee, and as we have demonstrated earlier, an honest employee is the best employee. Many lectures, articles, and books are dedicated to proper interviewing techniques, and they express a wide array of opinions. Various techniques can be successful so long as they find candidates who are honest, but no technique will work beyond a level of dumb luck unless it focuses on honesty. Honest employees are best found by looking expressly for them. We'll discuss specific interview situations in Chapter 12, The All-About-You Interview. Here, we focus on the broader concepts and fundamental purpose of interviewing.

Think of all the preparations a good candidate makes prior to meeting the interviewer. The well-prepared candidate will have studied the company, noting factors such as size, corporate structure, and products. He or she will have compared the job posting or job description, if it has been made available, to his or her education and work history. The company's reputation as a fair, honest and trusting prospective employer will be considered. Things like driving time to and from work, traffic, and road conditions will have been investigated. How will this job mesh with family and private life? Pay and benefits will be balanced against those offered by other employers and against the candidate's personal economic considerations. On the day of the interview, proper grooming and attire, essential documents, parking, weather, and a dozen other issues will be resolved. When the office door opens and the interviewer rises to greet the candidate, all prior worries shrink by comparison as the actual interview commences. So, don't you think the candidate needs to be cut some slack?

What happens if you conducted an interview with the candidate of your dreams and you, your assistant, or the receptionist treated him or her thoughtlessly or rudely? Maybe yesterday your competitor offered that candidate a compensation package similar to the one your company offered, but you kept the candidate waiting in the reception area without explanation, or you were daydreaming about spending your own paycheck and you forgot to explain the company's paid-leave program to the candidate. Because of your unprofessionalism, your competitor—not you—will likely employ the candidate of your dreams.

Make a good impression on job candidates. From the initial job posting and throughout the hiring process, the empathetic employer will treat every job candidate with respectful professionalism. From the tone of the wording on the job posting to the tone of voice during the interview, to the comfort of the candidate upon his or her arrival, to allowing time to relax and compose before starting the interview, to an enthusiastic and cheerful greeting, to the friendly smiles of your support staff, to an upbeat tone of the interview, to answering questions fully, to following through with promises, to conducting all correspondence in a timely manner, job interviews should show deference and respect to the candidates. It is important for the employer to understand that in the quest for top-notch honest workers it is a competitive arena. The way to attract such workers is by becoming the type of employer they want to work for. That way, all things considered, when you proffer the job, the candidate is more likely to accept it.

Research Candidates Before Interviewing Them

As we discussed in Chapter 10, Reading Resumes, it is better to scrutinize resumes, select worthy candidates, and interview fewer people than to waste time interviewing unworthy candidates. Using the Internet and whatever other resources are available, the interviewer should research the contents of the candidate's resume. Review the places of employment listed by the candidate. If the candidate lists awards, accomplishments, or associations, those should be researched and be familiar to the interviewer. If the candidate is a recent college graduate and lists campus sports and clubs, look up those organizations, check their rosters, and become familiar with their records and activities.

If a job application has been filed by the candidate, that application should be cross-referenced with the resume and any discrepancies noted, occasional typos and incidental errors excepted.

Note whether the candidate provides the names of supervisors on the resume or on an accompanying reference list, and, if supervisors' names are provided, are they provided for all recent jobs? Inconsistencies are worthy of discussion during the interview.

It is advisable to inform the applicant ahead of the interview that he or she will be asked for verification of education credentials. If the applicant then comes to the interview with supporting documentation in hand, such as diplomas, transcripts, or certificates that confirm the content of the resume, that's a good thing. If he or she begins the interview by handing the interviewer an amended resume with changes made to the education portion or refuses or fails to provide supporting documentation, that's a bad thing.

Social media provide unconventional sources of information about job candidates. Considerable time has been spent discussing and writing opinions about the ethics and utility of checking a candidate's Facebook, Twitter, LinkedIn, or other personal sites. It is the author's opinion that if the information is available in a public forum, it is not off-limits. To the contrary, if the information were available and not investigated, that would be irresponsible on the part of the hiring manager.

Charges of negligent hiring may result from an employer's failure to investigate adequately an employee's past. Many state's courts have punished employers for hiring an employee whose past provided evidence of questionable judgment, such as a pizza delivery driver who had been found guilty of armed robbery and reckless driving, or an accountant found guilty of embezzlement. Legally and morally, every employer has the responsibility to perform the basic background investigations that protect the public from the incompetent or harmful actions of employees.

During the Interview

As with causal conversation, the hiring manager encourages the applicant to talk, and subordinates him- or herself in the process. A good interviewer uses rapport-building conversational techniques to put the applicant at ease. Conversational inferences need to be sorted out and adapted to. Then, using the applicant's resume and the company's job description as guides, the ensuing conversation focuses on the applicant's past employment and future prospects. Each applicant's history is different, and the questions should be particular to that applicant and the prospective job.

The candidate needs to choose words carefully and to ponder salient points, so it is important not to rush him or her. The interviewer should provide encouragement with nods and rapport-building acknowledgements, and allow the talker some leeway in setting the pace. As we discussed earlier, those qualities that stem from personal honesty begat of humility manifest themselves and become apparent during a focused managed conversation. So the pace and demeanor of the interview should be in accord with the temperament of the interviewee.

Sometimes, through careless wording of questions or thoughtless disregard for the sensibilities of others, an interviewer will unintentionally trigger concerns of bias or hurtful insensitivity, such as when an interviewer persists in asking questions about a lapse in a candidate's employment timeline when that lapse was caused by a personal tragedy. It is important to avoid questions involving personal topics. In general, it is advisable—both socially and legally—to avoid any non-workplace related topic such as politics, race, religion, marital status, sexuality, age, and disabilities. If the interviewee initiates discussions on these topics, the interviewer should make a note of his or her doing so before continuing along that line of discussion. The interviewer can avoid most pitfalls by focusing on the applicant's resume, whereby the applicant, not the interviewer, has established the course of the interview.

Where special job skills and experience are required, HR professionals select honest applicants who suit the character of the company, and then defer to specialists within the various departments to judge the level of skill possessed by the applicant. Unless the skill specialists have the requisite training to identify honesty when selecting candidates, the HR person should participate in these follow-up interviews. When on-the-job training is provided, as in an entry-level position, special skills may not be needed, but honesty is still essential to job performance and job satisfaction.

The interviewer must make thorough notes during the interview. Care should be taken that note-taking does not interrupt the flow of conversation, but accurate documentation is essential. The interviewer will want to write down names, dates, and places mentioned by the candidate, and refer back to them.

The impressions a candidate makes upon the interviewer are not always apparent at the conclusion of the interview. It takes time for inklings to congeal into judgments. But at the end of the interview it helps to make a conscious effort to stop and reflect about the specific circumstances as well as the general impressions. Consider these:

Facts

- Did the candidate arrive on time?
- Was he or she well-informed about the company?
- Did the applicant use the correct names and titles of company personnel?
- Was he or she properly groomed and did he or she present him- or herself with professional poise?

- Did resume content match the statements made during the interview?
- Had he or she thoroughly read the job description?
- What impressions did the applicant make on others?

Impressions

- Was rapport established?
- Was the candidate polite, enthusiastic, positive?
- Did he or she acknowledge weaknesses and address them?
- Was he or she cooperative in explaining events and circumstances of work history?
- How did the candidate react when asked to explain the details of specific events?
- Did the candidate's demeanor change when asked about past supervisors?
- Were the candidate's statements consistent throughout the interview?
- Did the candidate's statements and questions focus more on the position and the company, or more on him- or herself and pay and benefits?
- Did rapport break down at any point?
- Did he or she end the interview with professionalism?
- At the end of the interview, did the interviewer feel he or she had been speaking to an honest person?

Follow through

- Did the candidate provide requested reference contact information?
- Did he or she thank the interviewer or others for the opportunity?

- Were other departing courtesies or salutations extended?
- When references were contacted, had the candidate made them aware of the impending call?
- Were loose ends tied up and promises fulfilled?

Immediately following an interview, the interviewer should ponder what has taken place and review the candidate's resume and the notes taken during the interview. If a confidante is available, a discussion about the interview may help shape and clarify impressions. If the interviewer promised to follow-up with actions such as emailing information about a benefits package, those actions should be put into motion.

Phone and Off-site Interviews

For jobs where off-site communications are important, such as traveling sales representatives, it is advisable to test the lines of communication to confirm they are open and efficient. In a job where an employee must be on call, or available for irregular scheduling, reliable access is essential.

Some hiring managers feel phone interviews are fairer than face-to-face interviews because one cannot be biased by appearance over the phone. But the Aalto study that we discussed in Chapter 4, Honesty in the Workplace, discovered that people are more likely to lie in phone interviews than in face-to-face interviews.[70] An interviewer who insists on a face-to-face interview may be performing a service for the interviewee by removing the added temptation to lie as well as removing distractions such as poor cell phone reception and other unforeseen intrusions like, say, when a parent is calling from a home filled with noisy children. Unless the job opening is for a telemarketing position or other phone-heavy tasks, phone interviews are generally less informative than face-to-face interviews.

Essential Questions   Must ask?

Most job applications contain certain legal disclaimers to scare the applicants into providing only accurate information. Resumes do not come with notations such as "All information provided here is accurate." So it is necessary for the interviewer to ask certain questions and make notes of both the questions and the applicant's answers. These disclaimer questions include:

1. Is everything on your resume up-to-date and factual?
2. Does this resume show all the places you have worked?
3. Why are you leaving your current job?
4. Does your employer know you intend to leave?
5. Do you fulfill all the requirements listed on the job description?
6. Are there any limitations that would keep you from performing all the duties of this job?
7. Have you been found guilty of a felony?
8. Are you legally allowed to work in the United States of America?
9. Do I have your permission to contact these references? (Name each reference.)

These questions may protect the employer if the applicant lied or misrepresented him or herself on the resume or job application. Questions 1 and 2 should be asked at the beginning of the first review of the applicant's resume. The questions relating to the current job and the current employer's awareness of the candidates impending departure are best asked during the work history portion of the interview. Questions 7, 8, and 9 should be asked upon completion of the initial review of the job description.

Standardized Interview Questions

Popular business books and trendy online fora are filled with advice about "tough, insightful" interview questions. These articles make boasts akin to "questions that reveal everything" about a candidate. One of my favorites is, "What's your superpower, or what's your spirit animal?"[71] Really?

When considering which questions to ask job applicants, I like to ponder, "How would George Costanza or P. T. Barnum answer this question?" If either of them could give a plausible answer, then the question is worthless.

For an interview question to be worth asking, it can be answered effectively only by the job candidate. Such questions focus expressly on the candidate's work history and job performance. Answers to these work questions lead to relevant follow-up questions.

For example, "What were your responsibilities at XYZ Company?" Followed by, "As production manager, what issues were most challenging?" After that, "How did you cope with the frequent breakdown of your widget machine?" Then, "How did management respond to your request for a preventative maintenance program?"

The ensuing discussion could touch on how the candidate presented the proposed changes. Did the proposal meet resistance? How was resistance overcome? Who among management sided with the candidate and why?

Within a few minutes, the interviewer will know a whole lot more about the candidate's actual workplace performance than would come from a rehearsed answer to a canned question pulled from some wonk's list. Besides, George Costanza is not stupid. Probably he will check information sources that show which questions are likely to be asked during your company's interviews, and hone his answers ahead of time.

Thwarting George Costanza in the Job Interview

In *Seinfeld*, America's most successful television comedy series, George Costanza was Jerry Seinfeld's best friend. George was entertaining and intelligent, but also unprincipled and deceitful. No employer wants George Costanza on the payroll, and no employee wants him for a coworker. How do we keep the Georges out there away from our businesses?

For George, lying is an industry, the instrument to achieve his life's ambition: "I was free and clear. I was living the dream! I was stripped to the waist, eating a block of cheese the size of a car battery!"[72] It's not surprising that George would lie and pull out all the stops to attain such lofty goals.

"We're just trying to come up with the best possible lie," George calmly explains to Elaine in the "Marisa Tomei/Cadillac" episode. He concludes, "That's what this is all about."[73] For a small but determined group of job applicants, that is precisely what it's all about. When asked questions during the interview, they're trying to come up with the best possible lie. So, why make it easy for them?

Many authors recommend that employers ask scripted or standardized questions.[74] While these standardized questions allow one candidate's answers to be compared to another's, they do little to disclose a candidate's level of honesty. The predictability of popular scripted questions allows candidates to rehearse answers, thereby reducing both spontaneity and the insight into the candidates' true nature. During the open-questioning phase of an interview, scripted questions can serve as platforms for additional veracity-testing questions, but the answers to scripted questions are of little value unless followed up with unscripted, spontaneous questions.

What if George Costanza were asked a popular scripted question, such as "Tell me about a time when you experienced professional growth."

He might answer: "One particular client argued with me and insulted my intelligence. Early on, I had made a minor mistake, which he harped on and wouldn't let slide. Eventually he accepted my apologies and we moved on. I grew professionally from that experience by becoming more patient, understanding, and careful in my communications."

This wordy answer demonstrates a willingness to accept criticism, an ability to mollify an irate client, and the adaptability to learn in the face of adversity. So, why wouldn't any deceitful character like George Costanza give that same answer? He's smart enough. He's devious enough. If successful, he's rewarded with a paycheck, so he's certainly motivated. George may be a bad character, but he knows which qualities of character are commendable, so he'll speak as though he possesses them.

With a few veracity-testing questions, the interviewer may gain a clearer insight into George's true nature.

"What mistake did you make?"

"What was your client's name?"

"So when you stopped using the inaccurate term 'latex' and started calling it by its proper trade name, polyisoprene, did Mr. Vanderlay become cooperative?"

"Is Mr. Vanderlay still your client?"

"How did your supervisor react when you lost Mr. Vanderlay as a client?"

"What was your supervisor's name?"

So, Mr. Vanderlay was not happy with George's performance, and ceased buying latex from him. That pertinent fact was not evident from George's initial answer, which, though eloquent, was also deceitful. Even a determined trickster like George has difficulty maintaining shams for more than a few minutes and a few layers of questioning. When a discussion begins slipping from his control, he may dodge questions, change the subject, drastically reduce his verbal output, or he may simply begin contradicting earlier statements.

If the candidate were honest, and not George Costanza, the interviewer might say this:

"What mistake did you make?"

"You said your client's name was Mr. Vanderlay from Isoprene Incorporated. After Mr. Vanderlay corrected your terminology, did he continue buying from you?"

"That must have pleased your supervisor. Did you say her name was Jennifer?"

George could be duplicitous enough to fudge his answers to veracity-testing questions, but that would be unlikely. An interviewer who asks for supervisors' and coworkers' names is probably going to crosscheck answers, so if George lied initially, he probably will be looking for a quick exit when the veracity-testing questions are asked. An interviewee who provides names willingly is essentially asking the interviewer to contact those named. One who provides supervisors' names reluctantly or not at all is likely seeking cover.

The goal of interviewing is to find honest workers, to expose dishonesty, and to oust George Costanza from the good-worker gene pool.

Summary

The goal of an interview is to find the most honest candidate for the job. The market for honest employees is competitive, so every employer should strive to make a good impression upon job candidates. Interviewers must conscientiously avoid provocative questions and topics. Before scheduling interviews, hiring managers should thoroughly research the resumes of job

applicants and sift out those that show inconsistencies and contradictions, as well as those from unqualified candidates, thus
providing more time for interviewing the best candidates. An
employer has a legal and moral responsibility to vet job candidates carefully. During the interview the candidate's answers and
comments should be noted for future reference. Every employer
should obtain from the candidate certain information that protects the employer in case the candidate is lying or omitting important information. Standardized and popular interview questions that are not specific to the candidate's work performance
furnish little insight into the candidate's honesty.

Part III

The Process

The interview is about to begin and the interviewer has assembled his or her tools. The tangible tools include the applicant's resume, the employer's job description, and the information accumulated by researching the resume. The intangible tools include managed conversation, interviewer advantages, the telltale clues of honesty, and the interviewer's judgment. Now we'll see how these tools are used to determine a job candidate's honesty—whether the candidate possesses the good-worker gene.

Chapter 12 The All-About-You Interview

Interviews are managed conversations, managed conversations are casual conversations with a purpose, and casual conversations are all about the other person. So an effective interview is all about the interviewee. It is an all-about-you interview.

We have already discussed that an effective conversation focuses on the other person. We learned that we can test veracity by cross-referencing known facts with information accumulated in that conversation. We know that a prolonged conversation provides more information for cross-referencing and veracity testing than a brief conversation. So, in the workplace where time is money, a balance must be struck that provides adequate time for accumulating information while not wasting money.

Interview Timeframe

This step-by-step interview process is designed to allow the best use of the interview tools discussed earlier. The time spent in each phase of the interview depends on circumstances. The length of the interview will vary depending upon many factors including time needed to sort out conversational inferences, the complexity of the job, and uncertainty in the mind of the interviewer.

The interview begins with rapport-building, which dominates the introductions and casual conversation. This phase of the interview allows the candidate to acclimate to the setting while the interviewer resolves the conversational inferences that could otherwise reduce the quality of communication. Information-gathering through the process of open questioning will dominate the next two phases: the first review of the candidate's resume and the first review of the job description.

Interview Timeframe

· Introductions and casual discussion   5 to 10 minutes
· First review of resume   10 to 15 minutes
· First review of job description   10 to 15 minutes

Summary decision about applicant

· Return to casual discussion   5 to 10 minutes
· Second review of resume   15 to 20 minutes

Assessed decision about applicant

· Second review of job description   15 to 20 minutes
  and conclusions

Total Interview Time 1 to 1 ½ Hours

After the candidate's resume and the job description have been reviewed in the open-questioning format, the interviewer should be able to make a summary decision about the suitability of the candidate. If the candidate is judged suitable and the decision to continue is made, the interviewer will return to a topic for casual discussion, which bolsters rapport in preparation for the more rigorous questioning to follow.

During the second review of the resume, the cycle turns from open questioning to intensive veracity testing with questions following upon earlier answers, digging deeper into the specific aspects and events of the candidate's work history, clarifying prior statements to determine if contradictions exist or if vital information has been omitted or glossed over. Contradictions and omissions provide the evidence of dishonesty that may result in the rejection of a job candidate. This phase provides the indicators of honesty that interviewers look for.

After the resume has been thoroughly reviewed for the second time, and the candidate's veracity established, the interviewer will make a summary decision about the hireability of the candidate. If the candidate is deemed worthy of further consideration, the interviewer will review the job description for a second time while focusing on the benefits and advantages of working for this particular company, and then conclude with a discussion of when and where the interview process goes from here.

Sample Interviews

In this section, I will insert segments from hypothetical interviews. Real life conversations consist of many short phrases, interjections, inducements, and acknowledgments, which, if included, would fragment the written dialogue. So those grunts and uh-huhs are mostly omitted from the dialogues that follow. However, the volume of words in a conversation often exceeds that which would be found in good literary dialogue. Here I've tried to make the dialogue readable while keeping it plausible.

Introductions and Casual Conversation

The first order of business is putting the candidate at ease. The general demeanor of the interview should be friendly and open. The interviewer strives to establish a tone of shared friendship and understanding.

If the receptionist has not already done so, offer the applicant something to drink or a few moments to relax and unwind. The interview will likely consume more than an hour, so physical comfort should be considered.

After the candidate is comfortable, the interviewer should look for a topic of causal interest linked directly to the candidate. It may be an item from the resume, a piece of jewelry or clothing, a throwaway comment, or an observation of the surroundings, but some incidental discussion needs to occur that establishes a common conversational thread between the interviewer and the candidate while conversational inferences are resolved. This important phase, which consumes five or ten minutes, establishes the baseline of communication that will be sustained throughout the interview.

Sample Introductions and Casual Conversations

We'll follow the job interviews of civil engineer Carter Johnfeld (see resume on page 126) and dental hygienist Jackie Kondin (see resume page 129), whose resumes we looked at earlier. They are applying for the jobs that were posted and reviewed in the chapter on job descriptions. Carter is being interviewed by Brownwell Engineering, who posted online a civil engineering position (job posting shown on page 109). Brownwell did not provide Carter a complete job description, so he is operating with only the information provided in the job posting. Jackie is interviewing with Chestnut Ridge Dentistry for the position of dental hygienist/assistant. Chestnut Ridge provided a proper job description (job description shown on page 111), so, if she read it, Jackie will know the requirements of the job.

My observations are found in the right-hand column. As you read these dialogues, please do not confuse my sentiments with those of the interviewers. In the end, the interviewers will make their hiring decisions, which may differ from my choice or yours.

As you read these dialogues, they may seem to drag on and their content may become tedious to you. Reading a dialogue is a fundamentally different experience from engaging in one. Actual participation is far more stimulating and engrossing. If you find yourself losing interest while you are reading, feel free to skip ahead. However, seemingly insignificant words may have major bearing on the direction of an interview, especially when they are accompanied by non-verbal indicators; so as you read, try to picture the setting and the physical presence of the participants.

Introductory Casual Conversation Between HR Professional, Pauline White, and Job Applicant Carter Johnfeld

Brownwell Corporation, typical of many large companies, has a human resources department that posts job openings, accepts applications, screens resumes, interviews worthy candidates, then maintains personnel files and payroll records for the company. Carter Johnfeld's initial interview will be conducted by Human Resource Director Pauline White, who will make her recommendation to hire or not. As with many large companies, after the HR department makes a recommendation to hire, the applicant's resume and accompanying notes are forwarded to the project's team leader, who will also interview the candidate, then confer again with HR before the hiring decision is finalized.

Pauline has worked for Brownwell for over twenty years, and for the past fifteen years she has been directly involved in hiring many of the engineers who are currently employed by this world-renowned engineering firm.

Candidate: Carter Johnfeld
Interviewer: Pauline White
Company: Brownwell Corporation
Position: Civil engineer, EIT
Introduction and casual conversation

Dialogue	Observations
Interviewer: Are those bicycles on your tie? Are you a cyclist?	Pauline picked bicycles on Carter's tie instead of baseball mentioned on his resume. Maybe Pauline is not a baseball fan, or maybe the bicycle tie was too dazzling to ignore.
Candidate: When I have time. The tie was a gift.	
I: What sort of bicycling do you do?	
C: Mostly mountain biking. I do it for exercise and fun.	
I: Mountain biking is popular now. Why do you think that is?	
C: Probably because you can ride mountain bikes anywhere: streets, trails, off-trail. They're versatile. And they don't have to be expensive. Walmart sells decent mountain bikes.	
I: But don't their frames need to be extra strong?	

Dialogue	**Observations**
C: If you're doing actual mountain biking—in serious mountain settings—it's a good idea to have the appropriate bike. But most people use them on packed trails in parks and places like that. My grandmother's old 3-speed can handle that.	
I: What type do you ride?	
C: I started out one level above Walmart, but when some friends and I started riding on more challenging terrain, I bought a better bike. It's not top of the line, but it's good enough for me.	Humility.
I: Where do you ride?	
C: Raccoon Creek Park is only a few minutes from my apartment, so I go there.	
I: I love Raccoon Creek Park. I board my horse on a nearby farm and I use the park's trails.	
C: Uh-oh. Cyclist versus horseback rider. I see a conflict brewing.	Could be risky for Carter to point out a potential conflict rather than steer clear of it.
I: (Laughs) Not with my old horse. He's the steady, sure-footed type. Bicycles don't bother him. Have you had conflicts with horseback riders?	
C: I haven't. I grew up around horses, so I know to slow down to avoid spooking them. But most cyclists don't understand horses, and a lot of horseback riders don't understand horses either. That's why they insist on riding their green horses on trails with bicycles whizzing by, scaring the horses and knocking the riders into the mud.	
I: (More laughs) Even if the horses don't know better, you would think their riders would. Mostly I try to ride Laponka, my horse, early in the morning. That way, the bugs aren't too thick and most of the hikers and bikers aren't out either.	Pauline appreciates Carter's little joke. Well played, Carter.
C: Laponka? That sounds like a good name for an Appaloosa. Is he?	When Pauline spoke, Carter was paying attention.
I: An Appaloosa? Yes. Are you familiar with that breed?	
C: From movies and books. The breed's history is fascinating. Does Laponka have spots over his haunches?	Now Carter is asking the questions.
I: He has some spots, but not the classic blanket pattern. I didn't buy him for his looks. I bought him because he's not afraid of bicycles, motorcycles, dogs, fly-fishermen, or anything else. He's just a good old trail horse.	
C: Fly-fishermen?	

Dialogue	Observations
I: It's a long story, and we have a job interview ahead of us. **C:** I'm ready. **I:** Is this resume up-to-date and accurate? **C:** Yes. Nothing's changed since last week when I emailed it to you.	I think Pauline wishes she had more time to chat, but time is money.

From this exchange it is apparent both parties are comfortable with their surroundings and with each other. Pauline and Carter have established an easy dialogue. If anything, Carter might be too familiar. It will be interesting to see if his casual manner continues through the interview, and if it does, whether he will benefit or be encumbered by it.

Introductory Casual Conversation Between Dr. Mingo Mauch, Owner of Chestnut Ridge Dentistry and Jackie Kondin, Job Seeker

Chestnut Ridge Dentistry is a small-town dental practice. Business is good. Dr. Mingo Mauch's staff of four has been with him almost from the start eighteen years ago, but now his dental hygienist is moving away. Because his business is thriving and his schedule is full, he does not have time to spend on the hiring process. He just wants to find somebody, hire him or her, and get back to fixing teeth.

Dr. Mauch posted the job opening on two popular job boards; from one he received a flood of resumes and from the other, nothing. The flood consisted mostly of click-through responses from browsers in other states. He invited three of these respondents to apply, but, apparently unwilling to live in rural Pennsylvania, none did. Two recent graduates from a nearby commercial school emailed their resumes, but Dr. Mauch is too busy working to train inexperienced hygienists. He prefers somebody with experience. Then departing hygienist Susan passed along the resume of Jackie Kondin, the daughter of a friend.

Dr. Mauch is successful, smart and friendly, but like many small-business people, he is inexperienced at locating and interviewing potential employees. In a manner that typifies many employers, he will interview candidates, but he is not sure what he is looking for in those interviews. He knows that he wants to hire an experienced dental hygienist/assistant who will come to work on time, get along with his patients, and be compatible with his staff. He knows he wants those character traits in his new employee. He doesn't know what indicators manifest those traits. He doesn't know to look expressly for honesty.

Candidate: Jackie Kondin
Interviewer: Dr. Mingo Mauch, DDS
Company: Chestnut Ridge Dentistry
Position: Dental hygienist/assistant
Introduction and casual discussion

Dialogue	Observations
Interviewer: Did you have trouble finding our office?	
Candidate: No. I pass here on my way to Pittsburgh. I've seen your sign.	
I: Do you drive to Pittsburgh often?	
C: I try to go to Steeler football games when I can. So, probably ten or twelve times a year, including shopping trips.	
I: How often do you attend games?	
C: I try to go to all the home games and at least one, sometimes two away games each year.	
I: Last year I tried buying tickets for friends who were visiting. I could not find them. How do you get tickets?	
C: Whatever way I can. If I can't buy tickets online, I try to buy them from one of the street hawkers. I know you're not supposed to do that, but sometimes it's the only way in. If we can't get into the stadium, we watch the game at one of the restaurants downtown or in Station Square.	Jackie fails to consider Dr. Mauch's need for tickets and talks about her own interests.
I: My friends will visit again this year. Maybe we'll try again. They are coming from Croatia.	

Dialogue	Observations
C: It's hard to get Steeler tickets.	Croatia? Why not ask about Croatia?
I: I'm more of a soccer fan, and I don't really understand American football. Why do they give six points for scoring only one time?	
C: Well, because those are the rules.	Logic?
I: Yes, but doesn't it seem strange to give six points for one score?	
C: I don't think so. If they gave only one point for each score, the games might end with scores like three to two. And I don't know what they would do about field goals—half a point maybe.	
I: In soccer, we call it football, final scores are often three to two, and the games are very exciting.	Jackie seems unenthused with a topic of someone else's choosing.
C: I've tried watching soccer. I can't get into it.	
I: Did you watch the World Cup?	
C: No. What's that?	
I: It's the biggest sporting event in the world.	
C: Oh. I thought the Super Bowl was.	
I: The Super Bowl is big only in America.	Dr. Mauch is not looking for common ground, not building rapport.
C: I heard it was popular in Mexico and England too.	
I: That may be, but it is not as popular as the World Cup.	
C: Everybody that I know watches the Super Bowl.	It's not about you, Jackie.
I: Everybody that I know watches the World Cup, but maybe we should look at your resume. Have you brought it with you?	Not about you, Dr. Mauch.
C: Yes.	

Here we have two people talking past each other with no regard to the interests or pleasure of the other. Strange as it may seem, this is not an atypical conversation. In workplaces and social settings, conversations often involve people who want to be heard but don't want to listen. Jackie wants to talk about American football, Dr. Mauch wants to talk about soccer, and neither is socially conscious of their own self-centeredness. If Jackie wants to find out what sort of person her prospective employer is, she should change strategies. If Dr. Mauch is looking for a reliable worker who will be on time, work hard, get along with her coworkers, and please her patients, we could have better luck throwing darts at resumes.

Because they don't know better, the participants don't mind the other's lapses. Let's see where this interview goes from here.

First Resume Review

The initial review of the applicant's resume should take from ten to fifteen minutes during which the interviewer will use open questioning to collect the information that will be explored more deeply later in the interview and again when speaking to references. The applicant's most recent work history should be thoroughly discussed, concentrating on job duties, supervisors' names, extent of interaction with those supervisors, challenging aspects of the work, favorite features of the job, and least favorite aspects of the job. These issues should be discussed in depth, with the interviewer pursuing the details of the applicant's past work experience and job performance. The interviewer should carefully make notes of the particular issues that the applicant raises as well as the names of supervisors and coworkers.

If the candidate lists several jobs or employers, the depth of the discussion of each should depend upon their relevance.

If a break in the timeline between jobs exists, the interviewer should ask about it. A break may have occurred for a sound reason, or it might indicate that the applicant held a job from which he or she was fired for reasons that would be relevant to a new employer.

After finishing the work history portion of the candidate's resume, move on to education and personal interests. Even if the candidate completed his or her education long ago, the interviewer should ask and make notes about the degrees earned and the dates they were completed. The frank question, "Did you fulfill the requirements and obtain your degree (or diploma)?"

may sound superfluous, but only candidates who have lied on their resumes will be offended by it.

If the candidate's resume lists hobbies or outside interests, engage in a brief conversation about at least one of these interests. In the "follow-up casual discussion," the interviewer may want to return to this topic.

Pauline's First Review of Carter's Resume

Carter Johnfeld and human resources professional Pauline White had an upbeat introductory conversation. No social or conversational obstacles were apparent. Now Pauline is beginning her first review of Carter's resume, so it is time to gather facts.

Pauline and Carter will discuss some technical matters, as would be expected when engaging in a conversation with an engineer about engineering work. Later in the interview Pauline may return to these topics and delve deeper into them to check Carter's veracity and to consider whether these topics would be worthy of discussing with selected references. Consider what direction you would have taken the discussion and what questions you would have asked Carter.

Candidate: Carter Johnfeld
Interviewer: Pauline White
Company: Brownwell Corporation
Position: Civil engineer, EIT
First review of applicant's resume

Dialogue	Observations
Interviewer: Is everything on this resume up to date and factual?	Obligatory questions.
Candidate: Yes.	
I: Does it show all the places where you have worked?	
C: Yes.	
I: How long have you worked for Tomlin Engineering?	
C: Almost three years. I still work there.	
I: Why are you thinking about leaving?	

Dialogue	Observations

C: I was hired when the company had two big bridge projects in the works, one in the construction phase and one in the planning stage. When I started I was working on the more advanced project, but after working on it for a few months, I was asked to work on the planning phase of the new project. The construction project is now complete, and we did not win the bid for the planned project. I'm concerned that I might be laid off. I would rather not wait for the ax to fall. That's why I'm looking for work now.

I: Does your employer know you're looking?

C: I haven't advertised it, but several of us are in the same boat and we're all concerned for our jobs. I think the firm expects us to be looking. But I have not discussed it with my project supervisor.

Frankness.

I: What is your project supervisor's name?

C: The senior engineer and project supervisor on this project is Imran Khan. The leader of my team is Scott Weaver. I work with Scott daily and with Imran a few times each week, mostly for planning meetings on Tuesday mornings.

Forthcoming with names.

I: How many engineers are on Scott's team?

C: Four engineers, two drafters, and occasionally we'll have one or two interns. We farm out a lot of the site issues. Early on, we had an architect.

I: Does your team focus primarily on bridges?

C: Single span, mostly arch bridges. No suspension or trusses, so far. Scott's team was formed specifically for long single spans, steel arches, like the New River Gorge Bridge, but not that big and not 876 feet high. They don't make many like that.

I: Have you been to the New River Gorge?

C: To people in my business that bridge is like a shrine. I've driven across it, walked across it, and jumped off it.

I: You jumped from it?

C: On Bridge Day five years ago. I was still in college. A couple of friends and I base-jumped from it—with parachutes of course. I started parachuting when I was at sophomore at Lehigh. You know, my supervisor, Scott Weaver bungee jumped from it about twenty years ago. They don't allow bungee jumping there anymore. It's an awesome bridge though.

I: Is it really 876 feet high?

Dialogue	Observations
C: Yes, and about 3000 feet long. They built it with COR-TEN steel. It's the special alloy used in the construction of the US Steel Building here in Pittsburgh. It rusts to a point, then the alloy creates an impervious surface that prevents further corrosion. You probably know all that.	Enthusiasm and depth of knowledge.
I: I don't. Did you say it's called COR-TEN steel?	
C: Yes. COR-TEN. Since it was developed in the 1960s, it's been used on some of the world's biggest construction projects. It's an alloy of manganese, nickel, and chromium mixed with iron. Because of its strength and durability, it's ideal for bridges.	Helpfulness. In depth knowledge.
I: How strong is it?	
C: Do you mean yield strength?	Respects accuracy.
I: Yes, yield strength, tensile strength.	
C: As best I can remember, yield strength is about 50ksi and tensile is around 75…that's 75 thousand pounds per square inch. It's strong, but its resistance to corrosion is a major benefit, and it's the main reason we recommended it for the Tampa Bay project.	Does he really know this stuff, or is he posing? Check for accuracy.
I: What's the Tampa Bay project?	
C: That's the project we didn't get. Tomlin bid on a three-mile long bridge near Tampa Bay, Florida, that would have consisted of two single-arch spans, each 1,250 feet long, that would have risen 230 feet above the water. Our team, with Imran as project engineer and Scott as team leader for the two arches, bid the project with COR-TEN A-588 steel. We lost out to Vulcan International who used a heavier but less expensive steel. Their bridge will cost less to build, but much more to maintain. If we'd won that contract, I wouldn't be looking for work today.	
I: Whose idea was it to use COR-TEN?	
C: I don't think Scott and Imran ever considered any steel but COR-TEN. We put together a great bridge proposal, as lean and streamlined as any project I've ever been involved in, and a couple of the older engineers said the same thing. We just didn't win the bidding war. It's a competitive field.	Not really an answer. Maybe unwilling to blame Scott or Imran.
I: Has all the time and energy spent designing this bridge gone to waste? Is there nothing you can do with the plans?	
C: Oh, yeah. Imran is shopping them to the city of Perth, Australia, and also in Indonesia. I don't think those plans will collect dust for long.	
I: Will that preserve your job?	

Dialogue	**Observations**
C: It might, but it might not.	Impatience?
I: Don't you want to wait around and see?	
C: If the plans are picked up by another buyer, it will be the talk of the industry. I'll hear about it. At Tomlin, I'm a bridge engineer, and while I like bridges, I would love to work on other things: buildings, mining, energy, railroads, airports. . . . I'd even like to try something in aerospace if I could find it. That's why I'm applying here. Brownwell is a much more diverse firm and I have heard that you encourage multidisciplined experience.	Maybe malcontented— maybe healthy ambition. Complimentary of Brownwell.
I: We do that for the right people. Do you think you're ready to try a different engineering arena?	
C: There's always plenty to learn in every aspect of engineering. That's what's so compelling about this field of work. I could spend every day studying, planning, and building bridges and never learn all there is to know about it, but I'm twenty-six years old, and I would like to test other waters and see where I fit in best.	
I: Are you afraid that your attitude might be regarded as reflecting latent discontent or impulsiveness?	
C: (Laughter) I guess so, but it's not that. I'm as committed to my team, my work, and my employer as anybody. But when I see SpaceX launch a satellite-bearing rocket, or hear talk of bridging the Bering Strait, or think about superconducting maglev trains moving at 500 miles per hour, it makes me say, "Wow." Doesn't it do that for you?	Inclusiveness. Enthusiasm.
I: (Laughs) Yeah, I guess it does, but probably not the way it excites you. How do you think Scott and Imran would rate your ability as an engineer when they compare it to other engineers in your position, hired out of college and working on their first major project, a big one, like the Tampa Bay project?	
C: I think they would give me good ratings. We didn't win the bid, and that fact weighs heavily on the team, but I'm confident they would say I performed well.	Realistic.
I: Did your performance always meet their expectations?	
C: Always? That's hard to say, but if I didn't provide what they wanted when they wanted it, I always had it for them shortly after I understood their directions.	
I: Can you give me an example when you maybe did not meet their expectations?	

Dialogue

C: Yes, I think so. Early in the planning phase, I overestimated the effects of thermal expansion on the bridge joints. My math was off because I plugged in expansion coefficients for COR-TEN A-242 instead of A-588. Scott caught it. He told me that on cold days sports cars would be falling through the cracks in my bridge. I fixed the mistake. There were other times too where my errors and miscalculations had to be corrected.

I: Really? Like when?

C: When I started working at Tomlin, I was working with Aasta's team—Aasta Parvadi was the team leader on my first project—and I showed my calculations to coworkers and they helped me with some of the math. I had made dumb mistakes.

I: Dumb mistakes?

C: Yes, dumb; not fatal. That's why we work in teams, to catch mistakes before they become flaws.

I: Did you find mistakes made by your coworkers?

C: Of course. We checked each other's work and helped each other out. As I mentioned earlier, I think our bridge plans were as good as anybody's, and teamwork is the reason for it.

I: You mentioned Scott as your team leader, Imran as the project engineer, and three other engineers on your team.

C: Yes, Carl, Tej, and Vickie.

I: Did you get along well?

C: We had a good team. As time went on we all sort of settled into our own areas of expertise. Ironically, I ended up handling most of the stress and expansion calculations and related aspects. But I would not hesitate to count on anyone of them in a critical matter. We all know we did a good job.

I: Did you enjoy working with anyone more than the others?

C: If you're asking about personality, Vickie had us laughing all the time. If you want to know the most serious, diligent worker; I have to say it's Tej.

I: What are you and your team doing right now, since Tomlin's bid for Tampa Bay has been rejected?

C: We're adjusting the plans to other potential applications. I mentioned Imran is talking to the city of Perth. He has asked us to examine the conditions of the harbor there, and revise our Tampa Bay plans to fit that situation. We're doing the same thing for Indonesia.

Observations

Pauline will probably return to this topic later. Good reference-check topic.

Note supervisor's name.

I wonder if Carter's coworkers agree with his assessment of his mistakes.

Note coworkers' names.

This might come up again in discussions about Carter's math ability.

Dialogue	**Observations**

I: Are those changes difficult to make?

C: The geology is quite different from Tampa to Perth. Perth has better rock under it, so that saves some money on the pilings and footers. Surabaya on Java, Indonesia, is a seismically active area. It may not be an ideal application for an arch bridge, but we're working on some novel ideas for foundational support.

Pauline asked about Carter's internship with Jacobs Engineering to confirm that this constituted real work experience and was not just an academic rubber stamp.

Otherwise, Carter doesn't meet the three-year experience requirement.

I: A couple of loose ends… How is your driving record?

C: Do you mean tickets and accidents, or are you asking about the types of licenses that I have?

I: Do you have your CDL?

C: No, I have a motorcycle endorsement.

I: How about tickets and accidents?

C: I have had one speeding ticket and I've never had an accident.

Get Carter's answers on record because they can be checked through testing and reviewing public records.

I: No others tickets…just one speeding ticket, ever?

C: No, just the one ticket.

I: Tell me about the speeding ticket.

C: I was going 56 in a 35 zone. It was at the edge of town, and I didn't realize the speed zones had changed.

Check this with an MVR.

I: Did you lose your license?

C: I was given three points against my license, but they remove a point every two years of clean driving, so by now I should have a clean record as far as the state of Pennsylvania is concerned. I was in high school then. Would it be beneficial if I had a CDL? I was thinking about taking the classes and getting one. I took the written test online, so I only need to pass the driving and air brakes tests.

Industriousness.

I: It can't hurt. Even if you're not the driver, it always helps to know what others on site are thinking and doing. Do you have any objection to taking a SAMHSA-10 pre-employment drug test?

C: No. I'll have no problem passing any drug or alcohol test you want me to take.

I: Good. Have you ever been convicted of a felony?

C: No. Never.

I: Let's talk about the openings here at Brownwell. ….

Well, Carter certainly is an interesting person. Few would be so frank and open in a job interview. Maybe it's just his nature, or maybe he's not really interested in the job and consequently is willing to risk a casual demeanor. Early on, he stated that he likes working at Tomlin, but that he is exploring new ground.

On the other hand, if he proves to be as confident and friendly as he seems, wouldn't he make a great addition to Brownwell's staff? It will take further questioning to determine if his competence lives up to his other qualities.

Pauline has compiled a list of names of supervisors and co-workers as well as a log of events that she can return to later in the interview when Carter is tiring and his guard is down.

Dr. Mauch's First Review of Jackie Kondin's Resume

Jackie and Dr. Mauch had an odd introductory conversation. Neither was willing to show deference to the other, which is less surprising on Dr. Mauch's account than on Jackie's. As they share a lack of social grace, the missed opportunities might not deter either one. Maybe, since they suffer similar failings, they will discover commonality. We know they have something in common: he needs to hire a dental hygienist and she is a dental hygienist.

Candidate: Jackie Kondin
Interviewer: Dr. Mingo Mauch, DDS
Interviewing at Chestnut Ridge Dentistry
Position: Dental hygienist/assistant
First review of applicant's resume

Dialogue	Observations
I: On this resume, is everything up to date and completely accurate?	Obligatory questions.
C: Yes.	
I: Does this show all the places where you have worked in the past five years?	
C: Yes. Well…no. Right after finishing at Bradford, I had a job for about two months. It was mostly just a training position. I didn't bother to put that on my resume.	Why was that employer omitted?

Dialogue	Observations
I: What were you training for?	
C: For dental hygienist, but I got a different job.	
I: What was that employer's name?	
C: It was a small office in Kittanning called Allegheny Dental. I think they've moved their office.	Possibly evasive. Why mention office move?
I: Was your departure your own choice?	
C: Yes. I got another job. A better job.	Reference question.
I: Are you currently working at Loyalhanna Dental Associates?	
C: No.	Contradicts resume.
I: When did you leave there?	
C: About a month ago.	Check timeline.
I: In July then. Why did you leave?	
C: The talk was that Dr. Sengji was going to leave and start his own practice because he wasn't seeing enough patients. He specializes in pediatric dentistry. If he leaves, I suspect they would cut back on support staff. Rather than wait around, I quit.	Weak reasoning. Return to this later.
I: Did you discuss Dr. Sengji's plans with him?	
C: No. But everybody knew what was going on.	Hearsay, gossip.
I: What did you do at Loyalhanna?	
C: I clean teeth, take X-rays, advise patients on proper brushing and flossing techniques, inform the dentists about any problems the patient might be having, and I keep records.	
I: How many dental hygienists were employed there?	
C: Three. Two of us, Judy and I, were mostly full-time hygienists, and Ken works as a dental assistant most of the time and occasionally cleans teeth. Sometimes Wanda fills in.	
I: What is Ken's last name?	Note for possible reference.
C: Ken Hartford.	
I: Do you prefer hygienist work or assisting?	
C: I'm a better hygienist than assistant. I enjoy dealing with patients one on one. So, I prefer hygienist work.	Frankness.
I: Do you dislike working as an assistant?	
C: I don't dislike it, but I would rather just clean teeth and not have the pressure of the dentist watching over my shoulder.	Possibly insecure about job performance.
I: At Loyalhanna, was it standard practice for the dentists to check your work after you performed a cleaning?	

Dialogue	Observations
C: Typically, when I finished a cleaning I notified Dr. Murkowski and he examined the patient's mouth and asked about nagging issues such as sore teeth or gums.	
I: Was he ever critical of your work?	
C: Sometimes I would miss a problem and he would catch it, but most of the time he was not openly critical.	Understanding and supportive.
I: Can you give me an example of an instance when your work was criticized?	
C: I nicked a patient's gum with a curette and it bled. The doctor saw the nick and he asked me about it. It was not long after I started at Loyalhanna, and after that, I was more careful.	Interesting. Doctor saw it . . . she didn't tell him? Come back to this.
I: How many patients' teeth did you clean on a typical day?	
C: It varied with the workload, because I also helped with recordkeeping and chart filing. If I just cleaned teeth, then six or seven, sometimes eight.	
I: How much time did you spend filing and recordkeeping?	
C: Wanda rarely asked for my help, but if she missed a day or two of work, or if we were very busy, I would spend a couple hours helping her. Ken often handled the office if Wanda was off. Occasionally, he needed my help.	Above, it sounded like filing was a time-consuming task. Not now.
I: Were you expected to keep to the one-patient-per-hour schedule that most offices maintain?	
C: We talked about that a lot. To do the job properly, I feel that more than a full hour was needed, sometimes an hour and a half. Ken and Wanda wanted me to stick to the one-patient-per-hour schedule. I think Ken was trying to impress Wanda so he could get a pay raise, and I think Wanda just wanted to push as many patients through the doors as possible. If you're doing a good and thorough job, I don't think anybody can keep up that pace.	Seems to be a contentious issue. Return to this later in interview.
I: Is Wanda, Wanda Murkowski?	
C: Yes, Wanda Murkowski is the office manager. She's Dr. Murkowski's wife.	Note as possible reference.
I: Did the dentists also expect you to adhere to the one-patient-per-hour schedule?	
C: They wanted us to, but Judy and I got together and explained to them that we couldn't do it.	Factious?
I: Who's Judy?	

Dialogue	Observations
C: The other hygienist.	
I: As office manager, was Wanda Murkowski responsible for scheduling your work hours?	
C: Yes.	
I: When did this dispute over the number of cleanings per day occur? When did it come to a head?	Return to this topic later.
C: In May.	
I: In May? And you left there in July?	
C: I left in May, but that wasn't the reason that I left. They just don't treat their hygienists well.	Timeline problem and contradicted reason given earlier for leaving.
I: Was Wanda Murkowski involved in the dispute over scheduling one-per-hour cleaning patients?	
C: Yes.	
I: Was this dispute resolved to your satisfaction?	
C: I don't think it was handled well.	Return to this topic later in interview.
I: Before working for Loyalhanna Dental Associates, how long did you work for Conemaugh Family Dentistry?	
C: For two years.	Check timeline.
I: Why did you leave there?	
C: One of their hygienists had been on maternity leave. When she came back, I was let go.	Incongruous. Omission?
I: How long was she on maternity leave?	
C: Six months, I think.	Inconsistent with duration of employment
I: Who was your main supervisor at Conemaugh?	
C: Dr. Reilly. I think maybe Connie was off for a year for maternity.	Return to this later. Note Dr. Reilly for reference.
I: Was Connie the dental hygienist on maternity leave whose return coincided with your dismissal?	
C: Yes, I think she was gone for a year.	Incongruous.
I: Did you work with her before she went on maternity leave?	
C: No…maybe, yes. She was there when I started, then she took time off to have her baby.	Vague, confusing.
I: What was Connie's last name?	
C: I don't remember. I think she got married.	Evasive.
I: Does Conemaugh Dental Clinic have a website?	
C: I think so.	Evasive.
I: Yes, here it is. A Connie Wickham is shown as dental assistant. Was Connie's last name Wickham?	Non-supportive.

Dialogue	Observations
C: Yes.	
I: Did Connie work as a dental hygienist and a dental assistant?	
C: Yes, but mostly as a hygienist.	
I: How many dentists were employed by Conemaugh Dental Clinic?	
C: One. Dr. Tim Reilly. His whole operation was him, a dental assistant, a hygienist, and the receptionist. Occasionally Dr. Reilly's mother would work in the office too.	Thoroughness.
I: It looks like the practice has expanded. The website shows two hygienists, two assistants, and another dentist—a doctor Jeneen Galloway. Was there talk of expanding the practice while you were there?	Revisit later. Deliberate omission?
C: I knew it would expand.	Disingenuousness. Check timeline against resume.
I: So you graduated from Bradford, then worked at Allegheny Valley Dental for a few months, then you worked at Conemaugh Family Dentistry for one year and three months, then you worked for Loyalhanna Dental Associates from February last year until last month. Did you start working at Conemaugh Dental Clinic immediately after leaving Allegheny Valley Dental?	
C: There were a couple months between my departure from Allegheny Valley and my joining Conemaugh.	Openness. But also contradicts earlier statement that Jackie left Allegheny for a better job.
I: How about Kiski Farm Supply?	
C: I worked there in the summers during high school, then for almost a year after I graduated from high school. I started at Westmoreland County Community College in January and completed one semester there before starting my dental training at Bradford.	Enduring working relationship.
I: On your resume you list Cynthia Holt as a reference. Who is Cynthia Holt?	
C: She's a friend of my mother. She's like an aunt to me. She owns Vintongrift Grocery, and she's a very successful businesswoman. She knows Susan, your hygienist who's leaving. That's how I learned about this position.	Sometimes it pays to live in a small town.
I: Oh, yes, that's right, I know Cynthia. She helped organize the Relay for Life and she's active in Habitat for Humanity.	Coincides with Jackie's resume.
C: Yes, and I worked with her on those projects. Cindy's a hoot.	

Dialogue	**Observations**
I: I see her at the club all the time. Her husband . . . Jordon? . . . Yeah, Jordon is a great golfer . . . always plays with an unlit cigar in his mouth.	Will this discussion help determine if Jackie is a competent dental hygienist, compatible coworker or reliable employee?
C: She and my mother have been best friends since they were little.	
I: Have you worked for Senator Don Whire, who you also show as a reference?	
C: I babysat his kids.	
I: Where they well behaved?	
C: Hellions, more like it.	
I: I thought so. But he did earmark the funds for the new streetlights on Main Street.	
C: My mother helped with that.	
I: How so?	
C: She knows the people who own the company that installed the streetlights.	How did that help?
I: Senator Whire did great things for this district.	
C: And his kids weren't really hellions . . . imps, maybe.	
I: Okay. Let's review our job description.	

Between the broken timelines, the damaged gums, and the omission of an employer, it is likely that Dr. Mingo Mauch would find numerous problems with Jackie's resume if he checks further. Maybe he is going to pursue those matters later. Jackie seems weak on the things related to job performance, but she is connected to the community. I think if Dr. Mauch were actively looking for honesty, this interview would have taken a different tack.

Almost from the beginning, Jackie's credibility was questionable. She seemed to have trouble admitting that she omitted Allegheny Dental from her work history, then she contradicted the timeline on her resume which shows that she is presently working at Loyalhanna Dental, when in fact she ceased working there months ago. Later she had trouble explaining her departure from Conemaugh. One lapse may be forgivable, two questionable, but, to me, three lapses would be terminal. Maybe Dr. Mauch is more patient than I am.

Review of Job Description

After discussing the applicant's work history, it is time to review the job description. This portion of the interview should take from ten to fifteen minutes. It is important for the interviewer to make the applicant aware of the rigors and complexity of the job. Though the tone of the interview to this point should have been very cordial, the interviewer must make clear that the employer requires serious dedication from all employees.

This is a good time to get a feel for the candidate's sobriety. In every job, a crunch time occurs when workers must work later, harder, or faster, and it is important that when presented with that reality, the candidate will respond professionally. The review of the job description is a good time to make that point and to record the candidate's reaction. Some interviewers make the mistake of attempting to sell the job to the applicant, but this is not the time for that. It is better to wait until the interviewer has determined the applicant's suitability for the position.

In reviewing the job description the interviewer will want to fully explain the job's duties and then discuss the details with the applicant. As each duty is described, the interviewer should ask about experiences, skills, and education regarding that duty. Answers to these questions can be compared to earlier discussions spawned by the applicant's resume.

The job's prerequisites should be discussed and the applicant's qualifications should be matched to each requirement. The matching of qualifications to job requirements can become important if it is learned that the applicant has falsified qualifications or experience. Proper note-taking in this stage of the interview will provide support in case a dismissal is required after the applicant is hired.

Pauline White's First Review of the Job Description with Carter Johnfeld

Pauline is not an engineer, and the job requirements include items such as, "Evaluate, select, and apply standard engineering methods, procedures, and criteria using independent judgment, adapting and modifying when necessary," which would require engineering expertise for a thorough assessment. So Pauline will review the job description in generalities as she looks for evidence of Carter's personal honesty.

Candidate: Carter Johnfeld
Interviewer: Pauline White
Company: Brownwell Corporation
Position: Civil engineer, EIT
First review of job description

Dialogue	Observations
Interviewer: Carter, did you carefully read the job posting for Civil Engineer Bridge Project?	Obligatory questions.
Candidate: Yes.	
I: Do you meet all the qualifications listed there?	
C: Yes, though it asks for three years of experience, and to fulfill that requirement I must include my three-month college internship with Jacobs Engineering. Otherwise, I'm just short.	Frankness, honesty.
I: So long as your work with Jacobs was compensated, hands-on engineering, it will count toward your work experience requirements.	
C: That's good.	
I: Are there any reasons that you would not perform the duties asked for on the job description?	
C: No.	
I: What do you know about Brownwell Corporation?	Rhetorical, ice-breaking question.
C: I have been on your website and I have spoken to two employees, one in engineering and one is accounting. Both enjoy working here.	

Dialogue	Observations
I: Glad to hear that. As you read on the job posting, we're looking for a civil engineer for a specific bridge project, but we have several projects for which you might qualify, so I would like to ask you if you would consider working on a project other than the one for which you applied.	
C: Sure. I'd be happy to consider any project, even non-bridge work.	Flexibility.
I: Some of our senior engineers are more strict than others, but you can expect everybody will operate at a high level of professionalism and expect the same from your team members. The supervising engineer is Kendall Swartz, and he has a reputation for being a stickler for promptness and accuracy. He's been with this company for over twenty-five years. He's a good one to learn from, but he's been known to be a harsh critic of newcomers and young engineers who may not be familiar with some aspects of engineering that he thinks are important. Are you willing to work under those conditions?	Impress candidate with sober assessment of professional requirements and seriousness of the position. Also, prepare candidate for obstacles and difficult conditions incumbent to the position.
C: Yes. It sounds like what I'm used to. Imran is the same way. From your description, I suspect Kendall Swartz has a similar management style to Imran Khan.	
I: On the current project, we have financial incentives for coming in under budget and completing early. That's where Kendall is a bear. He loves those incentives. When there's a bottleneck in a particular aspect of the planning or execution, he really puts on the pressure…even if he just thinks there might be a bottleneck.	Warn candidate of potential difficulty with personality of supervisors.
C: I respect that. When you look over my resume, where, specifically, do you think I would fit into a project like this?	Deference to employer.
I: I'm not sure. That's up to Kendall. Sometimes he likes to keep new hires close to him to monitor their skill and productivity. Since Kendall generally works as project manager, neophytes often end up in procurement and acquisition where they can prove their ability to spec-out materials, monitor quality and estimate quantities. Other times he plugs them in where he knows they have experience. In your case, that might be thermal expansion and stress loads. After he sees that a person performs well, he gives them a little more freedom and a lot less monitoring. Then he'll hand them off to another team leader. In your other jobs, did you earn safety certifications?	Making candidate aware of hierarchy and pressure associated with inexperience.

Dialogue	**Observations**
C: At Tomlin, I fulfilled numerous safety requirements in the form of classroom instruction, online courses and hands-on demonstrations. I have certificates for most of them. If you'd like to see them I can present them at our next meeting, or I can scan them and email them to you.	Cooperativeness. Initiative.
I: I'll let you know about that. Do you have a copy of your EIT license?	Veracity.
C: Yes. It's here.	
I: Have you worked with ANSYS or GT STRUDL?	JD requirements.
C: Yes, with both of them, but mostly with GT STRUDL and their arch and bridge design modes, integrated with CADWorx Steel Professional. I've used ANSYS Mechanical and ANSYS Fluent.	Familiarity with required tools.
I: Can you provide training certificates or samples of your work?	
C: Yes. I have those certificates here. My college transcripts show that I took a two-credit course in GT STRUDL software use, ENG-353. Also, at Tomlin we used it extensively. I have used ANSYS, but I haven't taken the certification tests.	Veracity.
I: ANSYS Fluent will be needed for this project.	
C: I have used it, and I am proficient at it, but not certified. I can brush up and take the certification tests if needed. I'm confident I will have no problem passing them.	Acknowledgement of personal limitations. Humility.
I: That's something we can take up at a second interview when you'll meet engineers who will ask the technical questions. This interview serves to make sure you're the type of character that we want to employ. During the second interview, they'll confirm your professional expertise.	
C: I understand. That's good.	
I: In procurement and acquisitions we use a version of Deltek accounting software. Are you proficient with Deltek?	
C: I did not see that listed on the job posting. I'm sorry to say I have not used it. At Tomlin, I used enterprise resource planning software in purchasing, but not Deltek.	
I: What accounting software have you used?	
C: Sage 300 ERP.	

Dialogue	Observations
I: I'll make a note of that. Kendall may question you about it. Before we go further in this interview, I want you to know that Kendall is one or our tougher project managers. He expects professionalism and he's unforgiving of those whom he feels don't perform at a level in keeping with the seriousness of the project.	A reminder of this job's difficulty and the sobriety of the company.
C: Thank you for making that point clear. You mentioned it earlier. I too am serious about engineering, that's why I'm in this field and that's why I'm here today. The fact is I prefer the company of serious professionals far more than with the casual Tuesdays, cupcakes at 2:15 crowd. On weekends I dress casual and eat all the cupcakes I want.	I can be a hard-nosed engineer too.
I: I think you'll get along well with Kendall. Would you like something to drink or a minute to relax?	

Does Carter seem honest? Though Pauline did not question him closely, nothing Carter said indicated any effort to evade answers or hide information. Pauline drove home the point that Carter will be working for a strident boss, but that didn't seem to bother him. In fact, he casually rebuffed Pauline's warnings. I see no problems for Carter so far.

Dr. Mauch's First Review of the Job Description with Jackie Kondin

In contrast to Pauline, who lacks the specific knowledge to test her candidate's engineering skill, Dr. Mingo Mauch is fully aware of the intricate knowledge that his candidate, Jackie Kondin, needs to perform her dental hygienist/assistant duties. Dr. Mauch can directly challenge Jackie's knowledge of her field.

Please excuse the arcane language.

Candidate: Jackie Kondin
Interviewer: Dr. Mingo Mauch, DDS
Company: Chestnut Ridge Dentistry
Position: Dental hygienist/assistant
First review of job description

Dialogue	Observations
Interviewer: You're probably tired of talking about your resume, so let's change the subject.	
Candidate: Okay.	
I: Have you read the Job Description for the position of Dental Assistant/Hygienist at Chestnut Ridge Dentistry?	Obligatory questions.
C: Yes.	
I: Do you feel that you fill the requirements shown on that job description?	
C: Yes.	
I: Do you have any questions about the requirements or the duties mentioned on that job description?	
C: I wanted to let you know that I practiced full-mouth ultrasonic debridement in school, but I haven't used such a debrider since then. At Bradford we were shown how to use it, which I did during my externship, but only once and I feel I will need a refresher.	Humility and conscientiousness. Shows she read job description.
I: We expect that. Our machine has not been installed yet. But it is the latest model, the integrated Cavitron Touch, Steri-Mate 360. The company provides on-site training. Do you recall the model of the machine that you trained on?	
C: I don't remember, but I believe it was a Cavitron model. It was not integrated; it was tabletop. Also, there were issues with the cable length. We had to swivel the chair when working on patients who were particularly tall.	Professional concern. Familiarity with relevant technology.
I: That's peculiar. I wonder why they didn't install a longer cable.	
C: It was a tabletop unit and I was told to move the unit closer if the cable didn't reach the patient, but the counter was so cluttered that to move it would have required rearranging the whole setup. I was only there for one day. It was easier to swivel the chair.	Attentiveness. Flexibility.
I: Did Loyalhanna use ultrasonic scalers and debriders?	

Dialogue	Observations
C: No. We used handheld Gracey scalers and curettes. But I understand that they now use ultrasonics.	Aware of proper terminology and dental tools. Knew that Loyalhanna updated systems, but unaware of expanded staff? Hmm.
I: Are you certified in CPR and external defibrillators?	
C: Yes. I brought those certificates.	Good.
I: Do you wear contact lenses?	
C: No corrective lenses at all. My eyes are fine.	Eyesight and manual dexterity are important to this line of work.
I: How about your hands?	
C: No problem. I have full range of movement.	
Dr. Mauch spends a few minutes reviewing office protocol and office hours, stressing the importance of promptness and accurate record-keeping.	
I: We switched the entire office to Dentafix software about a year ago. Now, all record-keeping and dental procedures are integrated into one system, including imaging. Have you used Dentafix software?	
C: At Loyalhanna we used Dentafix, but imaging was not automatically integrated into the filing system or into billing.	.
I: How did you file and track images and X-rays at Loyalhanna?	
C: The old-fashioned way: manila folders and handwritten notes.	
I: What did you use Dentafix for if not to manage files?	
C: We used the software to manage files, but not images. It was an older version.	
I: I wasn't aware there was an older version. I thought it was a new product. Are you sure you used Dentafix?	Wait a minute.
C: Did you say Dentafix or Dentrix?	
I: We use Dentafix, not Dentrix.	
C: I'm sorry. I have used Dentrix.	Reasonable mistake, probably.
I: So, are you saying that you have not used Dentafix?	

Dialogue	**Observations**
C: That's correct. Do you know if Dentafix is substantially different from Dentrix?	
I: I don't know. I have never used Dentrix.	
C: This is confusing. I assure you that I had no problem learning Dentrix Software, and I don't think I will have a problem learning Dentafix. I suspect I'll be up to speed after a few minute's instruction. If imaging and billing are integrated into the software, then it should be easier than I'm used to.	Sensible, positive.
I: I agree. Most of these software packages are similar, so you shouldn't have a problem. How do you set up your dental tray for cleaning?	
C: I'm left-handed so my tray is setup backward from most hygienists. My mirror is on the right and my forceps on the left. If I'm assisting, of course, I arrange the tray the way the dentist—the way you—would like it.	
Dr. Mauch asked Jackie about specific procedures related to her hygienist duties and duties as a dental assistant. He returned to a topic brought up when reviewing Jackie's resume.	
I: How often did you work as an assistant to Dr. Murkowski?	
C: Only a few times in two years. Maybe six or seven. Mostly Ken did that work…Ken or Judy.	
I: Who assisted Dr. Senji and Dr. Johnston? With three dentists in that practice, there must have been times when they needed three assistants.	
C: Usually Ken and Judy would handle the assisting, sometimes Wanda helped, and as I mentioned, I also helped. Wanda scheduled appointments so that it worked out. We were busy though.	
I: Earlier, didn't you say that Dr. Senji was not getting enough patients to stay busy?	
C: That's just what I heard. I don't really understand business.	
I: Do they need three assistants or not?	Dr. Mauch seems to be getting off track. What does this have to do with Jackie?
C: Much of the time Dr. Murkowski and Wanda aren't there. They have an estate at Arrowhead Lake and a condo in Myrtle Beach. When they're away, and Dr. Senji and Dr. Johnston take over, things slow down.	

Dialogue	**Observations**
I: Before we go further, I think you should know that I struggled to establish this practice in a small town. I could have moved to the city, joined a practice with other dentists, and had my choice of work hours and a fat profit sharing plan, but I chose to live here. And I'm very successful and happy here in Vintongrift.	Does Dr. Mauch have a jealous streak?
C: I've heard you have a beautiful house on Caton Hill.	
I: I only bring that up because it takes dedication to stay in business and I expect my employees to share in that dedication. Now, do you have any questions about the job description?	
C: Yes. How much does this job pay?	Premature question.
I: Between twenty and twenty-five dollars per hour. That will be decided after we review each applicant's experience and skill level.	
C: How much time off and vacation am I allowed?	Slow down, Jackie.
I: Vacation and personal leave time are compiled at the rate of 0.0385 hours PL for every hour worked on site. If you work typical workweeks, that amounts to ten days of personal leave per year. Also we have ten unpaid holidays.	
C: If we work on a holiday, for instance, Labor Day, are we allowed to take a different day off at another time?	Strange question.
I: We're closed on those holidays. If a holiday, say Christmas, lands on a Saturday or Sunday, usually we'll be closed on the following Monday. Does that answer your question?	
C: I was hoping to have some time off during football season to attend the away game at Denver. I try to get to at least one of the Steelers' away games each year.	Impatience. Self-serving.
I: If you have accumulated enough PL, it sounds possible. Do you have other questions?	
C: Was Susan good at her work, I mean as an hygienist?	Another strange question.
I: Yes. She worked here for many years. Our patients loved her.	
C: How do you think they'll take to me? They don't know me.	
I: If you're a good hygienist and you're friendly, you'll have no problem.	

This was supposed to be a discussion about the job description, but it took a strange turn near the end when Dr. Mauch adopted a harsh tone and began touting the success of his business. Maybe he was frustrated with Jackie's answers and, lacking adequate communication skills, he vented emotionally rather than rationally. Or he could be an irrational person. Jackie should keep that in mind if she is offered this job.

Jackie seems to have a grasp on the methods and technology of a dentist office. The confusion over software may have been a simple misunderstanding, though it would be worthwhile for Dr. Mauch to take Jackie to the office computer and have her demonstrate exactly what she knows about dentistry software. At the end, Jackie began asking questions that should have been held for later. This sort of impatience augurs badly for honesty and worse for personal tact.

I'm beginning to question the honesty of both Jackie and Dr. Mauch.

Summary Decision

To this point, the interview has consumed a half hour or more and, under most circumstances, the interviewer will be able to judge if the candidate is unfit for hiring. If the candidate is not suitable, the interviewer should thank him or her for his or her time and either frankly state reasons for not continuing, or end the interview with an expeditious statement of, "We will continue to interview for this position and contact you if we decide to schedule a second interview." While such a statement may smack of insincerity, employers are rightfully tasked with filling openings, not with consoling unsuitable applicants.

Summary Decisions on Our Two Candidates

After completing the rapport-building and open-questioning phases of their interviews, both Carter and Jackie deserve further consideration. Neither said nor did anything that demonstrated flagrant dishonesty or inexcusable uncouthness. Carter comes across as very honest. Some of Jackie's answers are questionable, but not to the point of disqualification.

The interviewers have very different approaches. Pauline is experienced and direct in her questioning, which gives Carter excellent opportunities to demonstrate his social skills and his honesty. Dr. Mauch lacks conversational skills, which diminishes his ability as an interviewer, so he is learning less about Jackie than he could. If Jackie is smart, she will pay close attention to Dr. Mauch's commitment to honesty.

Follow-up Casual Discussion

The second half of the interview begins with a return to the casual topic touched on at the beginning of the interview or with another non-work-related topic. As far as the applicant is concerned, the first portion of the interview had focused on the usual aspects of any job interview. Now for a brief time it will shift to the less demanding personal interests of the applicant. It was noted that early in the interview, the interviewer was to look for a topic of personal interest to the applicant: a sport, an item of clothing, an interesting movie, something mentioned on the applicant's resume, so long as the topic is spawned by the applicant. For the next few minutes, the interview should return to that topic.

While delving deeper into the selected topic, the interviewer should contemplate how the conversational inferences have evolved during the first half of the interview, and consider if any communication barriers would likely hamper the veracity-testing phase of the interview. In essence, the interviewer resets the scales of communication to accommodate his or her familiarity with the candidate's mode of communication.

Follow up Causal Conversation with Carter Johnfeld

Pauline thinks Carter is an excellent prospect for Brownwell. The veracity-testing phase of the interview can strain the relationship between interviewer and interviewee, so before going there she wants him to relax while she confirms their rapport. Pauline will ask about bicycling again.

Candidate: Carter Johnfeld
Interviewer: Pauline White
Company: Brownwell Corporation
Position: Civil engineer, EIT
Return to casual discussion

Dialogue	Observations
Interviewer: Do you need to relax for a minute or two?	
Candidate: I'm fine, but if you need a break please take one.	
I: Thank you. Do you have any bike trips planned?	
C: My wife and I are going with some friends to the Allegheny National Forest next weekend. We'll probably camp there and return home on Sunday afternoon.	
I: How many cyclists will go with you?	
C: Probably six or seven. Not everyone will camp. Some will just stay for the day.	
I: Does the Forest Service require permits for biking in the National Forest?	
C: You need a permit to camp, but not to ride a bike. The camping permit costs, I think, fifteen dollars per campsite.	
I: Do you encounter horseback riders in the park?	
C: Sometimes. In the National Forest you never know what you'll run into. But I want to hear your fly-fisherman story. You mentioned that your horse, Laponka, is not afraid of fly-fishermen. There must be a story connected to that.	Carter turns the interview around. He makes it about Pauline.

Dialogue	**Observations**
I: There is, but it's sort of long.	
C: I'd love to hear it. Give me the shortened version.	
I: I was riding Laponka along Raccoon Creek, thirteen…fourteen years ago, and it was in the spring so the water was high and rushing over the rocks. I noticed a man fly-fishing at one of the pools, but I didn't stop or pay much attention. I rode past.	
C: The fishing is great in Raccoon Creek. It's loaded with native brook trout.	
I: I wasn't aware then, but I know it now. A little later, Laponka started shaking his head and flicking his ears, the way a horse does when a horse fly is bothering it. So I'm looking around, hoping for a chance to swat the annoying fly, then I heard, "Ma'am, Ma'am, pardon me Ma'am." I looked back and the fisherman is trotting down the trail behind me, reeling in his line as he went.	This story is more suitable to a casual setting than the workplace, but maybe it is Carter's intention to establish a casual relationship with his interviewer. It is hard not to like somebody who is interested in your personal stories.
C: Was he dragging the fishing line behind him?	
I: No. He was reeling me in. His fly, his hook, was caught on Laponka's ear. He snagged the horse on his back cast, and I didn't see it. The hook was so small and his line, the leader was transparent.	
C: The horse didn't stop?	
I: He would have kept going, but I reined him in. Jim caught up and carefully removed the hook. Laponka just lowered his head and let him do it.	
C: What did the fisherman say?	
I: Jim? Well, he apologized profusely, and I married him. Fourteen years and two kids later, we still fish there. To the boys, it's "Mom and Dad's fishing spot."	
C: I don't know what surprises me more: that the horse didn't panic at having a fishhook stuck in its ear, or that a man actually, physically used a pickup line that worked.	
I: You can imagine the bad jokes we have endured over the years.	
C: Do you mean like: Did that fishhook affect Laponka's herring?	
I: Yes. That's a perfect example of the bad, really awful jokes that I carp about. We'd better take another longer look at your resume.	Painful.

By revisiting Pauline's throwaway comment about fly-fishing, Carter flipped roles and took control of the conversation. That move was a bit audacious. Is it indicative of his character or his mode of leadership? Did he just forge a personal bond with his interviewer that will help him land a job with Brownwell? He and Pauline seem to share a penchant for bad jokes. But when the puns get this bad, obviously, it's time to move on.

Dr. Mauch's Follow up Causal Conversation with Jackie Kondin

In their introductory conversation, rather than establish rapport and work out conversational inferences, it appeared as though Dr. Mauch and Jackie Kondin were going to grapple over their chosen sports. The interview has had its ups and downs, but since neither person has social skill or conversational grace, the interview goes on. Maybe Dr. Mauch will give football another try.

Candidate: Jackie Kondin
Interviewer: Dr. Mingo Mauch, DDS
Interviewing at Chestnut Ridge Dentistry
Position: Dental hygienist/assistant
Return to casual conversation

Dialogue	Observations
Interviewer: It sounds like you are an American football fan.	
Candidate: I'm more of a Steelers fan than a football fan. I enjoy the excitement and hoopla surrounding the games as much as the games themselves. I know the rules, but I don't care as much about them as I do about the fun and friends associated with the event.	Jackie's chance to ask about soccer or Croatia.
I: When did you become so interested in the Steelers?	Dr. Mauch is trying.

Dialogue	Observations
C: It's odd. I wasn't a sports fan in high school. It wasn't until later, when some friends started talking about the games, that I got interested. I like reading about the players and keeping track of their stats. I joined a fantasy football league and, when I won it, I really was motivated to follow players' careers, and I had a reputation to uphold.	Jackie is talking about her favorite topic: Jackie.
I: Fantasy football, is that what I see advertised on TV, where you pick teams and use statistics to evaluate your picks?	
C: Yes. After the games are played, each player's performance is rated, and then you accumulate the ratings to learn how your team did.	
I: We have a similar thing for soccer. Some of my friends are fanatical about it. Have you ever heard of fantasy soccer?	An invitation to discuss Dr. Mauch's favorite topic.
C: No. Last year there were twelve of us in my fantasy football league. Each of us ante up fifty dollars, then at the end of the season, it's winner take all. I won, but as the winner, I was expected to host our Super Bowl party, which cost me a big chunk of the pot. It's all for fun.	Oh well.
I: One of my friends won a lot of money with his fantasy soccer team. Sometimes I wonder how much they lose. They don't often talk about their losses. Have you noticed that?	Example of parallel monologs between two self-centered people.
C: I know a guy who bet a thousand dollars on the Steelers-Jets game last season. He lost it all.	
I: It's wasteful, don't you think?	
C: When I won, except for what I spent on the party, I used the money for a new tattoo on my calf. So, that worked out for me and for my tattoo artist.	
I: How much does a tattoo cost?	
C: I got a great deal: twelve colors, a custom design, and it covered a scar from burning myself on a motorcycle's exhaust pipe, and it cost only two hundred dollars.	
I: All that from winning in fantasy football. I'm impressed.	
C: I was lucky.	Humility at last.

This illustrates polite conversation at its unproductive worst. It goes like this: I say this about me, then you say that about you, and that reminds me to mention this about me, which prompts you to say something else about you. . . . Dr. Mauch started by politely asking Jackie about football, but even after he injected soccer into the conversation, Jackie failed to take the bait. Then Dr. Mauch broke the cycle with a follow-up question in direct response to Jackie's mention of her tattoo. Maybe he wants one, or maybe he became interested in conversing with Jackie. Either way, the conversation ended with commendable civility. Time to move on.

Second Time Through the Resume

This is the make-or-break segment of the interview, the veracity-testing stage, when the interviewer delves deeply into statements made earlier and compares them to those made now. For the next ten to fifteen minutes the interviewer will return to the applicant's resume, revisiting issues that caused concern, reopening discussions of problems acknowledged by the applicant, and reevaluating strengths and weaknesses. Moreover, we're more than forty minutes into the interview and the candidate has been speaking most of this time. By now, the candidate will be burdened by what psychologist John Sweller called cognitive load, the mental effort exerted to maintain memory.[75] If the candidate has made false statements, nuanced distortions, or lies of omission, his or her memory is likely to be muddled as to the exact nature of those untruths.

When an honest person answers a question for the second time, he or she has only one answer to give. As dishonest candidates realize their contradictions and consequent predicament, they will usually speak less voluminously or stop making a determined effort to provide thorough answers. Such otherwise subtle behavioral clues often become more pronounced during the second review of the resume as physical and emotional strain weakens mental defenses.

If contradictions are found, discussing them can cause even more strain for both the interviewer and the candidate. But the process is just entering its definitive stage, so the interviewer must maintain a positive tone and prevent antagonism so the candidate will continue providing information to an interviewer whom he or she sees as a compatriot and not an adversary. This requires the interviewer to provide the candidate every opportunity to explain the discrepancies.

For instance, during the first review of the resume, maybe the candidate mentioned a difficult relationship with his or her former boss, and that the candidate said this difficulty stemmed from the boss's chronic failure to answer emails in a timely manner. The interviewer should return to that problem, delve into the details again, and cross-check the statements, names, and resolutions against those made by the candidate during the first resume review. If discrepancies appear, the interviewer should allow the applicant to resolve them, giving the applicant adequate opportunity to explain how the situation could have been variously interpreted.

If it appears that the candidate is having problems resolving conflicting statements, the interviewer might ask how the boss would have explained the tardy emails. Answers to such questions will indicate whether the candidate wanted to resolve that particular problem honestly, or if he or she is merely scapegoating the former boss.

Also, this is the time when the interviewer compiles the list of individuals who will be contacted as work references. As the details of various workplace events and disputes are discussed, the interviewer should ask for the names of those involved with each occasion. Then the interviewer should integrate those names into follow-up questions, giving the interviewer a better grasp of the workplace relationship between the candidate and the reference, while conditioning the candidate to the notion that this reference may be contacted.

The question, "Would you mind if I spoke directly to . . . ?" is likely to spawn discussion that will provide further insight. A candidate who presented the situation fairly and accurately may say, "Go ahead." Or the candidate may suggest not making contact and give sound reasons for that decision. Generally, a less than forthright candidate will claim not to have the contact information or refuse to provide it. Since the interviewer can generally obtain the contact information from some other source, the candidate's refusal to provide it is reason enough to disqualify him or her from the job.

It is essential for the interviewer to accurately notate the contradictions or falsehoods and keep those notes for future consideration when contacting references.

Second Time Through Carter's Resume

To this point in the interview, Carter has shown few weaknesses, so Pauline will dig deeper into his engineering aptitudes and attempt to gain a better understanding of his relationships with his coworkers. After all, he is looking for another job and he had mentioned that a supervisor had recommended that he move to another department. She wants to learn more about his error on calculating the expansion rate of COR-TEN alloy. Was that mistake indicative of a tendency toward mathematical errors? On her first perusal of Carter's resume Pauline had wondered about his grade point average. At 3.14, it is lower than what she is used to seeing from recent college graduates. She'll ask about this.

Candidate: Carter Johnfeld
Interviewer: Pauline White
Company: Brownwell Corporation
Position: Civil engineer, EIT
Second review of applicant's resume

Dialogue	Observations
Interviewer: You said you were hired at Tomlin to work on an active construction project, then you moved to the planning phase of the Tampa Bay Bridge project. Why did you move from one project to the other?	
Candidate: I asked to be moved over. One of the planners had been reassigned, which left an opening. I thought the planning project would be more long-term and interesting, so when the opportunity arose I moved to the Tampa Bay project.	Discuss with reference.
I: How did you get that position?	Earlier Carter had said his team leader has recommended the move.
C: At Tomlin they post an internal job opening, then you apply for it. If a supervisor is satisfied that a qualified candidate has been found, the posting is removed. I learned about the Bay project opening from Aasta, my supervisor at the time. She introduced me to Scott and I applied for and got the job. It was handled in Tomlin's normal way.	Clears that up.
I: Why did your original supervisor recommend that you leave her team? What did you say her name is?	
C: My supervisor was Aasta Parvadi. We had talked about the Bay project, and when she saw I was curious, she asked if I wanted to move to it. At Tomlin this sort of thing happens often: personnel shuffle from one project to another. It's one of the things that I really like about the company.	Check with reference.
I: Can you spell your supervisor's name for me?	
C: It's A-a-s-t-a P-a-r-v-a-d-i, Indian, I think. If you would like to contact any of my managers or coworkers, I'll provide their phone numbers or emails. But, may I ask that you let me tell them that you might call? I don't want them to hear that I might be leaving from anyone else.	Openness.
I: No problem. I would like to get Aasta's phone number from you. Scott Weaver's too. Scott was your team leader on the Tampa Bay project, correct?	

Dialogue	**Observations**
C: That's right.	
I: Was it Scott who discovered your mathematic error in calculating the expansion of COR-TEN A-588?	
C: Yes, he found it. He's amazing that way. I don't think he spent more than ten minutes perusing my numbers, and he found that error. He said it was a "beginner's mistake." We laughed it off, but I have to say, I was embarrassed.	Complimentary. Humility.
I: I see on your resume that your GPA was 3.14 at graduation. Were there particular subjects that were difficult for you?	
C: I made a tactical error during my freshman and sophomore years at Lehigh. I got ahead of myself and took a couple courses in advanced mathematics for which I was ill-prepared. I got a C in one and a D in the other. That lowered my cumulative average, and I played catch-up for the next two years. As I moved ahead in engineering I remained weak on some fundamental math.	Plausible.
I: Did you confer with your academic adviser?	
C: She had advised against taking the advanced courses during my freshman year, so she was not sympathetic to my plight.	Interesting.
I: Are mathematics still a problem for you?	
C: I'm competent, but not completely confident. When I'm working with people whom I trust, I like to have them check my calculations.	Question for references.
I: Did you quit the baseball team because of your struggles with these courses?	
C: Baseball was taking up too much time and I needed to study. I didn't want to quit, but I knew I had to.	Mature decision.
I: Besides the Tampa Bay project, are there other projects at Tomlin that interest you?	
C: Oh, yes. We have other smaller engineering projects in bridges and in other road projects. There is some talk about getting into airport construction. I feel sure that we'll land major projects in the future.	
I: Then why are you looking for work?	

Dialogue	**Observations**
C: Because it makes sense now. Tomlin Engineering is a good company. It's not big, but it's growing and I like the culture. I could be happy there for a long time. But if I could find my dream job now, I would take it. And if I leave Tomlin now, when we're in a business lull, I won't feel I abandoned the company when they really needed me.	Reasonable, maybe discontented.
I: You said you were looking for new challenges. Most tasks within major engineering projects are focused on a singular aspect of the overall project, which often reduces any one engineer's involvement to a simple, sometimes tedious assignment. How would you avoid becoming bored on the job?	
C: It's not in my nature to be bored. It's a requirement for all engineers to see both the forest and the trees. Sure, any one assignment can become boring. That goes with the engineering territory. But at the end of the day, you're building a bridge, or launching a rocket, or producing electricity to light a city. Not many careers give a worker that level of satisfaction, accomplishment.	Optimism, industriousness.
I: How much does your mistake concerning the coefficient of expansion influence your decision to leave?	
C: Not at all. I only mentioned that incident because it is indicative of how we work as a team at Tomlin. I have made plenty of errors and mistakes in my almost three years there. And I corrected mistakes made by others too. I'm just being as frank and honest as I can be.	
I: Would Scott and Aasta agree with that assessment?	
C: I think so. You're welcome to ask them.	
I: How about Tej, would he agree?	
C: Tej? Yes, sure, call Tej. Ask him about his recommendations for the thickness of the concrete base for the arch supports on the Tampa Bay project.	
I: What about them?	
C: On his first calculations, he used the geologist's preliminary assessment, not the final one, and consequently he overestimated base requirements by a factor of two. Scott and Imran would surely have seen it early and fixed it. It wasn't a big mistake—concrete and fill aren't that expensive. But I caught it before he showed his report to them.	

Dialogue	**Observations**
I: Is there an atmosphere of backbiting at Tomlin?	
C: No. Quite the opposite. The overwhelming attitude there is one of teamwork and cooperation. We work together, which means foregoing egos and short-term self-interest and striving to achieve our mutual goals. We are all better off if we jointly produce the best possible product. To accomplish that end, one must cover for the failings of others and bear the humility of having the light shown on our own shortcomings. I don't consider that to be backbiting. I consider it a healthy attitude for a productive workplace.	Magnanimous, humility, earnestness, giving credit.
I: Was Imran aware of your mistake with expansion coefficients?	
C: I don't know. I doubt that something of that nature would have gone beyond the team leader. Scott might have mentioned it to him, but I doubt it.	
I: How would Imran react if he knew you were looking for work elsewhere?	
C: He's the one person I would worry about. I'm afraid he might see it as a personal slight if he knew I was talking to you. He's pushing hard to sell the plans that we prepared for Tampa Bay. If he thought I was thinking of leaving, he might feel betrayed.	Prudence? Or afraid to allow Pauline to speak to Imran?
I: Do you have a good rapport with him?	
C: Yes, quite good.	
I: Would Scott agree with your assessment of Imran's reaction?	
C: Yes, I'm sure he would. He knows how Imran is. I have no problem with you conferring with Imran if you're seriously considering me for this position. But, for the time being, I would rather let that sleeping dog alone.	Ask Scott about Imran's opinion of Carter.
I: Yes, certainly. Let's talk about the opportunities at Brownwell.	

Carter confirmed most of his earlier statements. He provided a plausible explanation for interviewing at Brownwell and he was open to allowing Pauline access to his coworkers and supervisors, with the reasonable exception of Imran Khan. He invited Pauline to check his thermal-expansion story with his supervisor Scott

Weaver. Carter provided a credible explanation for his relatively low GPA. If Pauline felt his grades needed further investigation, she could ask to see his college transcripts. I can see no reason to question Carter's honesty.

Carter's willingness to grant Pauline access to his current supervisors and co-workers is unusual. Most job seekers who are presently employed would be wary of letting their current employers know about their efforts to find work elsewhere, but not Carter. Maybe he is brash and bold, or maybe he wants his current employer to know that he is a marketable talent. In either case, he seems confident in his decisions.

Second Time Through Jackie's Resume

Even a quick review of Jackie's resume reveals timeline gaps and inconsistencies. After the first time through it, Dr. Mauch should want to know why Jackie omitted her employment at Allegheny Valley Dentistry. Why was she dismissed from Conemaugh Family Dentistry when they were in the middle of expanding, and why does her resume show that she is presently working at Loyalhanna, when she was laid off from there more than a month ago?

Dr. Mauch has not been using managed conversation well. He has been friendly, but self-centered, so he's talking about himself when he should be listening closely and following up with Jackie. Jackie's apparent inability to work at the standard professional pace is puzzling. Likewise, Jackie has failed to volunteer information that would clarify matters related to the nicked gums incident. She should try to be more cooperative, unless she is not being fully honest. Let's see if Dr. Mauch can figure this out.

Candidate: Jackie Kondin
Interviewer: Dr. Mingo Mauch, DDS
Interviewing at Chestnut Ridge Dentistry
Position: Dental hygienist/assistant
Second time through the applicant's resume

Dialogue	Observations
Interviewer: When did you stop working for Loyalhanna Dental Associates?	
Candidate: In May.	
I: When did you last update your resume?	
C: When I first thought about leaving Loyalhanna.	
I: Is that why your resume shows that you are working there presently?	Contradicting information.
C: Oh, I'm sorry. I should have updated that.	Contrition.
I: At Loyalhanna, were Ken and Judy able to maintain the one-patient-per-hour schedule?	
C: Ken did. At first, Judy agreed with me that, to do a good job, one cleaning an hour was too short a time. Later, it didn't seem to bother her. Ken was prone to rushing through patients. I don't think he was very thorough. Judy, I think, decided to go along to get along.	Balkanization, checkable with reference.
I: How did Ken's "rushing through the schedule" affect his work?	
C: I don't think his patients were given their proper due. His work was sloppier than Judy's or mine.	
I: Did Dr. Murkowski check Judy's and Ken's work the way he checked yours?	
C: Dr. Murkowski checked every patient's mouth after a cleaning.	Checkable.
I: Was Dr. Murkowski ever critical of Judy's or Ken's work?	
C: Not openly. Dr. Murkowski never was openly critical.	Contradiction.
I: Then how did you know Ken's work was sloppy?	
C: I don't. But I do know he didn't spend enough time with each patient to do it right.	Jackie's annoyance is showing.
I: When Dr. Murkowski criticized you for nicking a patient's gums, were you upset by his criticism?	Dr. Mauch switched topics.

<u>Dialogue</u>	<u>Observations</u>
C: I wouldn't say I was upset, but I think he handled the matter unprofessionally. I had only been working there for a couple weeks and I was still getting used to their curettes. I don't think it was fair what he said to me.	Defensiveness.
I: What did he say?	
C: That the patient would be justified in complaining about my work, and that I should call the patient the next morning and ask how she felt. If she was having pain, I was supposed to ask if she wanted Dr. Murkowski to look at it again. If she didn't want that, I was to recommend an over-the-counter pain medicine, like ibuprofen or acetaminophen.	
I: Did you call?	
C: I didn't have time. She called the office that afternoon and complained about an open wound on her gum. Dr. Murkowski went to her house and applied some analgesic and gave her Advil. It wasn't an open wound. I think everybody overreacted.	Omitted from earlier discussion. Discuss this with Dr. Murkowski in reference check.
I: Did others on staff hear about Dr. Murkowski's criticism of your work?	
C: They couldn't help it. The whole affair got completely out of control. When Dr. Murkowski left the office, everyone was asking what was up. I had to tell them. I was very embarrassed.	
I: Were there any comments from the staff?	
C: Wanda, of course. She asked me if I wanted to switch my curettes for a more comfortable brand.	Persecution complex?
I: Did you think it was a reasonable suggestion?	
C: Of course not. She only asked that to humiliate me.	Presumption, pettiness.
I: Did you continue using the same curettes?	
C: I switched out my anterior Gracey, just to make Wanda happy.	Pettiness.
I: Were there any more such incidents?	
C: I was much more careful after that. It's probably why I have trouble keeping up the one patient per hour pace.	Non-answer.
I: When you left Loyalhanna, did you and Dr. Murkowski have a good professional rapport?	

Dialogue	Observations
C: Yes. We always got along, even during the incident over the lady's gums.	Despite him acting "unprofessionally" and everybody overreacting?
I: Was that also true of Wanda Murkowski?	
C: We were never close, but we were friendly.	Indicates professionalism.
I: Would you mind if I called them and spoke to them about your job performance?	
C: No. There should be no problem. I told you why I could not stick to their schedule.	Less than enthusiastic go-ahead.
I: Was your need to spend extra time with your patients part of the reason for your departure?	
C: Not really. I just don't think the future at Loyalhanna looks promising.	Denial.
I: Is that because, as you mentioned earlier, you think Dr. Sengji is leaving Loyalhanna?	
C: Yes.	
I: Is Dr. Sengji still working at Loyalhanna?	
C: I believe so. I haven't heard that he left.	
I: But you think that he will be starting his own practice, correct?	
C: If he doesn't, I think he should. The Murkowskis don't present a child-friendly atmosphere. It will take years to build a pediatric clientele if he stays there.	Questionable expertise
I: You worked at Conemaugh for almost two years, correct?	
C: Yes. More than a year.	
I: Please tell me again why you left there.	
C: They were remodeling the building. Everything was in turmoil. I knew they were looking for another hygienist, and I didn't know if I would have a job. Then when Connie came back to work, I thought I would be let go.	Contradicts contention that she wasn't aware of expansion.
I: Why did you think that?	
C: I had a feeling. They loved Connie there. All the patients asked for her.	Diversionary answer.
I: They were remodeling with plans to expand. Didn't you think there would be enough work for both of you?	

Dialogue	**Observations**
C: There was enough work for both of us already. Together we could barely handle all the patients, even before the remodel was finished. We were often overbooked and sometimes I had to work overtime. Some days, Dr. Reilly would stay late and clean patients' teeth himself.	Breach of logic. Apparent that they were expanding and Jackie was not part of those plans.
I: Did Dr. Reilly ever ask you to work faster and see more patients?	
C: He asked me to work late a few times, which I did when I could.	Evasion.
I: Did he ask you to work faster?	
C: Not exactly. Sometimes he asked how much longer it would be until I could see the next patient.	Reference-check topic.
I: Did you interpret that as a criticism of your rate of work?	
C: I interpreted it as they scheduled the cleanings too close together.	
I: Have you found that you are able to work faster if you use particular instruments?	
C: I have tried several brands. When I finally get to use the new ultrasonic equipment, my rate of cleaning will increase considerably.	Presumption.
I: Why do you think that?	
C: I have talked to other hygienists about it. Some of the blog sites say the same thing. Also, I ran into Colleen from Conemaugh Family Dentistry, who told me that the new equipment is much faster.	
I: Have you ever used it?	
C: As I said earlier: I used it while in school, but never in practice. I think I would be good at it though.	Defensiveness.
I: But you feel confident your performance as a dental hygienist would improve significantly if you were trained in the use of the ultrasonic scaler and debrider, correct?	
C: Yes.	
I: The installation of our new Cavitron device is scheduled for next week, and the manufacturer's training program is scheduled for the following week.	So Dr. Mauch better hurry and find a dental hygienist/assistant.
C: I look forward to training on it and using it.	

If Dr. Mauch were searching for an honest candidate, his line of questioning would have been different. He might have delved deeper into the nature of the damage to that poor patient's gums, and he might have pried into her dismissal from Conemaugh. But, even without those answers, it is evident that Jackie makes judgments for which she is ill-informed (Dr. Senji's departure), bears resentment against her critics (Ken and Wanda), attempted to sow discord among her coworkers (fellow hygienist Judy), has distorted the timeline on her resume (time spent at Conemaugh, Loyalhanna, and Allegheny), and refuses to acknowledge that she is unprofessionally slow in her work. Taken together, these denote dishonesty.

But dishonesty is not recognized unless it is expressly sought. Dr. Mauch seems impressed with Jackie's desire to start working with new equipment. And he has the deadline imposed by the manufacturer's training schedule hanging over his head. His decision whether to hire Jackie is based on the wrong criteria.

Assessed Decision about Applicant

At the conclusion of the second review of the candidate's resume, the interviewer should have a clear perception of the candidate's level of honesty. If veracity testing showed few or no contradictions of earlier statements, if resume timelines have been confirmed, if workplace relationships with supervisors and coworkers are suitably portrayed, and if the candidate has willingly assisted in disclosing and explaining past experiences, then the interviewer will want to advance the candidate toward the next steps in the hiring process and possibly recommend the candidate for hire.

If the candidate failed to establish a suitable level of honesty, the interviewer may want to end the process now.

Assessed Decisions on Our Two Candidates

Carter has done an excellent job and Pauline wants to move to the next step in the interview process. Dr. Mauch has concerns about Jackie, but he thinks they are manageable and he needs a new hygienist right away.

Second Review of the Job Description and Conclusions

The candidate has passed muster and the interviewer wants the candidate earnestly to consider accepting the job. During the first review of the job description, the interviewer stressed the rigors of the job in order to make the candidate aware that his or her future employer will demand outstanding performance. During the second review of the job description, the focus is more on the needs of the applicant and on how the employer can accommodate those needs. Essentially, the interviewer is trying to rebuild rapport while encouraging the applicant to accept the job, if proffered.

The second review of the job description and conclusion usually takes ten or twenty minutes, but this is largely determined by the candidate and the number of questions asked.

The interviewer needs to make sure that all the candidate's questions about the job are answered fully and accurately, so now is the time to review workplace details with additional emphasis on the corporate demeanor, pay and benefits, and opportunities within the company or garage start-up.

By this time the candidate is likely to be mentally fatigued and anxious to end the interview. Sometimes a candidate is too shy or too tired to ask important questions. The interviewer should protect the candidate by instigating appropriate questions and volunteering pertinent information. The focus of this portion of the interview is to affirm that the company and the candidate want to follow the same path into the future.

The interview should terminate with a reconfirmation of the next step. Take a few minutes to explain where the process goes from here, how long it will take to make a hiring decision, maybe how many other candidates are being considered, and a quick assessment on how this candidate stacks up against the competition. The contact information of the selected references should be confirmed, and the candidate should be reminded to alert those references to the impending phone calls. A timeframe for second and subsequent interviews should be discussed.

Second Review of Job Description and Conclusions with Carter Johnfeld

Pauline will try to convince Carter to accept a job at Brownwell.

Candidate: Carter Johnfeld
Interviewer: Pauline White
Company: Brownwell Corporation
Position: Civil engineer, EIT
Second review of job description

Dialogue	Observations
Interviewer: Brownwell Corporation has a legacy that stretches from the Hoover Dam to the Hong Kong Airport to the Kuwaiti oil fields. Our superior engineers are the reason for our success and for our outstanding reputation. The Huron project is a big one, even by Brownwell standards. It is a combination of transportation, power production and energy transmission. Anybody who takes part in this project will have a distinguished achievement to brag about. The two-thousand-acre artificial island will serve as a transportation hub and a port of entry for the United States and Canada. It will be accessed by bridges for road and rail transportation and serve as a shipping port for Great Lake vessels. The docking facilities will handle bulk materials like ores, grains and coal, and liquids like oil and ethanol, and it will serve as a container port. You will be working directly with Kendall Swartz, project engineer for the land transportation, including bridges and roads. And he is considered by many to be the best in this industry. Have you read or heard anything about this project?	Sales pitch.

Dialogue

Candidate: I have heard rumors. But even the rumors are dwarfed by what you're telling me now.

I: That's good. We wanted to keep it quiet until the feasibility studies were completed. Now that they are, and both governments have signed off, we have a tentative go-ahead.

C: How tentative?

I: You never know how the public and various political groups will react to a project of this magnitude. So we'll have to wait and see how the environmental studies are received and how the news is greeted among local communities. While those issues are being decided, Brownwell's planners will continue working out the details so that when final approval comes, we can break ground without delay.

C: How long is the final approval likely to take?

I: Sometimes these matters drag on for five or more years, but that's about how long it would take us to complete our plans anyway.

C: What happens if we get three years into the planning and we're forced to halt the operation?

I: Those things happen. Fortunately, Brownwell is large enough that we can usually absorb the excess workforce into other projects. Let me tell you about pay and benefits. As an EIT with three years of experience, you will fall into the range of $80,000 to $100,000, depending on how your fellow engineers rate you. We provide health insurance, a 401(k), substantial year-end bonuses, and a liberal vacation schedule. Do those terms appeal to you?

C: Yes. They are quite generous.

I: Do you have any questions for me?

C: I am hoping you can fill me in about the Brownwell corporate culture.

I: What do you mean by corporate culture?

C: Every company—every institution of any kind— has a group culture. Can you give me an idea of what is expected of Brownwell employees that is unique or peculiar to this company?

I: I can't say that I've been asked that question before. What sort of peculiarities are you referring to?

Observations

Pauline brings up pay and benefits in general terms that are not specific to him. I don't think Carter should read this as tacit job offer.

Interesting that Carter chooses to discuss corporate culture instead of pay and benefits. Does it indicate farsightedness or shortsightedness?

Dialogue

C: Well, for example: Do your engineers wear ties to the office? In conferences with superiors, are free-ranging, open questions the norm or are these meetings generally more reserved? Are newcomers, like myself, warmly received and made to feel a home or are we expected to keep a low profile until somehow we have proven our worth? Does the CEO always win when golfing with employees? Those sorts of peculiarities.

I: Some of our senior personnel are set in their ways. But it's more social custom than professional obstinacy. It is likely that some of them would feel that open questioning in a conference setting would constitute a breach of etiquette, that such an open challenge would undermine their authority and their standing within the company. We're a big company with all types of people, personalities, backgrounds and cultures, and I feel sure some of our staff would react in ways that could be deemed peculiar. But I can assure you that "peculiarity" is not the norm at Brownwell.

C: I'm inquiring about those norms which might constitute peculiarities in other venues.

I: Our norm is one of conscientious professionalism and reliability. That's how we have remained at the forefront of the engineering world for nearly a century.

C: I understand that. I'm asking you about corporate character and personality. You are aware that General Motors, Intel, IBM, and Goldman Sachs have celebrated, in some cases notorious, unwritten codes of conformity. What are some of the quirks and conventions common to Brownwell?

I: Quirks and conventions?

C: Yes, quirks and conventions. Frankly, your line of questioning about backbiting has me concerned. You interview many engineers, but if the concept of cross-checking and correcting each other's work is foreign to you and to the hierarchy at Brownwell, this might not be the best place for me to work. Does it indicate lockstep conformity within the company? That's what I'm getting at. Brownwell has a commendable history with monumental achievements; I don't question it. But is this a place where creativity and ingenuity thrive, or is Brownwell just rolling along on a road smoothed by its storied past?

Observations

Now we're getting insight into Carter's thinking. Is this likely to help him land a job?

Is Pauline offended, thrown off her game, or is she enjoying this back and forth with a prospective employee?

Rote. Irrelevance.

Offended?

Persistent fellow.

Dialogue

I: Carter, I have worked in Brownwell's Human Resources for fifteen years. I admit that I do not know the nuts and bolts of our engineers' daily routine. It might be "lockstep," but I doubt it. I suspect it's as freewheeling and unfettered as any engineering company on the planet. That atmosphere is usually the most productive and our history, as a company, has been very productive and creative. You might be the person to find out what our corporate culture actually is; and when you find out, I want you to let me know what you have found. Such insight would help me do my job better. I will recommend you for hire, highly recommend, actually. Your next interview will be with the engineers in the Lake Huron Project. Find out for yourself what type of corporate culture prevails at Brownwell. When you question them, please be as direct and frank as you have been with me. Then please fill me in on what you have learned. This discussion fascinates me.

C: I might accept your challenge.

I: I would like to schedule your meeting with Dr. Swartz and his team for next Tuesday. The meeting usually takes about two hours. If you pass muster with them, then an additional interview will be scheduled, during which any final questions and issues will be resolved. If you get to the third meeting, you'll find it is basically an onboarding procedure, unless something unexpected appears in your background check, drug tests, or reference checks. Do you have other questions?

C: Yes. What is Dr. Swartz's full name and title? And if you can provide the names and titles of the other attendees of my impending interview, I would thank you for it.

I: I will email that information along with confirmation of the finalized date, time, and place of the meeting.

Observations

Has Carter's frank openness garnered Pauline's respect? Would she tolerate his audacity if he had not first joked with her and established a personal rapport?

I wonder if Carter noticed how quickly Pauline changed the subject when he asked what will happen if the project is cancelled. Could he be jumping from one indefinite future to another? After getting over her initial shock, Pauline responded positively to Carter's blunt questions about corporate culture. I wonder if Pauline would have tolerated such a grilling if she had not first established a rapport and become familiar with Carter's conversational inferences.

Second Review of Job Description and Conclusions with Jackie Kondin

Despite Jackie's lapses and inconsistencies, Dr. Mauch is considering hiring her. He has not used managed conversation effectively to determine her honesty. He seems more interested in peripheral matters, such as her social connections.

Some of the concerns that Dr. Mauch might have about Jackie's past job performance have been mitigated by the possibility that she will improve that performance after she is trained on the latest equipment. We also learned that the training is scheduled to begin in two weeks. That's not much time to shop around for more applicants. Hence, Dr. Mauch makes the classic small-business mistake: not allowing enough time to find and vet job candidates.

Candidate: Jackie Kondin
Interviewer: Dr. Mingo Mauch, DDS
Interviewing at Chestnut Ridge Dentistry
Position: Dental hygienist/assistant
Second review of Job Description

Dialogue	Observations
I: I would like to contact some former employers and coworkers.	
C: I don't have a problem with that, though I can't promise that Wanda will answer your questions.	Skepticism.
I: Does Dr. Murkowski have a policy against answering interview reference questions?	
C: Not that I'm aware of, but Wanda can be difficult.	
I: Do you think it would help if you called her and told her I would be calling?	
C: Yes, that might help.	

Dialogue	Observations
I: So, do I have your permission to contact Dr. Murkowski, Wanda Murkowski, Dr. Melanie Johnston, Dr. Reilly, and possibly other coworkers and employers about your workplace performance?	
C: Are you planning to call Dr. Reilly? It has been over two years since I worked there.	It seems Jackie would rather he didn't talk to Dr. Reilly.
I: I would like to speak to him.	
C: That's all right, I guess.	
I: Good. My schedule is crammed right now, but I'll try to call them within a few days. That will give you time to let them know that I'll be calling.	
Dr. Mauch reviewed pay, benefits and vacation with Jackie. He also reconfirmed the company drug policy.	
I: Do you have other questions for me?	
C: No. Not right now.	
I: After I talk to your references, I'll let you know what I have decided. Should I use the email address that appears on your resume?	
C: Yes. I want to let you know that I am excited to start using your ultrasonic scaler/debrider. I think I'll be very good at it.	Finally, some enthusiasm.
I: Oh?	
C: I love new technology and gadgets. If I am given a chance to learn ultrasonics, I'm sure I'll improve as a hygienist. At Bradford I only used it one day, but I really enjoyed it and it will be so much faster and simpler than a tray full of curettes.	
I: Most offices are going ultrasonic, but some patients prefer the old-fashioned way. Some claim that ultrasonic is painful.	
C: I won't throw away my old instruments.	
I: Good idea. We will be starting with a new procedure and a new hygienist at the same time, so our patients will likely see the change as an upgrade to our overall operation. Do you understand that you would be part of that upgrade?	
C: I understand and I promise you'll be glad you hired me.	
I: Good. Thanks for coming in today. I'll contact you in a few days.	

Jackie made a strong appeal at the end. Whether this was the result of desperation or inspiration, it seemed to get a positive response from Dr. Mauch. We know, but Jackie probably doesn't know, that Dr. Mauch has been unsuccessful at attracting qualified applicants.

Summary

Using the applicant's resume and the employer's job description as the framework, over a timeframe of one to one-and-a-half hours, the interviewer employs managed conversation to ascertain the applicant's level of honesty. Early in the interview and until the candidate is comfortable, rapport-building dominates. Then during the initial review of the resume and the job description, the focus shifts to open questioning and information gathering. The third phase focuses on intensive veracity testing. This phase peaks during the second review of the resume when statements made earlier by the candidate are cross-referenced and explored with follow-up questions and referrals to coworkers and supervisors. Though this entire interview process is protracted, it accomplishes the purpose served by any meaningful, casual conversation with a stranger: to determine if the person deserves trust.

CHAPTER 13 CONTACTING REFERENCES

A separate chapter is dedicated to contacting references because this part of the hiring process is too important to go under a subheading. Reference checks benefit the interviewer in two vital ways. First, they provide a veracity testing tool. Second, during the interview, the mere idea that the interviewer will be talking to past or present supervisors and coworkers is enough to persuade an interviewee to provide thorough and honest answers. This second benefit is available whether or not the interviewer finally contacts the potential reference.

Sometimes businesses, especially small businesses, skip this vital step in the hiring process. They think: Why spend the time talking to unknown people about a person who has already been interviewed and deemed worthy of hiring? Because George Costanzas and P. T. Barnums are out there, and it is worth taking an extra few minutes to keep them off your payroll. A short discussion with a candidate's former employer can be very revealing, and it can reverse a favorable opinion of a job candidate, preventing a significant hiring mistake. More likely, it will simply reaffirm the employer's positive opinion and thereby provide reassurance.

The problem with references is that their level of honesty has not been vetted. References may unfairly malign a candidate, or they may corroborate a candidate's lies. Personal grudges or favoritism may affect what a reference says. These issues are partially mitigated by selecting the references during the interview rather than accepting the candidate's prepared list.

Ultimately the interviewer must judge the honesty of the reference as well as the honesty of the candidate. This is the reason for contacting more than one, usually at least three separate references. The interviewer can compare the different recollections and reactions to gauge the true nature of the candidate.

Since a potential employer would only spend time checking the references of those candidates being considered for hiring, it should be expected that those references will provide positive statements. In many cases the interviewer will not have a chance to do much more than identify him or herself before the reference begins praising the candidate as an outstanding, reliable worker. That's a good thing. It is natural for a person to shower praise on a praiseworthy person. Still, a few specific questions should be asked of every reference.

The interviewer should confirm the dates of employment, the job title, the specific job duties of the candidate, and the official nature of the reference's working relationship with the applicant. Ask the reference to quantify the candidate's performance on a scale of one to ten, or as a percentage grade compared to other workers. If, during the interview, the candidate mentioned a particular work-related incident, discuss it with the reference and compare the ways the incident was presented. To spawn insightful discussions, ask questions such as "Did Joe's coworkers find him talkative?" or "Was Jane willing to work diligently to meet deadlines?" or "How do you think Pat will do in this new job?"

Reluctant References

References are sometimes wary of making judgmental statements about past or current employees' job performance, so rapport must first be established. This can be done in the usual way, by commenting on a casual topic: "Your website says you graduated from Marquette . . ." "I passed one of your trucks on the highway . . ." "Did you watch the Pirates play on Saturday?" If, during the job interview, the candidate provided a personal tidbit about the reference, such as she raises tomatoes in her backyard, use it.

Let your correspondent know that this need not be a formal discussion: It can be a simple chat about a common acquaintance, the job candidate. Then, from such humble beginnings, nurture the conversation with friendly assurances while the topic of the candidate's job performance is broached. If the reference remains reluctant, that too is valuable information.

References who are reluctant to talk can sometimes be persuaded with a reminder of an anecdote from the applicant's interview. For example, the candidate may have mentioned a particular event, and the interviewer can say to the reference, "Sally told me about the time when. . . ." Often the memory of the familiar topic will spawn a conversation. When interviewing a candidate, it is helpful to note such events in case they are needed for this purpose.

Broach problematic questions tactfully. This reference may have sparred with the candidate over those tardy emails. The interviewer should be sensitive to the candidate's position and pose questions in a non-accusatory tone. If the candidate is not offered a job from this company and has to use the reference again, the interviewer's tactlessness could damage the candidate's career opportunities. Or, if the candidate decides to return to his or her current company, the interviewer may have needlessly weakened the candidate's standing with that employer.

The reference might contradict the candidate's version of events, maybe even declaring the candidate was at fault by being tardy in returning his or her own emails. If such contradictions occur, it may be advisable for the interviewer to ask the candidate for the names of additional references who could validate his or her side of the story. It is important to remember the purpose of checking references is to determine without prejudice if the candidate is honest.

Most reference interviews take five or ten minutes, but sometimes the reference asks about the company where the applicant is applying for work. These questions may come from idle curiosity, or they may help the applicant's former employer to evaluate his or her relationship with current employees. Since the reference has been willing to sacrifice his or her time in answering the interviewer's questions, it is fair that the interviewer return the favor. Often the informality of this line of questioning reveals important information about the honesty and character of the candidate and the reference.

The trend toward emailing a list of questions should be discarded since the reference may be less than willing to answer the questions if that list looks like a homework assignment. Also, emails create a written record that may cause the reference to sanitize his or her opinions.

To avoid legal entanglements, some companies refuse to provide work references on their present or former employees. If this is the policy of a particular company, most employees are aware of it, and it is likely the candidate mentioned it during the interview. In other instances, to avoid the complications of providing a negative comment on a particular employee, former employers will claim they do not provide work references. Ask the question, "Do you ever provide job performance information on any of your past employees?" A yes answer could indicate the former employer has a negative opinion of this particular candidate.

Summary

Work references are contacted to provide insight into the candidate's honesty. References serve this purpose in two ways: Talking to a candidate's former coworkers validates that candidate's claims, and the awareness that the interviewer might contact those coworkers encourages the candidate to speak truthfully during the interview. The interviewer, not the interviewee, should determine which references will be contacted. Reference selection is an important aspect of the interview as the interviewer considers who among the candidate's work history is likely to provide insightful information into the honesty of the candidate. When conferring with references the interviewer must be attentive to the reference's concerns about making defamatory statements and to preserving the job candidate's reputation and position in the workforce. Some employers need to be coaxed into providing information; others flatly refuse. Generally a former employer's refusal to provide a reference statement can be interpreted as a negative statement.

Sample Reference Conversation Between Pauline White and Scott Weaver, a Former Coworker of Carter Johnfeld

Scott was Carter's team leader at Tomlin Engineering. Because of their close working relationship, Pauline wants to speak to Scott about Carter's job performance.

Candidate: Carter Johnfeld
Interviewer: Pauline White
Applicant at: Brownwell Corporation
Reference: Scott Weaver, PE, Candidate's former supervisor
Company: Tomlin Engineering
Reference phone call

Dialogue	Observations
Interviewer: Scott Weaver, this is Pauline White from Brownwell Corporation. I'm calling to ask you about a coworker of yours, Carter Johnfeld, who has applied to work at Brownwell. Do you have a few minutes to answer some questions?	
Reference: Pauline, may I call you right back? I'm a bit busy right now. I can call you in five minutes.	
I: Okay. I'll wait for your call at this number.	
A few minutes later.	
R: Thank you for allowing me to call back. I was with our project engineer and he probably shouldn't hear this call.	
I: Are you referring to Imran Khan?	
R: Yes. I suppose Carter told you that Imran doesn't like losing his employees. He's possessive that way.	Confirms Carter's sentiment.
I: I wanted to ask you about that. Is that typical of him?	
R: Oh yes, that's Imran. He's a little high-strung. **I:** So I should not consider Carter's reluctance to let me talk to Imran as a negative comment on Carter's ability as an engineer.	
R: Imran would tell you Carter is an outstanding engineer. That's what would bother Imran. He wouldn't want to lose Carter.	
I: How long have you worked with Carter?	
R: He came over to the Tampa Bridge Project about two and a half years ago. I've been his team leader since then.	Confirmation of timeline.
I: Would you say Carter is a good engineer?	
R: I would say he's an outstanding engineer and a great coworker. If you have a chance to grab him, you should take. You won't find a better person in this industry.	
I: How long have you been in the industry?	

Dialogue	Observations
R: Thirteen years. Eleven years with Tomlin Engineering and before that, two years with American Bridge.	Affirm Scott's credibility.
I: With that much time in engineering, you must have worked with a lot of good engineers. How would you rank Carter against others that you have worked with?	
R: At or near the top. I'm not sure what makes Carter such a good worker, but he's as good as they get. He has a way of asking questions and getting to the core of any problem that is both unusual and invigorating. He wasn't in my crew for a week before people were deferring to his opinion. Even when he made mistakes he turned them around and used them.as a way to pull us all together and get better results.	Carter's mistakes are brought up.
I: Was one of those mistakes Carter's failure to properly calculate the rate of expansion on the Tampa Bay project?	
R: Exactly. Take that example. Here this young guy, Carter, only with us a couple weeks, makes a mistake, which I quietly bring to his attention. Instead of doting over it or becoming upset about it, he walks over to Tej and shows it to him. The day before, Imran had found a mistake in Tej's work, so Carter lets Tej know we all make mistakes. Keep in mind that Tej has been an engineer longer than I have. Carter is a natural-born leader.	Not everybody earns praise from their mistakes.
I: He told me about the Tampa Bay bid being rejected. How did that affect his job performance?	
R: We were all disappointed with that, Carter as much as anybody. Did he mention to you that he had recommended to Imran that we should submit two quotes, one with Cor-Ten steel and the other with a cheaper product? Imran declined to do it. Had he taken Carter's advice, we probably would have won the project.	This is new information to Pauline.
I: He didn't mention that. He talked about working with Aasta Parvadi. Have you discussed Carter's job performance with Aasta?	
R: Aasta works down the hall. Our team and hers share office space, projects, pizza, so yes, I have talked to her about Carter. But I can't speak for her.	
I: Carter almost sounds too good to be true.	

Dialogue	**Observations**
R: Well, it won't bother any of us if you don't hire him. We want him to stay right here. He'll have his master's degree next year. Then he'll sit for his Professional Engineer's license. Already the higher-ups have been conferring with him on personnel as well as management issues.	
I: I wanted to ask you about management. Carter inquired about Brownwell's corporate character. He was strident about the topic. Why do you suppose that is?	
R: I really can't say for sure, but the issue seems important to him. He's very polite and gracious in front of other people, but he is not intimidated by seniority and management in the least. In fact, he challenges it. But he goes about it in such a way that the company officials turn around and ask him what they should do. That's why Imran is pursuing the Indonesia project with these bridge plans. When management was ready to toss the whole thing, Carter stands up at a department meeting and starts asking questions. The next thing we know, the project is back on center stage, and we all have Carter to thank for it. He's going places. We won't mind riding on his coattails.	Pauline has experienced Carter's direct questioning for herself. Does she think such tactics are acceptable at Brownwell?
I: Thanks for your time, Scott.	

Pauline just heard a ringing endorsement of Carter's professionalism and his character. Typical of the reaction from a friendly coworker, Scott heaped praise on Carter. Pauline's concerns about Carter's directness were allayed. That trait seems to spawn admiration among his coworkers. Nothing that Scott said would cause Carter's honesty to be questioned.

Sample Reference Conversation Between Pauline White and Aasta Parvadi, a Former Coworker of Carter Johnfeld

At Tomlin Engineering, Aasta was Carter's first supervisor, then she recommended that he move to another project and leave hers. As Carter explained it, the move was not a demotion or negative comment on his performance: it was the result of Aasta seeking the best opportunity for Carter. Let's see what Pauline finds out.

Candidate: Carter Johnfeld
Applicant at: Brownwell Corporation
Interviewer: Pauline White
Reference: Aasta Parvadi, PE, Candidate's former supervisor
Company: Tomlin Engineering
Reference phone call

Dialogue	Observations
Interviewer: Aasta, this is Pauline White with Brownwell Corporation. Carter Johnfeld has applied for a job with us, and I would like to ask you a few questions about Carter's job performance.	
Reference: Please, go ahead. Carter mentioned that you might call.	
I: How long did you work with Carter?	
R: I worked directly with him for about six months. But he has been employed in our department for almost three years. He transferred from my team to his current team quite a while ago.	
I: About two years ago?	
R: Yes, I think, about that.	
I: Why did he leave your team?	
R: I recommended him for another department, one where he could get more experience and work with more challenging aspects of engineering and work directly under Imran.	
I: While he worked with you, would you say he was a good worker?	

Dialogue	Observations
R: After he got used to his surroundings, he was an excellent worker.	Aasta is not as quick to praise Carter as was Scott.
I: Did he have some difficulty getting used to his surroundings?	
R: I wouldn't say difficulty. "Cautious" might be a better word. Carter took some time before he opened up. Once he did, though, he excelled.	
I: Can you tell me how Carter exhibited his caution in his job?	
R: I don't want to give you the impression that Carter is anything but a good worker. I mostly bring up his slow start because one never knows how a worker will perform until some time passes and you get to know him better. Carter was one of those. I thought he was unsure of himself or maybe extremely shy because he was so deferential and polite. But he was simply determined not to make mistakes. When I gave him one of his first assignments—I think it was estimating stress load on truss supports—he took longer than the typical newbie and he went around asking others on the team to check his work. I'm used to recent grads flying through their work, trying to impress me with their smarts and confidence; not Carter. His goal was professionalism, not showing off.	Is this answer Aasta's attempt to cover for Carter? Let's let it stew a little then try it again later.
I: Was he a slow worker? Did he take more time than the other engineers?	
R: He did on his first couple assignments. But that changed within a month or so. He soon proved to be quicker and more precise in his projections than most of his coworkers.	
I: So why do you think he was slow in the beginning?	
R: That's just Carter. He takes his time and learns things. After that he's as good as anybody at getting things done, better than most.	
I: Has there been any issues with Carter's assertive nature, or even a belligerence around others?	
R: Those are interesting questions. Assertive, yes, belligerent, no—absolutely not. Why do you ask that?	
I: I was under the impression that he might have a tendency to grandstand in front of others. Did he ever confront a senior member of management in an open forum?	

Dialogue

R: Carter asks a lot of questions at those meetings. It's his way of doing things. He doesn't seem to care if his coworkers or supervisors think him ill-informed or ignorant. He just asks questions; but not dumb questions. It's Socratic in a way. He's nonconfrontational—even coming across as naïve, then, before anybody realizes it, he's skillfully introducing the proposals that become the action plan for the department. That's what happened with the Tampa Bay project.

I: Is that the project for which you were outbid?

R: Yes, but thanks to Carter it's still being shopped around, and Scott's team is still working on adaptations to make it suitable for other settings.

I: Can you think of a reason that Carter would consider leaving Tomlin Engineering?

R: He's young and adventurous, sort of a risk taker. He's probably looking for broader opportunities.

I: Can you tell me something about his shortcomings?

R: Yes, like I said, he's young and adventurous, sort of a risk taker....

I: Okay, I get it. Any other workplace faults?

R: None that come to mind.

I: You mentioned that his slow start and attributed it to professional caution. Were there any other factors involved there?

R: Maybe he isn't as mathematically adept as he could be. He bogs down on some of the more complex calculations.

I: What do you mean?

R: His math skills are weaker than some of the other engineers, and that becomes apparent over time.

I: How apparent?

R: Look, here's what I did—and I would appreciate it if this never got back to Carter.

I: You have my word.

Observations

Again, praise for Carter's questions and his ability to work with others.

Pauline tries again.

Does this confirm Pauline's suspicions about Carter's low college GPA?

Dialogue	**Observations**
R: Good. I couldn't judge whether Carter was inaccurate or extra-cautious, so I thought Imran was the guy to make that decision. That's why I recommended Carter for the Tampa Bay project—so he could work directly with Imran, who is a great mentor for young engineers.	Interesting bit of insight.
I: And, what does Imran think?	
R: After our last department meeting, Imran told me Carter is the most impressive raw talent he has encountered in recent years. Coming from Imran, that's as high praise as an engineer can get.	Now, Pauline is thinking about how Dr. Swartz, Carter's new supervisor, will judge him.
I: But about his math skills . . .	
R: He gets around to the correct calculations, but often he depends on others' input to do it, that's all. When left to his own devices, he eventually comes up with the answer, but he is not always certain of himself.	
I: I understand that you are trying to help Carter. He'll benefit by my having an accurate opinion of his abilities. Otherwise, during the interview process he could reveal a fault that I could have helped him explain. I would really like to see Carter working for our company.	
R: Pauline, are you an engineer?	
I: No, I am not.	
R: Well, we engineers like to think of ourselves as artists with discipline and brains—well, at least with discipline. (laughter)	Is Aasta telling Pauline to back off?
I: Oh?	
R: (Laughs) You sound skeptical. But I just want to point out that art and discipline have as much to do with successful engineering as do the analytical skills. Carter has adequate analytical skill and he excels in art and discipline. Taken together, he has all the talent to be an outstanding engineer.	
I: But I think I hear you saying that you feel he lacks the smarts needed for the job.	But Pauline will not let go.
R: If I led you to think that, then I gave you the wrong impression. It's really nitpicking. Maybe I shouldn't have mentioned it. He's very smart.	
I: I think I understand. I think you are saying that your criticism is marginally quantitative.	

Dialogue	Observations
R: Yes, thank you. I only mentioned it because you pressed me to name a fault. **I:** Thanks, Aasta.	

Even when Pauline badgers them, Carter's coworkers will not say anything negative about him. After speaking to Aasta, Pauline is excited about the prospect of adding Carter to Brownwell's team. If he is even close to the quality of worker that his background indicates, and his coworkers claim, is appears that whoever employs Carter will be much better off for it.

Sample Reference Conversation Between Dr. Mingo Mauch and Dr. Jim Murkowski, Former Employer of Jackie Kondin

Dr. Mauch wants to know how well Jackie Kondin performed her job at Loyalhanna Dental. Specifically he plans to ask about her struggles with maintaining a standard working pace, since she apparently could not stay on schedule. Also he wants to know if Dr. Murkowski's staff had difficulty working alongside Jackie. Fortunately, Dr. Mauch and Dr. Murkowski are close friends, so establishing rapport and trust are not an issue.

Job candidate: Jackie Kondin
Applicant at Chestnut Ridge Dentistry
Interviewer: Dr. Mingo Mauch, DDS, owner
Reference: Dr. James Murkowski, most recent employer.
Company: Loyalhanna Dental Associates
Reference-check phone call

Dialogue	Observations
Interviewer: Hi, Jim, this is Mingo. I'm calling about a dental hygienist that recently interviewed for a job here. Do you have a few minutes to discuss Jackie Kondin?	
Reference: Yeah, Mingo. How have you been? Wanda and I missed you at the conference in Phoenix. We were hoping you would be there.	The Murkowskis and Dr. Mauch are friends. The candidate was apparently not aware of this.
I: My mother was in the hospital. If you're going to ADA's Charlotte conference this year, I'll see you there.	
R: Yes, Wanda and I are going. Let's plan to get together. So you're calling about Jackie Kondin.	
I: Yes. You probably know that my hygienist, Susan, is moving to Iowa to be near her grandchildren. I need to replace her, which isn't going to be easy.	
R: I remember Susan. She worked here for a couple years when her kids were in school. She is a great worker. Sorry you're losing her. So you interviewed Jackie for that position.	
I: That's right. Jackie seemed uncertain about how you would rank her abilities as a hygienist.	
R: She's is a tough one. Jackie's such a likeable person, and she's full of energy.	
I: I'm waiting for the "but."	
R: But, while working here, she did not show the empathy toward the patients that we felt was needed. She would rush through her work and, in the process, nick gums, drop tools, and spill things. I never had so many complaints from patients.	
I: Was she asked to keep to the one-patient-per-hour schedule?	
R: At first, we thought that was the problem. But when Wanda started spacing Jackie's appointments out to an hour and fifteen minutes, she performed no better. She's just sort of a sloppy worker.	Contradicts Jackie's interview statements.
I: So you don't think that if Jackie were given more time with each patient, she would do better.	

<u>Dialogue</u>	<u>Observations</u>
R: We tried that and got the same results.	
I: She mentioned an incident when she nicked a patient's gums and you left the office to see the patient at home. Can you tell me about that?	
R: I could, if I knew which incident you were asking about. It happened three different times that I can remember. And I don't know how many times I apologized to patients in the office.	Omission.
I: I see. We're installing an ultrasonic scaler and debrider. Do you think she would perform better on different equipment?	Grasping at straws?
R: I can't say, Mingo. I would like to think so, but it's impossible to know. The reason I haven't switched over to ultrasonic is that reports show that a high percentage of patients say ultrasonic is more painful than conventional cleaning and scaling. In Jackie's hands, such equipment could make things better, or make them worse.	
I: Did she leave voluntarily?	
R: Yes and no. Wanda tried everything she could to cover for her, but when patients started pointedly asking for Ken or Judy instead of Jackie, we knew we had a problem. One day Wanda had three patients refuse to go to Jackie. When Wanda mentioned it to her, Jackie grew noticeably upset then walked out of the office. So we dropped her from payroll.	This is not the way Jackie described her departure.
I: Was that the end of it?	
R: Yes. Jackie never filed for unemployment that we know of, so I assume she acknowledges that she left of her own volition.	
I: Thanks, Jim.	
R: It's a shame, because, as I said, she's fun to be around, she makes everybody laugh, she's smart and has plenty of friends around town.	Apparently, Jackie is a good friend to have, but not a good coworker.
I: Thanks. I'll see you and Wanda in Charlotte. Leave that checkered sports jacket at home. Please.	

If Dr. Mauch was looking for confirmation of Jackie's honesty, he did not find it. But I don't think he was thinking about honesty. In fact, he learned that Jackie misrepresented the nature of her departure from her former employer—another clear indicator that she is dishonest.

But Dr. Mauch needs a new hygienist right now, and he is desperate to find one. Maybe he is not familiar with the maxim: hire slow, fire fast. Judging by the tone of his conversation with Dr. Murkowski, Dr. Mauch seems willing to stake his hopes on the remote possibility that Jackie's job performance will improve if she practices with new equipment.

Sample Reference Conversation Between Dr. Mingo Mauch and Dr. Carl Reilly, Former Employer of Jackie Kondin

Jackie had worked for Dr. Reilly more than two years ago. When Dr. Mauch mentioned that he wanted to contact Dr. Reilly, Jackie was not enthused. That reaction made Dr. Mauch curious, so he called.

Job candidate: Jackie Kondin
Applicant at Chestnut Ridge Dentistry
Interviewer: Dr. Mingo Mauch, DDS, owner
Reference: Dr. Carlton Reilly, second most recent employer.
Company: Conemaugh Family Dentistry
Reference-check phone call

Dialogue	Observations
Interviewer: Dr. Reilly, my name is Mingo Mauch. My practice is Chestnut Ridge Dentistry in Vintongrift. I have interviewed a former employee of yours for a position as dental assistant/hygienist. Do you mind answering a few questions?	
Reference: No problem. Who is the employee?	Sounds willing to cooperate.
I: Jackie Kondin.	
R: Oh. She worked here as a hygienist for a few months. That was probably two years ago.	Not enthusiastic.
I: Would you say she performed her job well?	
R: I won't say that she performed poorly, because I don't want to risk a defamation lawsuit.	Really not enthusiastic.

Dialogue	Observations
I: I see. When did she work there?	
R: I would need to look it up in our employee files. I can't do that right now, so if you need that information, I'll have to get back to you.	
I: That's not necessary. I noticed that Jackie left your employment right around the time you were expanding your practice. Was her departure voluntary?	Dr. Mauch is getting the picture.
R: Honestly, I don't remember all the details. She left and we hired two new hygienists, and they are still here and we're happy with their work.	
I: Thanks for your time, Dr. Reilly.	Get me out of here.
R: You're welcome.	

Dr. Reilly is a typical noncooperative reference. He was friendly right up to the moment when he heard Jackie Kondin's name, then he soured. Apparently he was willing to talk about former employees, just not Jackie. Most employers would qualify this reaction from a former employer as a negative reference. Dr. Mauch, however, is desperate.

Analysis and outcome of Our Candidates' Interview Experiences

Carter Johnfeld

In many ways, Carter was the ideal job candidate. If he had interviewed with me, I would have hired him. His resume was simple, inclusive, and accurate. He treated his interviewer with deference and respect to the point that Pauline, the interviewer, was answering questions about herself at his behest. At no point during the interview did he contradict either his resume or his earlier statements. If anything, he omitted a few points that could have benefited him, such as his recommendation to submit an alternative to COR-TEN steel in the Tampa Bay project and his instigation of the Indonesian proposal.

Pauline pursued many issues with successive questions that would have tripped up most dishonest candidates, such as when she repeatedly asked about the events surrounding his switch to the Tampa Bay project and when she took him to task over his less than stellar college grades. When she followed up on his mistake in calculating the thermal expansion of the Tampa Bay bridge, Carter's story not only held up, but it was held out by his coworkers as evidence of his leadership and professionalism. Carter exemplifies the manner in which personal honesty extends to the other virtuous human characteristics.

Because of her experience as an interviewer, Pauline squeezed more from her reference calls than most. She cajoled Aasta into revealing her underlying reason for recommending Carter's move to the Tampa Bay project, apparently something even Carter didn't know. Also, after talking with Aasta and Scott, she was able to dismiss her concerns about Carter's tendency to question superiors in public. Accordingly, she learned that his questions were constructive and appreciated by coworkers and the superiors to whom they were directed.

Ultimately, the outcome was this: Pauline asked for and was granted the authority to raise Carter's contingent pay scale a notch above what his experience warranted. She emailed that information to Carter. The email included scheduling information for the upcoming professional skills interview with Dr. Swartz, project engineer for Brownwell's Lake Huron project. To Pauline's disappointment, Carter responded by cancelling the appointment and declining the job offer, stating, "I have decided the best place for me is right here at Tomlin Engineering. Thank you for your thoughtful consideration and your company's generous offer."

Ironically, Carter's decision to stay at Tomlin was based upon the support that his coworkers expressed when he told them about applying for a position with Brownwell. Scott told Carter about his conversation with Pauline, then said, "I hope you don't get that job." The ensuing discussion about the rising prospects of the bridge projects at Tomlin Engineering, and about the comradery and teamwork that they had established there, made Carter decide to stay with his current coworkers and employer.

Jackie Kondin

Jackie had problems from the beginning. I would have set aside her application and ended the interview shortly after learning that she had excluded an employer and falsely stated her dates of employment at both Conemaugh and Loyalhanna. But Dr. Mauch was using different criteria than me in his selection process.

Abundant evidence of dishonesty was there. She omitted one employer and listed incorrect dates of employment for the others. Her resume's timeline shows a seven-month gap between graduation and starting at Conemaugh (later, we learned that she was employed during part of this time, but failed to list it), then she was idle for four months between Conemaugh and Loyalhanna. (In the interview Jackie claimed she worked at Loyalhanna for two years, in contradiction to the one year and three months shown on her resume.) Finally her resume shows that she still works at Loyalhanna, when in fact she doesn't.

Throughout the interview, Jackie gave nebulous answers, engaged in hearsay, disparaged coworkers and omitted important work-related facts. When given the opportunity to build rapport with her prospective employer, she chose instead to talk about herself. Luckily for Jackie, her interviewer was neither pursuing personal honesty in her nor brimming with social skills himself. Instead, Dr. Mauch wanted a dental hygienist/assistant who could start within two weeks so that he could begin collecting revenue from his new ultrasonic scaler/debrider.

While going through the motions of contacting references, Dr. Mauch failed to connect the contents of the reference calls to the original purpose of discerning whether or not Jackie Kondin was a good worker. Indifferent to Dr. Murkowski's comments about Jackie's job performance, upon hanging up the phone Dr. Mauch went to his calendar and circled the date of the Charlotte convention. After speaking with Dr. Reilly, Dr. Mauch fumed at that man's rudeness. Dr. Mauch misread Dr. Reilly's curt conversation as disrespect toward him personally, instead of a commentary on Jackie's work performance.

Dr. Mauch did not view the interview process as a means by which an employer finds an honest worker. He, like many employers, is unaware of honesty's importance to the successful workplace. To Dr. Mauch, the purpose of interviewing was to meet a job seeker whom he hoped would, by some twist of fate, become a good worker, and there was no method to it.

But Jackie's plusses caught Dr. Mauch's attention. She gamefully bantered with him about football, which he enjoyed. She was well connected in the community. Dr. Mauch's outgoing hygienist recommended her because they had mutual friends. Jackie was close with Cynthia Holt, whose husband golfs with a cigar clenched in his teeth, and she babysat the children of the state senator whose political influence had bestowed new streetlights on Vintongrift.

I would not have hired Jackie, but Dr. Mauch offered her the job, and she accepted it. Then she asked to have the following Monday off because that was the day that the Pittsburgh Steelers played the Denver Broncos and she planned to attend the game. Dr. Mauch decided that one more day without a dental hygienist would not hurt. He felt somewhat sure that things would work out.

Chapter 14 Second Interviews and Pay Negotiations

Second interviews and pay negotiations are thrown together like pie and ice cream, not because they have anything structural in common, but because they show up together at the end of the affair. As any pastry chef will remind you, the final course makes or breaks the meal, and second interviews and pay negotiations can cement or undermine a well-orchestrated hiring plan. An employer who has invested heavily in finding honest workers needs to finish the process in a completely honest manner. Nothing leaves a bitter taste in a new employee's mouth like being promised dessert then being fed a baloney sandwich.

Second Interviews

As a matter of course, larger companies and those with human resource departments require second and subsequent interviews before proffering a job to a candidate. However, many small employers are too swamped with business or too disorganized to take the time. They just want to hire somebody, anybody, and get back to work. They skip the essential second interview and that can be a big mistake.

A second interview is necessary even if a candidate appears to be a shoe-in. More often than not, the extra half hour spent with a job candidate prior to offering the position will reveal a significant misunderstanding or allay an unfounded apprehension. Coming as it often does, a week or more after the original interview, the second interview takes place after the candidate has considered various aspects of the job's duties and benefits through the lens of time. Inevitably, this new perspective instigates new considerations. The second interview allows both parties to review the terms of employment, clear up any lingering doubts, and answer any remaining questions that have come to light since the first interview. Only after the second interview should the job be proffered.

Between the first interview and the second, reference checks should be completed. Comments from references may need to be discussed before a potential employer makes a hiring decision. If comments from references require further investigation, or if the candidate requires more information from the employer, the second interview may prompt the scheduling of a third meeting.

The second interview also provides an excellent opportunity to bring a third party into the process. The interviewer will witness the candidate's ability to interact with another person. The additional person may provide valuable insight into the candidate's qualifications. And the candidate may appreciate the chance to ask questions of someone other than the original interviewer.

If the job requirements include specific skills or specialized knowledge, subsequent interviews are the time to bring in specialists and perform testing. If the hiring manager will not attend these interviews, it is essential that those who participate be trained in the process of selecting for honesty. If a candidate has traveled a long distance to attend the interview, it may be necessary to perform the initial interview and the testing in one day. If this is the case, provide a recuperative break before beginning the second interview or testing process.

Pay and Benefits Negotiations

Since ancient times, oriental rug merchants have been stig-
matized as unscrupulous negotiators, and not without justification. Records of bad actors taking advantage of the public's lack
of oriental rug knowledge have been around since the days of
Homer. I spent twenty-eight years of my professional life buying,
importing, and selling oriental rugs. Yet I avoided the tedious
negotiations and the sometimes-heated exchanges that are associated with purchasing carpets. That is because I knew the
product, its quality, its availability on the market, its market value
at the producer's end, and its value at the consumer's end. So,
before asking the price of a rug, I would explain to the producer
that I will either accept the price and purchase the product or
decline and not purchase it. The producer got one chance to
quote his or her price. Using this technique, I was able to purchase fine carpets at competitive prices, save a lot of time, and
avoid aggravation.

This yes-or-no system is the standard marketing model in
established economies, but not in the world's freewheeling ba-
zaars and open markets where an ill-informed buyer can produce a windfall for an unscrupulous seller. The yes-or-no market
operates under this simple understanding: The price that a seller
puts on a product accurately reflects the value of that product.
This works in the market for tangible products and it works in
the market for labor.

A new employee's position in the labor market is not unlike
mine within the oriental rug market. The employee should have
a minimum acceptable pay in mind and be willing to reject the
job if that amount is not proffered. Realistically, this amount will
vary greatly depending on the experience, skills, education and
personal financial condition of each employee, but it is essential

that the job candidate has considered these matters thoroughly and honestly before entering the job market.

If an employer considers it sporting to battle with employees for the lowest-paying labor contract, then they are allowing the employees to manage the employer's labor costs. If on the other hand the employer has prepared a budget, projected payroll expenses, and calculated employee pay accordingly, that employer will know the amount of pay each employee can and should receive. Competent employers determine pay through analytical means, not through flea market negotiating games.

Though plenty of employers do it, arguing with an employee over a pay scale is clearly counterproductive. The intrinsic nature of such negotiations is that the employer speaks disparagingly of the quality or potential of the employee's work in order to lower the pay, and the employee's natural reaction is to defend or exaggerate his or her performance in order to warrant higher pay.

Conversely, the employee tells the employer how bad he or she is as an employer, and the employer says the business is barely staying afloat and the employee should be happy just to have a job. The underlying premise is one of distorted facts and dishonesty. Instead, the employer and employee should both have an honest idea of the where they stand, the position of the company within the current business climate, and the employee's job performance, and then they should reach a common understanding about pay.

All aspects of pay, vacation time, sick leave, personal time, health benefits, maternity leave, child care, pension plans, and any other form of compensation should be discussed in full before the applicant's acceptance is confirmed. It is not enough to assume that if the candidate does not ask, then he or she either is fully informed or is not interested in these matters. Many people lack the confidence, or are unsure of the proper protocol, and fail to ask the necessary questions. Among new employees, nothing causes more resentment than when they receive less compensation than they thought they would.

Employers who respect the honesty of their employees need to protect those employees from predatory management practices that would trample passive personalities. If an employer feels that pay scales are a trifling matter over which a negotiating game plays out, or if an employee feels compelled to fight for justly earned higher pay, fundamental honesty is missing from that workplace relationship.

Summary

Second interviews are essential, even if the candidate appears to be a shoe-in for the job. In a second interview, the interviewer should resolve issues that arose from reference discussions. If the position is offered, the employer should provide a complete and final compensation package, so the candidate can make a definitive decision of accepting or rejecting the job. Aggressive pay negotiations are counterproductive and indicative of distrustful employer/employee relationships. Employers drive away honest employees by participating in the sport of pay negotiation.

PART IV

THE APPLICATION

Now that you've decided to hire honest workers, how will you transition to an honest workplace? How will you manage those workers? What are the long-term prospects for the honest workplace, and how will it influence the lives of employees, employers, and society?

CHAPTER 15 SUPERVISING AN HONEST WORKPLACE

Honest workers, like honest friends and family, possess many subtle assets that are not immediately attributed to honesty. For instance, because they are honest with themselves, honest workers are not disposed to personality excesses that may interfere with workplace productivity. They are less likely to swing with fads, create public spectacles, and veer off course in their home and family lives, so they are less distracted at work. Some skeptics may claim these attributes are functions of boring personalities but I credit honesty, or as I like to call it, the good-worker gene.

From my observations as an employer who for over thirty years selected employees based on their high level of honesty, I have concluded that honest employees also tend to be non-smokers, moderate drinkers, good parents, reliable spouses, and safe drivers. Please, let me explain.

At Patusan Trading Company, over a span of twenty-eight years, I interviewed and hired hundreds of employees, men and women who—in addition to selling oriental rugs, physically managing heavy inventory, and working long hours in furniture stores—were regularly required to drive commercial trucks across United States and Canada. All together we logged more than ten million highway miles. During that time we had a total of one, single reportable accident in a company vehicle (damn it, anyway), and that accident, on a highway ramp in San Francisco, totaled slightly over $4,000 in vehicle damages with no injuries.

I did not hire employees based on their driving skills or safe driving records. I selected for honesty, and I got safe drivers. Most of Patusan's new hires were recent college graduates who, frankly, would have preferred jobs that didn't require driving trucks, but they were willing to tolerate the chore—at least until they could find better jobs. But, years later, most of them were still driving trucks, still selling oriental rugs, and liking it.

I did not deliberately select nonsmokers, moderate drinkers, good parents, reliable spouses, and safe drivers, but I that's who I got. I selected honest workers, and I got a highly diverse group of fun-loving, hardworking, reliable characters who made every workday a joy—with a few conspicuous speed bumps. Life does have speed bumps.

When Leslie and I became general managers at Triple Creek Ranch, in 2009, our first policy change was to establish new hiring practices. We instituted a program of hiring workers who were honest above all other selection criteria. Five years later, in 2014, the readers of *Travel + Leisure Magazine* voted Triple Creek Ranch "The World's Best Hotel" with our staff earning accolades for their charming personalities. When I reminded certain members of staff and management that they were selected for honesty, not personality, they joked that just because I have no personality, I shouldn't downplay theirs. Nonetheless, without honesty, our staff could have accommodated our guests, but they would not have been good employees. Honesty provided the platform from which our employees could showcase their charming personalities.

You will quickly recognize the following scenario because it is so emblematic of dishonesty in the workplace that nearly every employer can recall a similar experience. I have changed the names, but when I was told of this event, I thought I was listening to a rerun of one of the many similar stories that I have heard over the years. How many times have you been in a similar situation to Natasha's?

Natasha's call center desperately needed a full-time worker for the shift that included weekends. She hired Carl, a smart young man whose resume indicated he was more than qualified for the job. Natasha wondered about the gaps in his working timeline and about his explanation for leaving his last employer, but she was desperate. So she skipped the all-about-you interview and reference checks. She needed somebody now, and Carl said he would work weekends. With the hiring of Carl, Natasha promised her staff that finally they could return to their regular work schedules.

For a week the shift manager trained Carl. Schedules were adjusted with Carl taking the new shift and other personnel adjusting accordingly. Human resources built Carl's personnel files with W-4, I-9, state tax forms, resume, application, and background check. They contacted their insurer for the requisite liability and workers' compensation coverage. They processed health insurance coverage by opening a separate file, completing essential forms, and scheduling the necessary doctors' visits. Timesheets and payroll records were entered and activated. The act of hiring Carl was time-consuming and costly.

On the third week of employment, Carl told Natasha that he needed the upcoming weekend off for a long-ago scheduled family event. She wished he had told her about this earlier, but she went ahead and rearranged schedules to accommodate him. Two weeks later he asked for another weekend off, this time for his high school reunion. The next weekend he called in sick.

Natasha met Carl in her office. She reminded him that he was hired expressly to work weekends. Carl replied, "Are you suggesting that I'm lying, that I wasn't really sick?"

Carl's response elevated this matter to an ominous level; he used a health issue to leverage his broken promise. Of course, she questioned whether or not he was really sick, but she could not say so. No rational employer will comment upon or make a judgment about an employee's health. Doing so is occupational suicide. Natasha had begun doubting Carl's integrity when he asked for a weekend off after only three weeks of employment. If the family event was prescheduled, as he said it was, then he knew about it even while he was promising to work on weekends. She replied obliquely, "But you had taken two of the prior three weekends off."

"Well, you gave me permission," Carl responded.

And the downward spiral began. Not only did Natasha spend her days fretting over Carl's performance and the damage it wreaked on coworker morale, for two additional months her department toiled in limbo as she maneuvered to resolve the problem. After she built a case and finally dismissed him, she once again had nobody to work on weekends. All the time and effort spent on filing and processing employment credentials, on training, on enrolling him in insurance programs, was now lost. Months had been wasted, employees piqued, and money lost because Natasha hired a dishonest worker.

Honest workplaces spiral upward and dishonest workplaces spiral down. Recognizing the importance of workplace honesty, setting about establishing it, and then preserving it is as vital as any task assigned to an employer or manager.

Coaching as a Management Style

Supervising honest employees is exceptionally different from supervising a typical workforce. Most supervisors spend their time managing the damage done by dishonesty, such as tardiness, sloth, and theft. Within honest workforces, these vices are minimally present, and supervisors can focus their attention on improving job performance and productivity, which, if a supervisor is not used to the concept, requires a conscious change of management style. In the transition from a typical workforce to an honest workforce, supervisors' roles transition from bossing to coaching.

The difference between bossing and coaching is akin to the difference between supervising a chain gang and leading a football team. The chain gang does what it has been told because the boss holds the billy club and the workers have balls and chains attached to their ankles. The football team does what the coach demands because the coach and the players have set common goals, created a game plan that makes the best use of each team member's particular skills, and the coach and the players expect to share the benefits from a positive outcome.

Where honesty prevails, worker performance becomes a measure of the supervisor's ability to coach, which requires recognizing workers' strengths and weaknesses and using them to the best advantage. When performances do not meet expectations, the coach rightfully accepts blame, rather than assigning it wholly to employees. Then the coaching supervisor either provides appropriate training or reassigns workers to tasks for which they are better suited. The supervisor and the employees share common goals and mutual benefits, just like a coach and a team.

Managing with Managed Conversation

Friendly, open, and frequent managed conversation is as important to supervising employees as it is to hiring them. Managed conversation within the workplace allows supervisors and workers to develop and share the conversational inferences that are essential to effective communication, especially where precise terminology and fine-tuning of ideas are concerned. As employers and employees integrate conversational inferences, ideas and information move easily within the workplace.

From a supervisor's standpoint, managed conversations should communicate civility and personal concern, so that an employee receives the personal gratification akin to that enjoyed in casual conversation. While focusing on the sustenance providing affairs of the workplace, the managed conversation is about the employee, about what he or she knows, thinks, and recommends concerning his or her job duties. It should be the supervisor's goal, that when the managed conversation is over, the employee is left with a feeling of accomplishment verging on comradery with the supervisor.

For management and employees to establish and preserve workplace honesty and an atmosphere of fairness, open channels of communication are essential. Otherwise, natural curiosity will spur workers to seek information from unreliable sources that are often dominated by moderately dishonest components, ultimately dividing the workplace into cliques and factions.[76] Communication vacuums within a workplace are quickly filled with rumors, gossip and suspicion.

The Self-Policing Workforce

In discussing the good-worker gene, I mentioned its recessive nature: it is expressed only in the company of other workers possessing similar good-worker genes. As learned from the Sussex study conducted for the British government, these genes manifest their expression through the honest and accurate conveyance of information during managed conversations. As managed conversations become de rigueur, those managers and workers who are perceived as dishonest are either rehabilitated or expelled from the system. In this way employees police their own ranks.

The mode of self-policing varies. Sometimes factions briefly appear, indicating a dishonest person has been identified and workers are isolating the culprit for expulsion. Other times staff will simply fail to cover for a dishonest worker's poor job performance, tacitly bringing it to the attention of management. Sometimes leaders among the staff will confront the offender and demand either amended ways or a resignation. Still other times the supervisor will be approached and presented with evidence of dishonesty. Ultimately, though, the supervisor must effect the ouster of the dishonest party.

Within an honest workplace, staff tends to protect honest coworkers, even when those workers are under-performing. A supervisor must recognize these situations and assist staff, either by providing proper coaching or by reassigning the worker to more suitable tasks. Within an honest workplace, when such re-assignments are necessary, coworkers and the under-performing party generally welcome corrective changes.

Transitioning to an Honest Workplace

What happens when one day an employer, manager, or business owner decides to adopt this book's tenets, to accept and institute the precept that an honest workplace with honest supervisors managing honest workers provides the most productive and profitable business opportunity? How does this newly enlightened disciple set about making the switch from the ordinary workplace to the honest workplace? Follow this six-step process.

1. **Management themselves must adopt a policy of honesty.**

To recognize and maintain honesty, management must be honest. In a small company, a manager may accomplish this by simply making a personal resolution, such as "I'll be honest and surround myself with honest employees." In larger companies where management is tiered, supervisors should be selected and promoted based upon their commitment to honesty, then those supervisors must communicate that commitment to their workers. Management's commitment to honesty must extend beyond the Human Resources office to all supervisors.

2. **Make managed conversations the normal mode of communication between management and staff.**

Through a deliberate effort, either by scheduling regular one-on-one meetings, or by setting aside time during which managers visit and converse with employees at their workstations, managed conversations must commence. Once they have, they must become routine. Managed conversations serve to identify, reinforce, and promote honesty, and are thereby vital to transitioning to an honest workplace, as well as to maintaining one.

These managed conversations focus strictly on the work at hand. They are neither bull sessions nor social events; they are conversations that address work-related topics. While they are pursued in an upbeat and casual tone, the conversations address the various matters affecting job performance, productivity, and the common goals shared by workers and management. Managers need to make these conversations into regular events that become routine to daily operations.

3. **Make staff aware of the new policies.**

Staff is likely to catch on quickly that changes are afoot when they engage in their first managed conversation with a supervisor. It is prudent that the first managed conversation be about managed conversations, including a discussion about their methods and purpose. General announcements and group meetings are not the proper forum for instituting such a policy. Little would be accomplished toward the goal of ascertaining an individual's level of honesty by addressing the individual amid a roomful of people.

In preparation for individual managed conversations with staff, the manager should anticipate the questions that are likely to be asked, be prepared to explain the importance of open and honest communications, and use managed conversation to demonstrate that management will be interested in the opinions and concerns of the employees.

4. **Hire and promote honest employees.**

Begin by using the interview tools and techniques discussed earlier to hire honest new employees and to replace departing employees. At the same time, use managed conversation to evaluate the honesty of current staff, and as opportunities for promotion arise, grant those promotions to honest workers. As honest workers begin to fill the ranks, a tipping point will be reached when honesty surges of its own momentum.

The transition from an ordinary workforce to an honest workforce takes time, and during that time, honest workers will have difficulty facing the innate aggression of dishonesty. Therefore, supervisors must shelter honest workers and defend them from dishonesty. Management can do this by increasing the frequency and depth of the managed conversations that take place with the honest elements, preventing them from being overwhelmed by the remaining dishonest ones.

However, as newly hired honest workers are brought on-line and honest coworkers earn promotions, the honest workers among the remaining employees will tend to improve their job performance and assert their independence, further isolating the remaining dishonest elements. This eventuality is confirmed by the Aalto University study cited earlier.[77] Furthermore, as they recognize that new workers exhibit the subtle attributes of honesty, including friendliness, reliability, and competence, those honest employees currently on staff will dissolve preexisting workplace cliques and begin to communicate more openly with coworkers and supervisors. As this movement toward honesty infuses the workplace, newly hired workers will be accepted openly by existing staff.

5. **Recognize and reward honesty and good performance.**

If, prior to the implementation of an honest workplace, the environment had been one of entrenched distrust and dishonesty, it may take a long time before workers feel confident that supervisors and coworkers can be trusted. Patience is required until those stifled honest people feel confident enough to emerge from their refuges. Sometimes management will be surprised at just who these honest workers are. They may be poor-performing workers who, under pressure from or in a clique with dishonest workers, felt compelled to perform at a low level. Such people, when liberated to an honest workplace, may perform admirably. When they do, the parties should be rewarded with praise, promotions, or increased pay.

Sometimes people change. Perhaps it is because they never worked for an honest employer, or maybe it is because they grew up in an environment where honesty was never encouraged, or maybe it is because they deliberately rejected honesty on their first go-round, but some people who have acted dishonestly in the past become honest people. By making it clear to all workers that honesty will be rewarded, such people may be encouraged to change their ways and adopt an honest work ethic.

6. **Discharge noncompliant and dishonest staff.**

After it has been established that management and workers are expected to adhere to a code of workplace honesty, and after ample time has passed to allow that policy to become entrenched, those who violate the policy should be dismissed from employment. It is never pleasant when a person loses his or her job. Yet decisions must be made that insure the business can continue to provide the best products to the most customers at the lowest cost, and sometimes those decisions entail discharging workers.

Employees cannot be fired for being dishonest; they can be fired for acting dishonestly within the workplace. For example, a person can be dishonest as in the case of a worker known to be cheating on a spouse, for which he or she cannot be fired; or an employee could have provided a false excuse for missing work, for which he or she can be fired. Both cases involve dishonesty, but only the latter provides cause for firing as it is directly related to workplace actions. Before firing an employee, an employer should have a clear-cut reason that is directly related to the employee's job performance.

Before making the fateful decision, an employer must carefully judge the employee's actions and statements, and consider the particular circumstances. Though an employer should provide the coaching necessary to encourage optimal performance from each employee, including performance within the realm of honesty, when an employee has acted dishonestly on the job it is appropriate to fire that employee rather than coach him or her. Coaching a known dishonest person provides no guaranteed that he or she will become honest; instead it may make him or her more convincingly deceptive. While a well-intentioned supervisor tries to coach a dishonest worker, valuable time could be wrongly invested and dishonesty's disruptive impact could further infect the workplace. Better to invest the time in training and coaching those who show promise.

Discharging Failed Employees

What follows is a discussion of the proper way to discharge an employee while transitioning from a regular workforce to an honest one. This is not intended to be a comprehensive discussion of dismissal policies. Dismissal policies and laws vary widely from state to state and country to country, and each human resource manager should be familiar with the laws of his or her particular area.

It is typical of a workplace where dishonesty is rife to have a high rate of employee turnover, which may be used to the employer's advantage. If dishonest employees depart voluntarily, that trend may obviate the need for actively discharging them. Many times, when a new policy or program is introduced which interrupts the status quo, various employees will decide to depart voluntarily rather than endure the uncertainty brought on by the changes. When a new policy of honesty is communicated to the staff, those who feel threatened by that policy may begin looking for work elsewhere.

Dismissing a dishonest worker can be a challenge depending on the level of dishonesty. When a dishonest worker is caught red-handed, the process may follow routine procedures. However, most dismissals involve nuances, quantitative charges and subjective judgment. So long as the supervisor's judgment is sound, a staff of honest workers is likely to be thankful for the move. Once the decision has been made to fire an employee, it is best to set about the task without delay.

"At Will" versus "For Cause" Discharge from Employment

In America, most regions abide by "employment at will" precepts, in which either party may terminate employment at any time for any reason—meaning that an employee can be fired at the whim of the employer. A few states and some municipalities have "for cause" dismissal laws, where an employer must show "cause" before firing an employee.

Even in those states where "employment at will" is the law, employees may not be fired for reasons that are discriminatory. Discrimination has occurred if an employee is fired because of race, religion, gender, age, disability, or sexual orientation. Other reasons that an employee may not be fired include:

- for filing a safety complaint,
- for filing a worker's compensation claim,
- for participating in required military service,
- for serving on a jury,
- for reporting an employer's or supervisor's illegal activities, or
- for rebuffing an employer's or supervisor's sexual advances.

In "employment at will" states, it is also important for an employer to consider "good faith" dealings and "implied employment contracts." Good faith is violated when an employer lies to an employee, such as when an employee has been promised compensation for accomplishing a particular goal, and then when the goal has been reached, the employer fires the employee instead of paying him or her. An implied employment contract may exist where an employer generally provides a warning before firing employees for a specific offense, but changes that policy and immediately fires a particular employee. These matters are best clarified by labor attorneys.

In those states and municipalities where discharge "for cause" is the law, each employer should be aware of the local labor laws. In Montana, which is a "for cause" state, an employee may be dismissed for "legitimate business reasons," so long as those reasons are neither "false, whimsical, arbitrary, nor capricious," and so long as the reasons "have some logical relationship to the needs of the business." Being the first state to adopt "for cause" labor laws, Montana serves as a precedent setting legal template for many regions where such laws have been enacted.

Good Employees Depart Sometimes

Inevitably, the time will come when a valuable and honest worker will get the urge to move on, either in pursuit of better opportunities, or merely for the change of scenery. Within an honest venue, where the worker has received fair treatment and compensation, management can assume that the worker's move is not a negotiating ploy, but the result of a profound decision. Management will be best served to bid best wishes and a hearty farewell to such a worker and even go so far as to assist the departing worker's ambitions. These departures can hurt a supervisor's pride and create short-term difficulty, but pride is a form of personal bias that must be checked, and the difficulty caused by the departure of one honest worker can quickly be mitigated by the rise of another honest worker. Employees who depart with blessings from their former employers are often lifelong goodwill ambassadors to those magnanimous employers who set them on the path to success.

Sometimes it is difficult for those managing a tight-knit, honest workforce to recognize that the workplace serves a different role for workers than it does for management. Businesses are often the embodiment of management's creativity and intuition, and, therefore, management's emotional ties to a business are usually far stronger than are those of the workforce. Sometimes management misreads workplace harmony as an affirmation of familial ties between management and staff. Management should recognize that the workplace serves the role of providing sustenance to staff, sustenance that workers can enjoy and share with their friends and family far removed from work. As Dr. Harlow's laboratory experiments demonstrated, workers prefer the company of comfort companions to the company of sustenance providers. Management needs to allow workers to have inviolate private lives separate from their work.

Time for Trust

Trust is both the means and the ends to managing an honest workforce. Honest workers make decisions based upon objective evaluations, allowing supervisors to tweak performances as opposed to questioning motives. Where workers are honest, fretting and policing become ways of the past, and planning and projecting become the ways of the future. Supervisors who trust their employees are free to manage their businesses. Managing and participating in a trustworthy workforce is the quintessence of professional satisfaction. It is time for trust.

Sometimes old-school supervisors find it hard to let go— hard to trust their employees. The factory floor or the garage start-up is no Camelot, but to manage honest employees effectively, one must simply trust them.

The management lessons of *Hire Honesty* can be reduced to three precepts:

1. Be honest.
2. Hire honest workers.
3. Trust them.

No one of these precepts trumps another. All three are equally important; as such, each must be monitored and maintained to the highest degree. However, the importance of trust to the overall performance of an honest workforce is sometimes overlooked. It cannot be overstated. Trust is as essential to managing an honest workforce as honesty is to assembling it.

Trust allows workers to perform. It allows managers to manage, and it allows everyone to relax. When management trusts employees it is possible for workers to concentrate on job performance rather than on conforming to management's concocted regimen of expectations, especially when such a regimen has been established to prevent the sorts of dishonest acts that an honest worker would not perform anyway. Management must simply back off. Let honest workers do their jobs.

Honest employees are essential to every business. Businesses may survive with dishonest employees, but they will not provide the workplace atmosphere that allows creativity, the open exchange of ideas, and the general worker satisfaction that infuses and stimulates full business potential. Only within workplaces where employee honesty prevails will employers and employees reap and enjoy the fruits of their efforts.

By allowing it to blossom, trust expands the impact of honesty. A trusting employer sends a message to the employees that their honesty is recognized, their productivity and ideas are rewarded, and their private lives are inviolate. Trust, as mentioned earlier, is the means by which we navigate the ocean of truth. An employer reaps the benefits of honest employees if those employees know their honesty is recognized and preserved. Only then can an employer sail on the ocean of truth and visit all the fascinating and fulfilling ports of call on a successful voyage around the business world.

Summary

Honest workers require coaching instead of bossing. Coaching is most effectively performed through managed conversations that encourage workers to communicate freely and confidently with supervisors and coworkers. Such communication results in more accurate gauging of worker's abilities and integrity.

Transitioning from a typical workplace to an honest workplace is a multistep process. First, management needs to adopt a self-imposed policy of honesty. Then they must begin and maintain regular communications with staff. The new workplace model needs to be explained to all workers. New employees must be selected for honesty. Good performance is to be rewarded. Dishonest and noncompliant workers should be dismissed. Management must trust their staff.

In nearly every business, dismissing workers is unavoidable. No worker should be dismissed for reasons that are discriminatory or unfair. Labor laws vary from place to place, and every employer should be familiar with the local laws that regulate dismissing employees. It is disappointing and inconvenient when good workers move on, but it is also an opportunity within the workplace as other workers rise to fill the vacated positions and as the goodwill of departing employees can benefit their former employers.

Hire Honesty has three management precepts: be honest; hire honest workers; trust them.

Chapter 16 Conclusion

At the beginning of this book we set out to find the best employees and to pair them with the best employers, and we did it. Who are the best employees and the best employers? Honest employees and employers. Why are they the best employees and employers? Because they follow principles that are knowable, consistent, and productive. What makes honesty so useful in predicting the satisfactory performance of workers? By its fundamental nature, honesty is the moral equivalent of the good-worker gene.

We have seen that honesty is essential to personal fulfillment, societal trust, and workplace satisfaction, but what hope do we have for the future? Judging by the past, the outlook on average is good. It's good because even when society falters, when honesty is besmirched and truth derided, someone, somewhere comes along and corrects our course and puts us back on track. By their example, a way is cleared for others to follow and once again society is enlightened and moves forward.

Rarely are these advances heralded. They aren't greeted with fireworks and flashing lights. They are subtle, humble grassroots movements. The process may be as simple as a man or woman complementing another for a statement in support of truth. A bond is formed and trust flowers. And then another person joins their bond of trust, and then another. But none of these events are likely to garner much attention. More likely, they will be quiet, confidential undertakings, and it's better that way.

Mother Teresa said, "Never worry about numbers. Help one person at a time, and always start with the person nearest you." If we build our communities of honesty one person at a time, the numbers will increase of their own accord. Employers and human resource professionals are ideally positioned to begin the process of assembling honest people into workplace communities. One employee at a time, employers can bring honest people together, reward their honesty, and pave the way for shared prosperity. As honesty brings prosperity to a community, outsiders will ask the secret to the community's success. Maybe the outsiders will mend their ways and commit to trust, integrity, and honor, and the community of honesty will grow larger still.

As we have learned in the early chapters of this book, honesty encourages positivity because honesty is based on facts, and facts are the essential components of all optimism. Even facts that are distinctly negative, because they are nonetheless facts, provide the foundation for positive action, whereas untruths provide no guidance, and any actions based on them simply compound the problems that promote pessimism. But even as dishonesty pervades society and culture stagnates, human nature's quest for truth works beneath the surface as a root system that eventually reawakens, grows, and blossoms. It blossoms as one man or one woman possessed of optimism, one person willing to regard facts for what they are, refusing to hide from them, forging ahead with a confidence borne of reality, not falsehood. Such a person epitomizes optimism, not naiveté, because true optimism must be based on fact.

Pessimism is not new or indicative of this era. When I was in the tenth grade at Milton Hershey School, our literature teacher, W. Lyndon Hess, began one of his many memorable sessions by reading from the first chapter of Livy's *The Early History of Rome*, written 2,100 years ago, during the reign of Augustus Caesar. Livy began his monumental work by scolding his contemporaries:

> *I would have him* [the reader] *trace the process of our moral decline, to watch, first, the sinking of the foundations of morality as the old teaching was allowed to lapse, then the rapidly increasing disintegration, then the final collapse of the whole edifice, and the dark dawning of our modern day when we can neither endure our vices nor face the remedies needed to cure them.*[78]

In his next paragraph, Livy continues:

> *Of late years wealth has made us greedy, and self-indulgence has brought us, through every form of sensual excess, to be, if I may so put it, in love with death both individual and collective.*

Sound familiar? Livy's diatribe is not unlike many that appear in newspapers, popular media, and sermons in our everyday, twenty-first century lives. Ironically, Mr. Hess recited these gloomy passages from antiquity to cheer us up. We were a bunch of fifteen-year-old "wise fools" with raging hormones and intermittently useful brains. We were often derisively referred to as "kids these days . . .," and had just borne a particularly scathing tongue-lashing from our high school principal who conveyed all the "bitter curses" Livy laid at the feet of the young Romans.

"You see," Mr. Hess concluded, "Nothing's new. You're not so bad. Youth have always been derided by their elders. Livy was doing it two thousand years ago, and yet we survive. My parents did it to me, my peers do it to you, and you—goofballs that you are—will someday do the same to your children."

I don't remember how we reacted as a classroom. If the topic wasn't sex, sports (or drugs if that's your thing), or rock 'n' roll we usually didn't pay much attention. Since then, I've thought frequently about Mr. Hess's insight. Despite the doomsaying around us all, and the ebb and flow of current events, we tend to improve as a society; and society, as we have learned, is built on honesty. It seems someone somewhere is always willing to stand up and fight for truth.

To find good and trustworthy people, Mr. Sufian Ahmed from Ghosia, India, told me to look beyond religion, cultural diversions, and social castes. Answer this question, he counselled me: "Is this person honest?" Within his laconic counsel lay a moral path that trumped religion. It stifled most of the social ills afflicting the working world and virtually the entire civil structure of modern society.

Honest people attract like-minded people. Even when we feel alone in an ocean of dishonesty, truth keeps our heads above water until we can find another honest person to cling to and buoy our spirits. Together, we form a raft of trust. Then others clamber aboard, and the raft grows into an island. While waves and storms erode the beaches, the island continues to grow from the center out, pushing back against the forces of erosion and decay.

Islands merge and form continents of truth. From time to time, society unites to encode the freedoms that protect honesty. The First Amendment to the Constitution of the United States of America is one such attempt. The laws that protect free speech and press are essentially guarantors of honesty. People can say anything they please, and it is incumbent upon each member of a free society to discern whether what is said is truth or deceit, no trifling task. We pay dearly for our freedom when we decide wrongly. But the wisdom of the ages recognizes that, when any manner of speech is limited, truth will suffer first. The antidote to false speech is honest speech, and sometimes we must fight to have honest speech heard.

The First Amendment also protects the sanctity of the workplace with its "freedom of assembly" clause, which states, "The government shall make no law respecting . . . the right of the people peaceably to assemble, . . ." The workplace is nothing more than a place where people peaceably assemble to provide sustenance for one another. The right to assemble is guaranteed equally to each prospective employer and employee. We each have the freedom to choose where we work, with whom we work, and when we should part ways with our employers or employees.

As with our right to free speech, the burden of freedom lies in the choices we make. If we choose to work for thoughtless, irresponsible employers, we have the freedom to leave and look for better associations, or to remain and be unhappy. If an employer chooses to hire dishonest, unproductive employees, he or she has the freedom to endure the maladies of dishonesty, to discharge dishonest workers, or to fail as a business. The worst that can be said about an honest employee is that he or she did not perform well and needs better training. The best that can be said about a dishonest employee is that he or she has not been caught cheating yet. Freedom entails responsibility and we are each responsible for our own employment predicament.

As we have learned in the preceding pages, honesty not only makes workplaces better, it makes people better. The good-worker gene also works as a good-friend gene, good-character gene, good-personality gene, and good-citizen gene. The decision to hire honest workers and to assemble an honest workforce not only spawns successful businesses, it also sows the seeds for a better society. Employers, hiring managers, and human resource professionals need to recognize the magnitude of their assignment and choose their employees wisely. Recognize honesty. Reward honesty. Trust honest workers. Expand honest society.

"Where do you find these wonderful workers?" was the question asked at the beginning of this book, as it is asked by customers and clients of well-run companies everywhere. The answer is simple: "We find them where honesty thrives."

Sources

1   Flowers, Jennifer. "World's Best Awards, 2014." *Travel + Leisure*. August 2014 Ed.: Pg. 112.

2   *Jacobellis v. Ohio*. https://supreme.justia.com/cases/federal/us/378/184/case.html

3   Aristotle, quote. http://quoteworld.org/quotes/559

4   Carr, Winfred; Kemmis, Stephen; *Becoming Critical: Education, Knowledge and Action Research*; Pg 32. 1986, http://enotez.files.wordpress.com/2011/09/becoming-critical.pdf

5   Hume, David; *A Treatise of Human Nature*; http://www.davidhume.org/search. html?T1=on&T2=on&T3=on&A=on&L=on&ad=on&es=on&E=on&M=on&P=on&N=on&D=on&q=%22science%22+%22sciences%22 T 3.1.1.24, SBN 466-467.

6   Hume, David; *A Treatise of Human Nature*; http://www.davidhume.org/search.html?T1=on&T2=on&T3=on&A=on&L=on&ad=on&es=on&E=on&M=on&P=on&N=on&D=on&q=%22science%22+%22sciences%22, T 2.3.10.11, SBN 452-453

7   Shapin, Steven. *Social History of Truth*. pg. 11. Chicago; The University of Chicago Press, 1994.

8   Montaigne, Michel de, Montaigne's Essay "On Liars" www.tnellen.com/06iths/spring/liars.html

9   Garfinkel, Harold. *Studies in Ethnomethodology*. Pg. 35-53. UCLA; Prentice-Hall, 1967.

10 Conquest, Robert. *The Harvest of Sorrow*. Pg 340. Oxford; Oxford University Press, 1986.

11 Manvell, Roger; Fraenkel, Heinrich. *Doctor Goebbels, His Life and Death*. Pg. 266. New York; Skyhorse Publications, 2010.

12 Manvell, Roger; Fraenkel, Heinrich. *Doctor Goebbels, His Life and Death*, Pg. 73. New York; Skyhorse Publications, 2010.

13 Marx, Karl; Engels, Friedrich, *The Communist Manifesto*. Pg. 92. New York; Pocket Books, Simon & Schuster, 1964.

14 Alinsky, Saul; *Rules for Radicals*, Pg. 10. New York; Vintage Books, 1971.

15 Mussolini, Benito; *The Doctrine of Fascism*. Pg. 7. New York; Howard Fertig, 2006.

16 Feynman, Richard, quote, http://www.openculture.com/2014/03/richard-feynman-on-religion-science.html

17 Shapin, Steven. *Social History of Truth*. Pg. 17. Chicago; The University of Chicago Press, 1994.

18 Shapin, Steven. *Social History of Truth*. Pg. xxx. Chicago; The University of Chicago Press, 1994.

19 Montaigne's Essay "On Liars" www.tnellen.com/06iths/spring/liars.html

20 Shakespeare, William; *Hamlet* Act I, Scene 2. Lord Polonius to son, Laertes.

21 Burns, George; quote. http://www.goodreads.com/quotes/128348-sincerity—if-you-can-fake-that-you-ve-got-it

22 Johnson, Spencer; quote. http://thinkexist.com/quotes/spencer_johnson/ Spencer Johnson co-authored One Minute Manager.

23 Lee, Mi-Kyoung (2005). *Epistemology after Protagoras: Responses to relativism in Plato, Aristotle*. Oxford: Oxford University Press. ISBN 0-19-926222-5. From Wikipedia, "Protagoras"

24 Nietzsche, Friedrich. *The Viking Portable Nietzsche*. Quote; 'On truth and lie in an extra-moral sense,' pg.47, Walter Kaufmann translation. New York; Penguin Books, 1968.

25 Sowell, Thomas. *The Vision of the Anointed*. Pg 98. New York; Basic Books, 1995.

26 Lee, Mi-Kyoung (2005). *Epistemology after Protagoras: Responses to relativism in Plato, Aristotle*. Oxford: Oxford University Press. ISBN 0-19-926222-5. From Wikipedia, "Protagoras"

27 www.psychologytoday.com/blog/insight/201408/new-scientific-study-being-honest-improved-health?th=HomeEssentials.

28 Harlow, Harry; "The Nature of Love," http://psychclassics.yorku.ca/Harlow/love.html

29 Peter, Laurence J.. *The Peter Principle: Why Things Always Go Wrong*. New York; William Morrow & Co., 1969.

30 Smith, Adam; *The Theory of Moral Sentiments*, pg 300. Originally published, 1759. Printed, Lexington, KY, 2014.

31 Iñiguez, Gerardo; Govezensky, Tzipe; Dunbar, Robin; Kashi, Kimmo; and Bario, Rafael A.; Aalto University, "Effects of Deception in Social Networks"

Gerardo Iñiguez 1, Tzipe Govezensky 2, Robin Dunbar 3, Kimmo Kaski 1 and Rafael A. Barrio 4, 1

1. Department of Biomedical Engineering and Computational Science, Aalto University School of Science, FI-00076 AALTO, Finland
2. Instituto de Investigaciones Biomédicas, Universidad Nacional Autónoma de México, 04510 México D.F., Mexico
3. Department of Experimental Psychology, University of Oxford, OX1 3UD, United Kingdom
4. Instituto de Física, Universidad Nacional Autónoma de México, 01000 México D.F., Mexico

32 Iñiguez, Gerardo; Govezensky, Tzipe; Dunbar, Robin; Kashi, Kimmo; and Bario, Rafael A.; Aalto University, "Effects of Deception in Social Networks" pg 9, para 1.

33 Popper, Karl. *The Logic of Scientific Discovery*. New York; Routledge Classics, 2002.

34 Feldman, Robert. *The Liar in Your Life*. Pg. 14. New York; Twelve, Hatchette Book Group, 2009.

35 Iñiguez, Gerardo; Govezensky, Tzipe; Dunbar, Robin; Kashi, Kimmo; and Bario, Rafael A.; Aalto University, "Effects of Deception in Social Networks" pg 10.

36 Feldman, Robert. *The Liar in Your Life*. Pg 24. New York; Twelve, Hatchette Book Group, 2009.

37 Coleridge, Samuel, quote. http://en.wikipedia.org/wiki/Suspension_of_disbelief

38 Blake, William; Auguries of Innocence. https://www.goodreads.com/author/quotes/13453.William_Blake

39 Dean, Dizzy; quote. http://www.brainyquote.com/quotes/quotes/d/dizzydean379853.html

40 Scopelliti, Irene; Loewenstein, George; Vosgerau, Joachim; *Psychological Science*. "Miscalibration in Predicted Emotional Responses to Self-Promotion" http://www.cassknowledge.com/sites/default/files/article-attachments/Bragging_miscalibration_final_rep.pdf

41 Barthes, Roland; *Roland Barthes*.

42 Smith, David Livingston. *Why We Lie*. Pg 137-142. New York; St. Martin's Press, 2004.

43 *The Simpsons*, quote. "I didn't do it, nobody saw me do it, you can't prove anything." http://www.simpsoncrazy.com/episodes/moaning-lisa

44 *Leave it to Beaver*, quote. http://www.imdb.com/title/tt0050032/quotes Leave it to Beaver.

45 Barry, David; quote. http://thinkexist.com/quotation/a_person_who_is_nice_to_you-but_rude_to_the/199146.html

46 Gagarina, Amalia K., M.S., R.D. "Kernberg's View of Narcissistic Personality Disorder" http://www.health.am/psy/more/kernbergs_view_of_narcissistic_personality_disorder/ 2006

47 Ford, Charles V., MD. *Lies, Lies, Lies.* Pg. 123. Arlington, VA; American Psychiatric Publishing, Inc., 1996.

48 Hume, David. *A Treatise on Human Nature*, Book 3. Part 1, Sect. 1, Para. 9 Pg. 240 on .pdf.

49 Smith, David Livingston. *Why We Lie*. Pg. 3. New York; St. Martin's Press, 2004.

50 Montaigne, Michel de, Montaigne's Essay "On Liars" www.tnellen.com/06iths/spring/liars.html

51 Ekman, Paul. *Telling Lies*. Pg. 76-79. New York; W.W. Norton & Company, Inc., 2009.

52 Ford, Charles V., MD. *Lies, Lies, Lies.* Pg 91. Arlington, VA; American Psychiatric Publishing, Inc., 1996.

53 Ekman, Paul. *Telling Lies*. Pg, 29. New York; W.W. Norton & Company, Inc., 2009.

54 Smith, David Livingston. *Why We Lie*. Pg 107. New York; St. Martin's Press, 2004.

55 Washington Post. http://articles.dailypress.com/1994-04-29/news/9404290219_1_aldrich-h-ames-soviet-defectors-spy

56 Jump up ^ http://articles.dailypress.com/1994-04-29/news/9404290219_1_aldrich-h-ames-soviet-defectors-spy .

57 Central Intelligence Agency; https://www.cia.gov/library/center-for-the-study-of-intelligence/kent-csi/vol5no2/html/v05i2a09p_0001.html

58 Ekman, Paul. *Telling Lies*. Pg. 163. New York; W.W. Norton & Company, Inc., 2009.

59 Feldman, Robert. *The Liar in Your Life*, Pg. 44-48. New York; Twelve, Hatchette Book Group, 2009.

60 Smith, David Livingston. *Why We Lie*. Pg. 2. New York; St. Martin's Press, 2004.

61 Bond, Charles F., Jr; and DePaulo, Bella M.; *Psychological Bulletin*, 2008 by the American Psychological Association, Vol. 134, No. 4, 477–492 "Individual Differences in Judging Deception: Accuracy and Bias" http://postcog.ucd.ie/files/Individual%20differences%20in%20judging%20deception%20Accuracy%20and% 20bias..pdf

62 http://www.uiowa.edu/~grpproc/crisp/crisp14_9.pdf "LieDetectionIndirect.pdf"

63 Ekman, Paul. *Telling Lies*. Pg. 331. New York; W.W. Norton & Company, Inc., 2009.

64 Ekman, Paul. *Telling Lies*. Pg. 331. New York; W.W. Norton & Company, Inc., 2009.

65 Carnegie, Dale. *How to Win Friends and Influence People*. Pg. 85. New York; Pocket Books, 1982.

66 Ekman, Paul. *Telling Lies*. Pg. 167. Uses "a better baseline as acquaintance grows." . New York; W.W. Norton & Company, Inc., 2009.

67 Ormerod and Dando; "Finding a Needle in a Haystack: Toward a Psychologically Informed Method of Aviation Security Screening" *Journal of Experimental Psychology*, November 2014

68 Ormerod and Dando; "Finding a Needle in a Haystack: Toward a Psychologically Informed Method of Aviation Security Screening" *Journal of Experimental Psychology*, November 2014, pg. 8, col 2, para 2.

69 Horvath, Frank; Blair, J.P.; Buckley, Joseph P. "The Behavioural analysis interview: clarifying the practice, theory and understanding of its use and effectiveness." International Journal of Police Science and Management. 2008. Vol. 10 No.1, Pg. 101-118.

70 Iñiguez, Gerardo; Govezensky, Tzipe; Dunbar, Robin; Kashi, Kimmo; and Bario, Rafael A.; Aalto University, "Effects of Deception in Social Networks" pg 2. Re: 33, 34, 35.

71 Hayden, Jeff; "14 Questions That Reveal Everything" *Inc*. http://www.huffingtonpost.com/2013/03/04/14-interview-questions-th_n_2807438.html

72 *Seinfeld* "The Foundation" episode http://www.pkmeco.com/seinfeld/found.htm

73 *Seinfeld* "The Cadillac 2" http://seinfeldscripts.com/TheCadillac2.html

74 Pulakos, Elaine. "Structured interview" from Selection Assessment Methods, SHRM, Pg. 11-12

75 Miller, GA, Dr.; "Working Memory," http://www.instructionaldesign.org/theories/cognitive-load.html

76 Iñiguez, Gerardo; Govezensky, Tzipe; Dunbar, Robin; Kashi, Kimmo; and Bario, Rafael A.; Aalto University, "Effects of Deception in Social Networks" 2014.

77 Iñiguez, Gerardo; Govezensky, Tzipe; Dunbar, Robin; Kashi, Kimmo; and Bario, Rafael A.; Aalto University, "Effects of Deception in Social Networks" 2014.

78 Livy (Livius, Titus). *The Early History of Rome*. Translated by Aubrey De Selincourt. Pg. 34. New York; Penguin Classics, 1960.

Index

Reference —

Are they rethreable?
Would you rethere them?

CPSIA information can be obtained
at www.ICGtesting.com
Printed in the USA
BVOW01s2009071116
467169BV00002B/2/P